African Americans and Community Engagement in Higher Education

African Americans and Community Engagement in Higher Education

Community Service, Service-Learning, and Community-Based Research

Edited by

Stephanie Y. Evans,
Colette M. Taylor,
Michelle R. Dunlap,

and

DeMond S. Miller

Front Cover: "Self-Portrait Reflection from the Ground UP" by Brittany Ferguson
Back Cover: "People Speak" by Derek Dent

Published by State University of New York Press, Albany

© 2009 State University of New York

For information, contact State University of New York Press, Albany, NY
www.sunypress.edu

Production by Diane Ganeles
Marketing by Michael Campochiaro

Library of Congress Cataloging-in-Publication Data

African Americans and community engagement in higher education :
  community service, service-learning, and community-based research /
  edited by Stephanie Y. Evans . . . [et al.].
      p. cm.
  Includes bibliographical references and index.
  ISBN 978-1-4384-2873-4 (hardcover : alk. paper)
  ISBN 978-1-4384-2874-1 (pbk. : alk. paper)
    1. Service learning—United States.   2. African American college students.
  3. Community and college—United States.   I. Evans, Stephanie Y.
  LC220.5.A48   2009
  378.1'03—dc22
                                                                2008055627

                        10 9 8 7 6 5 4 3 2 1

Contents

❖❖❖

PART 2. COMMUNITY SERVICE-LEARNING

Michelle R. Dunlap

List of Tables

Preface

Using History, Experience, and Theory to Balance Relationships in Community Engagement

STEPHANIE Y. EVANS

In this edited collection, authors put race—specifically, African American identity—at the center of analyzing town/gown relationships. Beyond defining race as a problem to be solved, this collection demonstrates the rich dialogue that occurs when scholars and practitioners give race due attention for its role in relationship building and evaluation. As chapters in this book vividly demonstrate, race still matters, especially when developing community partnerships. In this text, authors reflect on how the race of faculty, students, and community partners impacts expectations and experience. Some commentators may argue that we have arrived as a nation and are entering a "postracial" moment. However, only a critical lens toward race reveals how we got "here" and how far we have yet to travel. I argue that race and gender studies in general, and Black Studies in particular, are more crucial now precisely because of the movement to erase race.

African Americans have been systematically subjected to social oppression such as racialized terrorism, sexualized violence (including generations of rape and lynching), legalized discrimination, political disenfranchisement, economic thievery, criminal injustice in law enforcement, and institutionalized social subjugation. Thus, the struggle for equal rights, equitable access to resources, and community empowerment has been an integral part of Black people's educational philosophies, program development, curricula, and pedagogy. *African Americans and Community Engagement in Higher Education* (which will be abbreviated *AACE* throughout) engages historic and current people, programs, and practices that provide a deeper understanding of how race impacts individual relationships and institutional partnerships.[1]

Though not duly recognized in mainstream contemporary scholarship, an attitude like that of Nannie Helen Burroughs, "we specialize in the wholly impossible," has been prevalent in Black articulations of community service and effective in furthering community-based education for racial and ethnic minorities in the United States. Given the definitive election of President Barack Obama in 2008, race in general and African American heritage, identity, and history are now again central to the national dialogue in a way as intense as in the Civil War and the Civil Rights Movement.

In this book, we focus on how African Americans have done much to "clean up" the dirty laundry of the United States and correct antidemocratic policies by contributing critical thought and constructive practices that demand and create social justice. Clearly, more research is warranted in this area.[2]

Community Engagement in Historical Context

Critical race analysis in community engagement has not earned significant academic attention in mainstream contemporary journal and book publications, but academics such as Carter G. Woodson, who began the *Journal of Negro History* (1916) and wrote *Mis-Education of the Negro* (1933), understood that race-centered scholarly definitions of justice movements were central parts of community engagement.[3]

In "Unrecognized Roots of Service-Learning in African American Social Thought and Action, 1890–1930," Charles Stevens documented historic African American theories and practices that are relevant to community service-learning. In his article, Stevens highlighted underresearched historic figures and then asked, "How might knowledge of this historical antecedent serve current service-learning programs?" One important answer to this question is that scholarship and community initiatives of the past can help us place race at the center of analysis and problem solving.[4]

Men such as W. E. B. Du Bois, James Baldwin, Medgar Evers, Martin Luther King Jr., and Malcolm X have been duly recognized as effective community activists. Women in the 1950s and 1960s Civil Rights Movement such as Septima Poinsette Clark, Ella Baker, Gloria Richardson, Dorothy Height, and JoAnn Robinson have been hailed as activists, but because they are women, they are not widely recognized as scholars as well. Activists' ability to produce scholarship based on community partnership must be appreciated by contemporary researchers who wish to address issues of academic relevancy, validity, and ethical production. It is no accident that many of these activists earned graduate degrees or were college professors who connected their work in their institutions with their work for social justice.

In this preface, I focus on Septima Clark's contribution to the Civil Rights Movement as an exemplar of principles present within contemporary *AACE* researchers' race-centered agenda. I focus on Clark not simply in the capacity of practitioner, but also as a leader in the formation of race-based thought about service, service-learning, and community-based research as imperative components of higher education. Now more than ever, with the struggling and shifting global markets, a clearer understanding of how race and gender complicate economic class will be key variables in problem definition and problem solving. History in general—as personified by Septima Clark—can be a useful guide.

Septima Poinsette Clark (1898–1987): A Biographical Sketch

Septima Poinsette was born on May 3, 1898, in Charleston, South Carolina. Her mother, Victoria, was born free and raised in Haiti and worked as a laundress. Her father, Peter, was enslaved on the Poinsette's plantation in Charleston and later worked as a janitor. She was the second of eight children. In her 1962 autobiography, *Echo in My Soul*, Clark recalled her education, teaching career, activism, and hope for America's future.[5]

She began teaching at the Promise Land School on St. Johns Island, South Carolina, in 1916 at the age of eighteen. She taught writing to the men of the Odd Fellows, a Black fraternal organization, and participated in women's sewing circles. She did not view these activities as "service," she simply saw this as community engagement. In 1918, she moved back to the mainland and taught sixth grade at her former school, Avery Normal Institute. She married Nerie David Clark and had two children, but only the son survived, and Nerie himself died in 1927. Septima taught in Columbia and Charleston, volunteered with the YWCA, mediated community relations between city officials and the police department, and was part of the campaign to equalize Black and White teachers' salaries. In the 1930s, she attended summer school at Columbia University and studied with W. E. B. Du Bois at Atlanta University. She received her bachelor's degree in 1942 from Benedict College in South Carolina and her master's in 1946 from Hampton in Virginia.[6]

In 1956, after teaching for forty years, Clark was fired from her job in South Carolina because of her activism. Clark had been involved with the NAACP since 1918 and suffered socially and professionally for her organizing efforts. Myles Horton, director of the Highlander Folk School, then located in Monteagle, Tennessee, immediately hired Clark to run educational workshops. Highlander was a racially integrated school founded in the 1930s to provide space for community empowerment workshops. Clark had begun attending Highlander workshops in 1954 and was there with Rosa Parks two months before Parks's famed one-woman sit-in that sparked the 1955 Montgomery Bus Boycott.[7]

In the mid-1950s, while on St. Johns Island, Clark worked with Easu Jenkins and he noted that community members kept articulating the desire to vote. At the time, there was a reading requirement for voter registration in most southern states, and the Black literacy rate was low, so the voter registration and participation was low. From that community-defined need of literacy for political involvement, Clark began teaching basic literacy to improve St. John's Island citizens' opportunity for democratic participation. She developed a culturally and politically relevant curriculum: instead of teaching an alphabet where the ABCs stood for "apple," "bat," and "cat," she taught the ABCs where *a* was for "attorney," *b* for "bail," and *c* for "citizen." In math, the problems included similar examples: "Ten students were arrested in the sit-in movement and were fined $75.00 a piece. How much fine was paid?" and "We sent eight people down to register each day for thirty days. How many people were registered?"[8]

In January 1957, under the auspices of Highlander, the first Citizenship School was opened on St. Johns Island, and Clark employed her cousin, Bernice Robinson, to become head teacher. Robinson owned a beauty shop, and while she had no teaching experience or credentials, she was respected and trusted by the community—she spoke Gullah, the local language, and she spent time talking and listening to community members. The Citizenship School's first students all passed the South Carolina literacy test, and the effectiveness of the program was duplicated in other southern states. In 1959, police raided Highlander to enforce segregation policies, and in 1961, the state of Tennessee forced Highlander out of the area. Again, Clark was out of a job. At the suggestion of Ella Baker, Clark moved the Citizenship School operation to Atlanta with the national Southern Christian Leadership Conference (SCLC).[9]

With the SCLC teacher-training program under her purview, Clark led the way for a national African American voter registration drive. The movement was furthered by the 1962 Voter Education Project, which involved a broad coalition of Civil Rights organizations. In the next four years, the coalition trained ten thousand teachers for Citizenship Schools and nonviolent resistance. By the eve of the 1965 Voting Rights Act, seven hundred thousand Black Americans had registered to vote. This movement was of monumental importance—the Black population united and garnered unprecedented political power. In response, White resistance was calculating and brutal. Numerous African Americans such as Fannie Lou Hamer became leaders in the Civil Rights Movement because of the violence, intimidation, and discrimination they encountered as they attempted to exercise their right to register and vote. Despite resistance, Clark constructed and administered an adult education curriculum based on the principals of active participatory democracy that stemmed from a community-defined need and an unflinching critique of race in America.[10]

Clearly, Clark left a legacy worthy of reflection and emulation. It should come as no surprise, then, that Septima Clark was a cousin of Dr. Donald Blake, who provides the Final Word to this book, and his brother, scholar–activist

Dr. Herman Blake of South Carolina. As Dr. Blake articulates, institutions of higher education must have a larger agenda in mind for their community work to be effective. Septima Clark's writing provides examples of what to look for in the chapters in this volume.

Clark's *Echo in My Soul*: Three Lessons for Contemporary Scholar–Practitioners

Septima Clark's *Echo in My Soul* is a twenty-chapter autobiography that she wrote in 1962 when she had just moved from Highlander to the SCLC. Her story seems written to sway those embattled in the Civil Rights struggle to continue to fight but also to humanize protesters and discredit law enforcement's slanderous portrayals of community-based political organizers. In significant ways, the problems that community practitioners face today differ greatly from the problems of the antebellum, the Reconstruction, the Great Depression, and the World War eras or the Civil Rights Movement. Yet, core tenets of effective relationship building in local and national problem solving (as demonstrated by the Obama campaign) hold steadfast. Of the many themes present in *Echo in My Soul,* three relevant to contemporary educators, administrators, and community partners stand out: (1) the import of community voice in defining problems and solutions; (2) the power of collaborative learning and collective investment in project outcomes; and (3) the centrality of race in understanding justice movements.

Lesson 1: The Import of Community Voice in Defining Problems and Solutions

Clark argued that the agenda of community engagement must be set by needs of community members. The St. Johns Island community desired to vote; those from Highlander were simply there to assist in furthering an agenda already articulated by community members such as Alice Wine, who knew well the disparity in opportunity. In current town/gown relations, too often the emphasis is placed on the students' perceived needs (such as learning outcomes, leadership training, or obtaining "real-world" experience) rather than seeking to develop a partnership in which the community gets to define its own needs. Listening to community definitions increases the chances that the activity college students undertake is more valued, sustainable, and valuable in the community.

An additional aspect of the citizenship school framework was teachers' ability to recognize what assets participants brought to their learning process. Often, teaching and community work in the Jim Crow South was done with a focus only on what Black residents did not have; Clark noticed the skills that they did have and built on those. For example, Clark noted that "most of those men, being unable to read, had unusually good memories and were adept at memorizing. You could read something to a Johns Islander, and he could repeat it back to you. They were, many of them, amazing that way." As observed in the African tradition of storytelling, elders often fostered a capacity to memorize lengthy stories in order to pass them down to the next generation. Though the adults on St. Johns Island were not advanced in their literacy, they demonstrated a superior capacity to memorize, comprehend, and critique constitutional passages regarding the meaning of citizenship.[11]

If, as often occurs, the community itself is defined as the problem, then agency to solve the problem is placed solely in the college students' or academic researchers' hands. When community partners are recognized as resources to define the problem and as possessors of skills to develop solutions, students' learning experiences are enriched. In Clark's model, community members are recognized as relevant partners who are central to the program in all stages of development—from conception to evaluation.

Lesson 2: Collaborative Learning and Collective Investment in Project Outcomes

Clark highlighted the significance of all participants engaging in the learning process—everyone had a role as teacher and student. She viewed learning as a collaborative effort. All constituents, whether they were local youth, students of traditional college age, adult learners, community activists, business owners, lawmakers, or Citizenship School teachers, were actively engaged in the teaching–learning dialectic.

In addition, Clark advocated learning for self-awareness and self-determination but argued that learning was necessarily a public and communal endeavor:

> The school in which the Negro must be educated is the shopping center he is boycotting, the city council chamber where he is demanding justice, the ballot box at which he chooses his political leaders, the hiring offices where he demands that he be hired on merit, the meeting hall of the board of education where he insists on equal education.[12]

Clark insisted on people's active and collective participation in their own educational process. She saw learning as inherently democratic, which meant that education had social foundations and collective implications. She also saw that understanding the dynamics of Black oppression was central to effectively engaging resistance strategies. When a faculty member constructs a situation in which there is one assumed group of learners and one assumed group of teachers—and cultural identity is absent from the discussion—there is a missed opportunity for a collaborative educational experience.

Clark claimed that for a program to be effective, all partners must have a compelling motivation and must be invested in project outcomes. She included herself in this mandate. For example, while she was neither a true "outsider" nor "insider" in the Sea Island community, she measured her achievement as a teacher by the level of growth in her community. Although she was not a permanent resident, she saw herself as directly affected by the success or failure of community programs. In her work to expand educational opportunities in various states, all partners, regardless of origin or resident status, were extremely invested in project outcomes.

Campus partners' investment in local communities is essential, particularly at affluent institutions located in economically deprived areas. Building relationships with communities can be difficult for students who are temporary residents or faculty members who are weighed down by the pressure of campus responsibilities. Often, the faculty "service" mentioned in the "research, teaching, and service" higher education mantra, means only administrative campus-based service. So, while students are encouraged to volunteer, faculty members generally are discouraged from activities that build relationships necessary to advance meaningful citizenship. New models must be offered where all partners in campus and communities are recognized to have something to teach and learn.

Lesson 3: The Centrality of Race in Understanding Justice Movements

In 1956, Clark was dismissed from her teaching position because of her NAACP membership; this was just one of millions of examples of the retribution visited on Black people when they tried to improve their social position. Clark notes many examples of the egregious violence and intimidation on St. Johns Island. She also recorded the struggle—and joined the fight—for equal teachers' salaries for Blacks and Whites in Columbia, South Carolina. At every level of education (positions on the local school boards, teaching salaries and class sizes, and physical resources such as school buildings or teaching materials), African Americans were denied access to equal resources or denied entry at all. Because Whites controlled education, they controlled the government, and vice versa.[13]

As a parent and a teacher, she was very aware of the social restrictions put on those adults who would join the movement. She was also aware of the tragedy of having to teach Black children that their place in society was limited to the bottom rungs:

> The Negro parent's dilemma is fearsome. There is nothing worse, believe me, I KNOW this, than bringing a child into the world and having to teach him that none of the pleasant things of life are for him, or few of them at most. How do you teach a tot where to sit, where to walk, where not to play, and where not to go . . . like the theatre, art gallery, city parks, and public libraries? A parent has a terrible time explaining why the native soil is such a hard place for the native to grow in. . . . I can testify out of the bitter school of experience.[14]

As a researcher, Clark painstakingly listed the many ways individuals, groups, and representatives of institutions operated to withhold rights to African Americans and poor people. In her role as a community member, she effectively organized groups of people to fight against these operations.

The selection of the chapters that appear in this book was largely based on the contributors' explicit discussion of race. This work is valuable because authors present their work in relation to tenants of engagement that are in line with movement activists such as Septima Poinsette Clark and thousands of scholar–activists at her side.

Conclusion: Engaging Race to Define a Critical and Adaptive Research Agenda

As a Black woman, my experience with service-learning has been very different from that of my White colleagues. Actually, my foray into Black women's intellectual history developed from a frustration with theoretical and philosophical frameworks in mainstream educational research that did not represent my cultural standpoint. That research resulted in my dissertation and eventually a book: *Black Women in the Ivory Tower, 1850–1954: An Intellectual History*. In that text, I reveal how Black women educators had four criteria for scholarship, especially as it related to community work: applied learning, primacy of cultural identity, critical epistemology, and moral existentialism. Each of these ideas (lived experience, standpoint, challenging the status quo, and social responsibility) provides a guide to how I serve, teach service-learning classes, or participate in community-based research projects. These are components sorely missing from much of today's university scholarship and community engagement programs. As scholar–activist Dr. Anna Julia Cooper argued, service must go beyond social change; it must advance social justice. Without understanding African American history and acknowledging Black presence, oppression, and creative resistance, justice work in America will be incomplete and education will fail to be "higher" in significant ways.[15]

Were it not for recognition by a few influential scholars and social justice workers, Septima Clark might be overlooked as a poor schoolteacher who merely was the daughter of a janitor and a laundress. This commonplace dehumanization, especially in university-based service situations where the economic and educational power differential is extreme, often blinds academics to the real "experts." Though she also was an academic person, Clark recognized the value of community members who, while not formally educated, were knowledgeable in defining and meeting their own needs. Her insight and organizing skills provide a much-needed paradigm for future community partnerships. Her contributions might be especially rich to African American and gender studies departments, which can be valuable centers of scholarship and activism.

Since Barack Obama's candidacy, America and the world has more carefully confronted ethnicity and heritage in addition to race. This national dialogue on race and engagement centered in this volume should not serve to essentialize African American identity. Rather, this collection represents an initial foray into a much-needed extended discussion of race, power, knowledge, education, activism, and equitable partnerships. Dr. Martin Luther King Jr. spoke in his Nobel Peace Prize acceptance speech of three evils facing the world: racism, poverty, and militarism. These are no less issues today and it is a terrible wonder how anyone can look back at the Civil Rights Movement and favor regressive legislation, policies, or politicians that embody the very ideals that bring about these very evils. In his "World House" concept, King provides a guideline for international discussion of these issues; this edited volume continues the discussion as it impacts campus–community relations, where those interested in "public service" and state or national leadership are usually trained.[16]

AACE challenges contemporary ideas of college–community relations by bringing to the forefront critical thinkers who understand the central points raised by Clark's work—that communities must be central in articulating definitions of social problems and central in attempts to solve those problems; that people learn better in collaborative communities where everyone is recognized as a learner and a teacher; and that race dialogue is central to healthy or productive communication about change and justice.

AACE editors and contributors seek to move this dialogue forward to ensure more balanced institutional relationships and more informed human relationships. There are many types of potential relationships represented here, including reciprocal service, invested partnership, and sustained community building. Whatever mode of engagement participants choose, Clark's principles are instructive. A theory is an explanation; this collection uses historical and contemporary arguments centered in race and theories grounded in the necessary discussions of race and gender to further the efficacy of experiential education. Without this approach, partnerships will remain inequitable and, thus, will not reflect equitable or effective engagement.[17] With a commitment to identity studies and critical race praxis, our students will be more prepared to develop meaningful collaborations and town-gown relationships can become more functional, sustainable, adaptive, and transformative.

Notes

1. L. Litwack, *Trouble in Mind: Black Southerners in the Age of Jim Crow* (New York: Knopf, 1998); N. Painter, *Exodusters: Black Migration to Kansas after Reconstruction* (New York: Knopf, 1976).

2. S. Shaw, *What a Woman Ought to Be and to Do: Black Professional Women Workers during the Jim Crow Era* (Chicago: University of Chicago Press, 1996).

3. C. G. Woodson, *The Mis-Education of the Negro* (1992 ed.) (Hampton, VA: U.B. & U.S. Communication Systems, 1933); V. L. Crawford, J. A. Rouse,

and B. Woods, *Women in the Civil Rights Movement: Trailblazers and Torch-bearers, 1941–1965* (Bloomington: Indiana University Press, 1993).

4. C. Stevens, "Unrecognized Roots of Service-Learning in African American Social Thought and Action, 1890–1930," *Michigan Journal of Service-Learning* 9, no. 2 (2003): 25–34.

5. S. Clark, *Echo in my Soul* (New York: Dutton, 1962); S. Clark and C. Stokes-Brown, *Ready from Within: Septima Clark and the Civil Rights Movement* (Navarro, CA: Wild Trees Press, 1986); B. Collier Thomas and V. P. Franklin, *Sisters in the Struggle: African American Women in the Civil Rights–Black Power Movement* (New York: New York University Press, 2001).

6. Clark, *Echo in my Soul*; Clark and Stokes-Brown, *Ready from Within*.

7. Clark, *Echo in my Soul*.

8. Eliot Wigginton, *Refuse to Stand Silently By: An Oral History of Grass Roots Social Activism in America, 1921–1964* (New York: Doubleday, 1991).

9. After two relocations, Highlander is now operating in New Market, Tennessee, and is still offering workshops on social justice issues.

10. Wigginton, *Refuse to Stand Silently By*.

11. Clark, *Echo in my Soul*.

12. Clark, *Echo in my Soul*.

13. Clark, *Echo in my Soul*.

14. Clark, *Echo in my Soul*.

15. S. Y. Evans, *Black Women in the Ivory Tower, 1850–1954: An Intellectual History* (Gainesville: University Press of Florida, 2007).

16. For a consideration of Dr. King's "World House" speech, see his papers collected at Morehouse and the international discussion begun on the fortieth anniversary of his assassination, April 4, 2008: http://www.morehouse.edu/worldhouse/media.html (accessed April 6, 2008).

17. F. Evers, J, Rush, and I. Berdow, *The Bases of Competence: Skills for Life-long Learning and Employability* (San Francisco: Jossey-Bass, 1998). I would like to offer special thanks to Dr. Nathaniel Norment of Temple University's African American Studies Department for his helpful dialogue about "community building" in addition to service, justice, and engagement. Each of these represent a unique set of variables in a relationship as well as ideological approach; all are useful, but the goal of balanced relationships depends on the nuanced understanding of the strengths and weaknesses of each.

Acknowledgments

Stephanie Evans

I am eternally grateful for the sisterhood and intellectual synergy of Colette Taylor. When we met for our first brainstorming session in September 2003, I knew we could change the world. In addition, this project could not have been completed without Michelle and DeMond—you both are blessings! The authors who contributed were infinitely patient and every bit as dedicated to this collective vision. May this work continue to bring us closer. Thank you to my mentors, colleagues, community partners, and family for their continued motivation. Thank you especially to my loving husband, Curtis D. Byrd, for making my family, social, work, and spiritual life complete.

Colette Taylor

One cup of java at a Starbucks in Gainesville, Florida gave birth to not only lifelong friendships, but the work of a lifetime with Stephanie Evans. I am forever grateful for your presence in my life. To our coeditors, Michelle Dunlap and DeMond Miller: I have been forever changed by your dedication, commitment, and insights. Thank you to the authors and my mentors, friends, and students who consistently strive to make our communities better. I am thankful for my mother, father, and sister who support my every endeavor. Most importantly, thank you to my children, Devin and Dylan, for giving me purpose, love, and reminders of what this journey is about.

Michelle Dunlap

I thank God; my family; the coauthors whom I now consider family; the contributors; my colleagues both inside and outside of my department and college; my students; the many community partners with whom I am engaged and by whom I am inspired; and the students and youth who allow me to serve and learn as an engaged mentor. All of these tremendous folks are reflected in my contribution to this work, and I am grateful that they are a part of my life and the work that I do.

DeMond Miller

I wish to thank God for the chance meeting of Stephanie Evans in England leading to the formation of this research collaborative that I share with folks I too consider family—Stephanie, Michelle, and Colette. Their work ethic and scholarly insight set them apart in a class of their own. Also, I thank my colleagues at Rowan University who support my quest to empower students to use "sociological skills." Thanks also to my students and community partners who constantly teach me what community means. Finally, to my mother and father who support my endeavors—but most importantly, to the late Reverend John W. Craft Sr., my grandfather. His life provided me with an example of enduring selfless service.

AACE Editors

Stephanie, Colette, Michelle, and DeMond sincerely appreciate the positive and professional administration and staff at State University of New York Press, especially Jane Bunker, Lisa Chesnel, Amanda Lane, Diane Ganeles, and Michael Campochiaro. We are indebted to Cindy Bush for her invaluable editorial services.

Introduction

❖❖❖

Characteristics of Engagement

Communicated Experiences of Race, Universities, and Communities

COLETTE M. TAYLOR

A democracy is more than a form of government; it is primarily a mode of associated living, of conjoint communicated experience. The extension in space of the number of individuals who participate in an interest so that each has to refer his own action to that of others, and to consider the action of others to give point and direction to his own, is equivalent to breaking down barriers of class, race, and national territory which kept men from perceiving the full import of their activity.[1]

The phrase "a conjoint communicated experience" should be foremost in the educator's mind when undertaking the work of community engagement. If higher education frames its work as a mode of associated living, which communicates institutional possibilities and constraints to those around them, these institutions must model citizenship in their daily practices. From the higher education perspective, the literature has focused on detailing effective programmatic features of various community engagement approaches such as service-learning, experiential education, internships, community-based research, faculty professional service and outreach, and student volunteerism.[2]

More recently, the literature has explored the components necessary to institutionalize community/campus engagement within an institution of higher education.[3] The vision of the present, expressed by the voices in this book, demonstrates how monolithic and ethnocentric the literature on community engagement and higher education has been. We hope this book will inspire a more diverse vision and future of community engagement in higher education. This book reviews the many ways contemporary researchers understand the role of African American community within the academy with a particular emphasis on how such a debate reshapes the very nature of community engagement work.

Engaging Universities, Communities, and Race

Engagement refers to an educational or research initiative conducted through some form of partnership and characterized by shared goals, a shared agenda, agreed-on definitions of success that are meaningful both to the university and to the community participants, and some pooling or leveraging of university resources and public and private. The resulting collaboration or partnership should be mutually beneficial and is likely to build the capacity and competence of all parties. To be successful, partnerships must be built on a reasonable understanding of the conjoint communicated experience or living arrangement. As exemplified by Willetts in chapter 1 of this book, successful partnerships with the African American community, such as the Community Folk Art Center and Syracuse University, could only be manifested through collaborative work and open dialogue.

Engagement is fundamentally different from *outreach*—a model developed in the early days of the development of the land-grant movement in the United States and originally supported by a series of cooperative extension offices and agents. Using outreach, institutions of higher learning apply their collective knowledge to problems brought to them by people in the community. Above all, outreach is the transfer of knowledge from a university to a client or community. It is solely a one-way experience rather than a shared endeavor. An excellent example of the kind of problem for which an engagement strategy is ideally suited is the improvement of elementary and secondary education. In the United States, this issue is being approached through the vehicle of partnerships between higher education and the leadership of elementary and secondary schools.

To create the conjoint experience, the engaged university is committed to direct interaction with external constituencies and communities through mutually beneficial exchange, exploration, and application of the knowledge, expertise, and resources of all participants. These interactions enrich and expand the learning and discovery functions of the academic institution while enhancing community capacity. The work of the engaged institution is responsive to (and respectful of) community-identified needs, opportunities, and goals in ways that are appropriate to the campus' mission and academic strengths. Colleges and universities stand to gain by fostering true collaboration among students, faculty members, and community organizations, as demonstrated by Hoffman and associates in chapter 6.

Engaged institutions, no matter what the foci of their interests or the pathways by which they arrive at substantial engagement, share some common characteristics:[4]

1. Civic engagement is articulated in the institutional mission and strategies. Public perspectives and needs consistently influence campus priorities.
2. The campus involves the community in continuous, purposeful, and authentic ways and listens carefully to community concerns.
3. The curriculum contains a variety of ways for students to learn and engages them in community concerns.
4. The campus carefully considers consequences of all of its decisions on its relationship with the community and its capacity to collaborate with the community.
5. The institution has a policy environment, appropriate infrastructure, and investment to promote, support, and reward engagement.
6. Individuals throughout the campus community play leadership roles in fostering engagement. This is especially important in order to ensure that a commitment to engagement will survive leadership transitions at presidential, provost, and decanal levels.
7. The campus approach to scholarship includes support of interdisciplinary work since societal issues do not come in "disciplinary form."
8. The campus honors and makes visible its engagement work, both internally and externally.
9. Engagement activities are held to high standards of excellence and are rigorously evaluated.

Analysis of the literature on community–campus partnerships reveals that the elements of effective collaboration are emphasized within community building and higher education literature, with scant attention paid to community voices and perspectives on these issues.[5] This is particularly true for literature representing multiple community voices and literature that highlights the costs and the benefits to community agencies and residents of participation in community–campus partnerships. It is reasonable to assume these components apply to the subset of community partnerships that are formed with higher education institutions as well as other kinds of partnerships. The literature suggests core elements that include the following:[6]

- Analyses and strategies that focus on community assets and strengths (rather than focusing solely, or primarily, on deficits and needs);
- Comprehensive strategies that cut across systems, sectors, issues, and disciplines;

- Acknowledgment of the roles that privilege, institutional and structural racism, and power differentials play in creating and maintaining differential community conditions;
- High quality and effective collaboration;
- Sustained, long-term action.

Because this list is fairly well-known among practitioners and researchers who work on community self-determination and improvement, it was particularly frustrating to community partners in African American communities that its elements are not better observed in collaborations between community organizations and higher educational institutions.

The lack of observation to these practices feeds the undercurrent of mistrust of institutions of higher learning and researchers that is deeply held with our communities. This mistrust goes way back—to the era of slavery, when stories were rampant of slaves being rounded up for special torture—and it moved like a poisonous snake through history until the Tuskegee Experiment, which broke the proverbial camel's back. The Tuskegee Experiment used 399 poor, illiterate black farmers in Macon County, Alabama, as guinea pigs in a torturous disaster designed to let them die of syphilis. Tuskegee's legacy adds to other barriers discouraging Blacks, Hispanics, and other minorities from getting involved in engagement activities. Many people do not know the particulars of what happened, but the bottom line is that they come away saying, "I'm not going to be a guinea pig." The African American community absorbed information about this unbelievable mistreatment, along with all the other suffering at the hands of medical and governmental entities, into the fiber of their culture, and whether they all know the specifics of Tuskegee, it affects their thinking about researchers—even those not associated with the medical field.

The stigmas of racial inequities and exploitation from the Tuskegee incident have not been erased from the minds of African Americans, particularly those in the baby-boom population. Engaging more African Americans in research requires careful consideration of the cultural roots of their thoughts and actions. Gaining trust is essential in getting more "buy-in" from the African American partners. An important part of this trust building, expressed by Vaccaro in chapter 8, is that colleges and universities that wish to require or encourage service-learning have an ethical obligation to safeguard communities of color from harm. To make service in any of its forms "truly ethical, aversive racism, microaggressions, and the structural oppression must be extinguished." In addition, the involvement of influential leaders, particularly from the African American faith community, adds credibility to the project. Sustained commitment to the community is critical.

Regardless of the engagement method, technology transfer, community-based or collaborative research, or public policy analysis and education— whether at the national, state, or local levels—the engagement is demanding and time-consuming. The faculty members require support and resources to be able to carry out activities effectively. Institutional and faculty resources are needed to make the outreach/engagement function an equal partner with on-campus teaching and research and to ensure that this happens even if there are no on-campus students involved. Entrepreneurial faculty who raise funds for outreach through grants must also commit additional time to outreach programs independent of their classroom teaching obligations, which may also contribute to their teaching activities. Of particular importance is the need to be relieved from on-campus teaching duties that conflict with the schedules necessary for successful off-campus outreach. To some degree, it is the question of serving one group of students or another group of students.

If there is a full commitment to engagement, then it is absolutely necessary to find the means to successfully serve both the registered campus students and the off-campus students whose identities are, at the start of such programs, more elusive and amorphous. For the university that wishes to encourage sustained engagement with the community, like the one demonstrated by Berea College in chapter 9, one of the most critical issues is to provide a way to sustain outreach activities over the long term. Developing and maintaining community relationships that are a *sine qua non* (i.e., an essential element) of a successful engagement program is time-consuming and demanding. The kind of support here envisioned will require administrative oversight and assistance of centralized campus outreach/service.

Centralized campus outreach/service offices can play a brokering role between the community and the faculty. Participants cited several strategies that institutions can adopt to improve their accessibility to potential community partners. At an administrative level, colleges and universities can provide a single point of contact for community members. For example, Virginia Commonwealth University's Office of Community Programs serves as a "one-stop shop" that connects community members with student and faculty outreach programs. Instead of having to approach a school or department cold, community members work with program staff to identify university programs that best match their specific needs. This "brokering" approach is a very efficient way to match community needs with academic research partners—if the institution has the resources and commitment to staff and maintain an office dedicated to this kind of work.

As authors have pointed out throughout this book, participants must feel that there is a vested interest in the advancement of the community. Not only do African Americans want involvement from those who can best identify with our cultural experiences, but we want to see ongoing, tangible results, such as development and implementation of new treatment strategies as well as documented solutions that are made available to our constituency in a format and language that is understood by the community. African American communities want to know that a positive, enduring investment has been made in their community as a result of the proposed research efforts and that these investments go beyond the limitations of the project period established by university Institutional Review Boards and offices of community service or service-learning. Culturally competent approaches, such as those defined by Briscoe and associates in chapter 13, should be utilized.

Providing culturally relevant and sound perspectives not only informs the discussion, it also adds greater depth and richness to the field as a whole, helping paint a more realistic and inclusive picture of the benefits of community engagement to this historically voiceless population. Engagement means staying attuned to the issues faced by people. Harkening back to the values of American democracy described by Dewey,[7] institutional greatness depends on the basis of how much of the university is engaged with America and with whom they engage. There is much to be done in renewing and fulfilling the ideals of the conjoint communicated experience.

The coeditors, all longtime practitioners of experiential education, feel that this text will connect historic and contemporary ideas of "service." If faculty, student, and administrators join with community partners and identify common motivations, then service, service-learning, and community-based research programs can be more effective and sustainable. These discussions of motivation, democracy, and equity simply cannot take place without addressing the historic and contemporary disparities in Black communities. More importantly, solutions that do not engage cultural identity will be ineffective at best and detrimental at least. The historical legacy of racial construction in America impacts generational relationships, health and safety, peer pressure, family structures, material culture, and educational quality. Thus, African American history underscores the limitations and promise of community engagement and partnerships. In this historical and intellectual context, it is also clear that both race and gender must be discussed in assessing and applying relevant scholarship.

Book Outline and Race-Centered Scholarship

This book is divided into three sections: Community Service, Community Service-Learning, and Community-Based Research. Each section contains unique chapters with a brief introduction that addresses salient issues present in each type of community relationship.

In part 1, "Community Service, Volunteerism, and Engagement," author discussions include the following: examples of an extension of Black Arts Movement legacies between a Black Studies department and a New York community art center (chapter 1); how race impacts community health and family medicine practitioners who work with African American rural communities in Florida (chapter 2); mentor motivations, attitudes, and experiences in low-performing urban Florida schools (chapter 3); and dimensions of prejudice in North Carolina university/community relationships (and often stark White–Black dichotomies) in service programs (chapter 4).

In part 2, "Community Service-Learning," authors contribute chapters covering myths surrounding community-based organizations and how strength assessments offer potential solutions for a range of Massachusetts educators (chapter 5); academic self-efficacy in a California community college setting (chapter 6); an African American male professor's perspective of developing learning partnerships in an urban Illinois environment (chapter 7); racial identity development analysis within the context of a small, private Colorado research university (chapter 8); and learning experiences of a White woman/Black man Kentucky teaching team during a service-learning trip to Katrina-ravaged Louisiana (chapter 9).

Part 3, "Community-Based Research," offers insight into stressors in Black women's health disparities in urban Georgia (chapter 10); university center partnerships with churches in Virginia (chapter 11); asset-based narrative research with Black homeless women in Michigan (chapter 12); practical models of cultural competency in Florida research (chapter 13); and implementation of cultural values in developmental programs for Illinois female adolescents (chapter 14).

The entries in this collection varies in many aspects: institution type; constituent and practitioner identity; theoretical frameworks; data sets; methodologies; program goals; urban or rural setting; and geographic location. However, the use of African American perspectives as a guiding force in praxis is universal. As a mosaic of Black experiential learning assessments, this collection must be read in historical context.

Chapter Outlines, Application of Historical Insights, and Contemporary Modeling

Authors in this collection readily apply principles learned by Septima Clark as outlined by Stephanie Evans in the preface. The principle of community voice is especially present in the following *AACE* chapters: "The Community Folk Art Center: A University and Community Creative Collaboration" (chapter 1), "Black Like Me: Navigating Race, Gender, Research, and Community" (chapter 10), "A Partnership with the African American Church: IMPPACT and S.P.I.C.E.S. For Life" (chapter 11), and "'I Have Three Strikes Against Me': Narratives of Plight and Efficacy among Older African American Homeless Women and Their Implications for Engaged Inquiry" (chapter 12). *AACE* chapters that demonstrate the value of collaborative learning and mutual investment are "An African American Health Care Experience: An Academic Medical Center and Its Interdisciplinary Practice" (chapter 2), "African American College Students and Volunteerism: Attitudes toward Mentoring at a Title I School" (chatper 3) "Sowing Seeds of Success: Gardening as a Method of Increasing Academic Self-Efficacy and Retention among African American Students" (chapter 6), "'We'll Understand It Better By and By': A Three-Dimensional Approach to Teaching Race through Community Engagement" (chapter 9), and "A Culturally Competent Community-Based Research Approach with African American Neighborhoods: Critical Components and Examples" (chapter 13).

Though all *AACE* authors address race, the following chapters make race the primary focus of program analysis: "Prejudice, Pitfalls, and Promise: Experiences in Community Service in a Historically Black University" (chapter 4), "Can the Village Educate the Prospective Teacher?: Reflections on Multicultural Service-Learning in African American Communities" (chapter 5), "A Service or a Commitment? A Black Man Teaching Service-Learning at a Predominantly White Institution" (chapter 7), "Racial Identity and the Ethics of Service-Learning as Pedagogy" (chapter 8), and "Community Engagement and Collaborations in Community-Based Research" (chapter 14).

From historic concepts of "race uplift" to contemporary debates about racialized perceptions of need and service efforts in Hurricane Katrina, African American identity offers a cogent platform to encourage the difficult (yet much-needed) inclusion of race in dialogues of national service and community engagement. Social change can happen more effectively through critically discussing assumptions, expectations, experiences, and perspectives that emerge when placing race at the center of town–gown communication and practice.

Notes

1. J. Dewey, *Democracy and Education* (New York: Free Press, 1916).

2. R. Stoecker, "Practices and Challenges of Community-Based Research," *Journal of Public Affairs* 6 (2002): 219-39; K. Ward, "Addressing Academic Culture: Service-Learning, Organizations, and Faculty Work," in *Academic Service-Learning: A Pedagogy of Action and Reflection*, ed. R. A. Rhoads and J. Howard (San Francisco, CA: Jossey-Bass, 1998); E. Zlotkowski, "Pedagogy and Engagement," in *Colleges and Universities as Citizens*, ed. R. Bringle and D. Duffy (Boston, MA: Allyn and Bacon, 1999).

3. A. Furco, "Institutionalizing Service-Learning in Higher Education," *Journal of Public Affairs* 6 (2002): 39–67; A. Vidal, N. Nye, C. Walker, C. Manjarrez, C. Romanik, P. Corvington, K. Ferryman, S. Freiberf, and D. Kim, *Lesson from the Community Outreach Partnership Center Program: Final Report* (Washington, DC: Urban Institute, 2003); M. J. Gray, E. H. Ondaaje, R. D. Fricker, and S. A. Geschwind, "Assessing Service-Learning: Results from a Survey of Learn and Servce America, Higher Education." *Change* 32: (2002): 31–29; G. Robinson, "Service-Learning at Community Colleges," *Horizons* (Washington, DC: American Association of Community Colleges, 2000) 2–4; B. Holland, "Factors and Strategies that Influence Faculty Involvement in Public Service," *Journal of Public Service and Outreach* 4, no. 1 (1999): 37–43.

4. R. G. Bringle and J. Hatcher, "Assessing and Planning Campus/ Community Engagement," paper presented at the conference University as

Citizen: Engaging Universities and Communities, University of South Florida, Tampa, 2001; B. Holland, "Toward a Definition and Characterization of the Engaged Campus: Six Cases," *Metropolitan Universities* 12, no. 3 (2001): 20–29; J. A. Ramaley, "Embracing Civic Responsibility," *American Association of Higher Education Bulletin* 52, no. 7 (2000): 9–13, 20; J. A. Ramaley, "Moving Mountains. Institutional Culture and Transformational Change," in *A Field Guide to Academic Leadership*, ed. R. Diamond (San Francisco, CA: Jossey-Bass, 2002), 59–74.

5. D. E. Giles and N. Cruz, "Where's the Community in Service-Learning?," *Michigan Journal of Community Service-Learning*, special issue, 2000.

6. R. J. Chaskin et al., *Building Community Capacity* (New York: Aldine De Gruyter, 2001); S. H. Leiderman, *Guide to Collaboration: Lessons from the Children First Initiative* (Philadelphia, PA: Center for Assessment and Policy Development, 2001).

7. Dewey, *Democracy and Education*.

PART I

Community Service, Volunteerism, and Engagement

STEPHANIE Y. EVANS, COLETTE M. TAYLOR,
MICHELLE R. DUNLAP, AND DeMOND S. MILLER

> We may have all come on different ships, but we're in the same boat now.
>
> —Martin Luther King Jr.

Many institutions of higher learning across the nation have begun responding to widespread criticism of higher education's disconnectedness to the needs of communities and recognizing a need to cultivate a student's civic capacity to fully engage in a democratic society. This attention to pragmatism is part of an ongoing cycle in higher education that dates back at least to the early nineteenth century. In rethinking their relationship to society, institutions of higher learning are reshaping their missions and implementing a variety of community outreach efforts. The need for such a relationship is particularly relevant today, as neighborhoods that are located adjacent to universities and colleges are struggling to deal with greater challenges, especially as the institution gains more prominence. The resources of a university, especially via community service, can help address urban decay, growing economic inequality, environmental hazards, and housing, health care, crime, and juvenile justice issues.[1]

Notions of community service vary across culture and socioeconomic status and vary from individual to individual and family to family. In mainstream American culture, community service is somewhat compartmentalized as distinct from everyday events of life. Under this model, we "do" community service. In many other cultures, this notion of community service is nonexistent, or at least not compartmentalized; it is subsumed within every aspect of individual and communal life. Under this alternate model, we "are" community service. Here, community service may take the form, for example, of ushering at church, rearing extended blood and nonblood kin, looking after neighborhood children before or after school, sitting in shifts at the hospital when friends and neighbors are sick, cooking food to bring to funerals and community events, and organizing the community for participation and activism in the municipal governing processes. To call such activities community service may seem awkward, unfitting, and even strange to those who find service and the giving of their time and energy to others to be a natural part of their cultural or familial legacy and survival. Having said that, we appreciate the value of examining examples of how community service looks or manifests in African American communities and/or when conducted by African Americans, even (or shall we say especially, given the purpose of this book) in more formalized educational contexts.

Experiential Education values individual and collective learning that is gained by lived experience. In "Foundations of Experiential Education," a groundbreaking article published by the National Society for Experiential Education, the practice is described as follows:

> ... captured by the philosopher John Dewey, who argued that "Events are present and operative anyway; what concerns us is their meaning." ...
> In its purest forms, Experiential Education is indicative, beginning with "raw" experience that is processed through an intentional learning format and transformed into working, usable knowledge.[2]

We argue that African American scholars—and non-Black scholars who acknowledge the centrality of race—can deepen the understanding of what it means to serve, work, experience, and educate. A racialized understanding of education (with perspectives of gender, class, and cultural identity) can broaden contemporary debates of how public service is defined and practiced.

Unlike some historic Black women educators who have written on community-based service and learning (most notably Anna Cooper and Mary McLeod Bethune), we do not argue that Black scholars in general (or Black women in particular) have a greater capacity or responsibility for social empowerment than does anyone else. However, if we are to improve service and learning, we must look to alternative models and acknowledge each service-learning partner's complex cultural identity.[3]

A theory is an explanation that helps provide a framework for understanding how, why, and under what limits and boundaries a concept, process, or phenomenon occurs. Explanations generated from academic course materials are often valued over explanations offered by local community members simply because the power differential dictates one knowledge source (faculty and students) as more credible than another (community agencies and local residents). Although many practitioners engage community partners as vital sources of knowledge, not enough community expertise gets incorporated into community service initiatives.

Reflection and reciprocity are important concepts in the field of service-learning; they are also useful in thinking about service relationships. Reflection on knowledge produced by "other" educational philosophers is essential in order to transcend ineffective homogeneous approaches to scholarship, teaching, or service. Reciprocity involves integrating values, norms, and expectations from disparate perspectives. Both reflection and reciprocity must allow all partners the creative power to define program or project goals, implementation, and evaluation.

As African Americans in our community life as well as in our life as civic engagement professionals, we use the phrase "giving back to the community" to express efforts at strengthening and sustaining civic life in Black communities. People have always assumed an understanding of what "giving back to the community" meant through the context of their conversations. By challenging the conventional idea of "giving back" or community service, especially as it applies to the needs of communities of color and other marginalized groups, campus partners can realize the opportunity to learn valuable intellectual and moral lessons from those with whom they engage in service. This work does not seek to romanticize the role of community agencies or residents, but rather underscores an asset-based community approach, the collaborative nature of learning, and the interconnectedness of human rights issues.

Part 1 draws on a long tradition of community service, volunteerism, and civic engagement in the African American community to address a variety of social ills. In chapter 1, "The Community Folk Art Center: A University and Community Creative Collaboration," Kheli Willetts discusses a collaboration that works with fourth- and fifth-grade students in developing photography skills. The chapter is an important contribution to this book because it discusses the role of an absence of community input, namely, parents; it also addresses how the project was established to overwhelming benefit to the university rather than the community. Moreover, it discusses the impact of implementing a program in an African American community without addressing the cultural, racial, and ethnic issues that shape the lifeworlds in which the participants live. As a result of reflection on experience, the chapter provides a series of lessons learned and ways to appear an overbearing community, which is imposed to true community collaboration. The author's guiding principles draw from a legacy of the Community Folk Arts Center's ability to be a "listening ear."

Next, in chapter 2, "An African American Health Care Experience: An Academic Medical Center and Its Interdisciplinary Practice," Kendall Campbell reviews the role of different mission components of institutions of higher learning and how those mission components impact the community services for medical care for underserved communities. The chapter's primary focus centers on the need to involve more diversity in medical education and ways to infuse service for underserved communities in the first two years of medical education. Campbell also raises issues of race in medical school faculty populations, which is an essential element in diagnosing community relations.

In chapter 3, "African American College Students and Volunteerism: Attitudes toward Mentoring at a Title I School," Joi Nathan focuses on Title I—the right for all children to have access to a fair, equal, and significant opportunity to obtain a high-quality education and have a chance to achieve on standardized tests. Because the hip-hop generation, as Nathan contends, does not have the experiences of the Civil Rights era, it is the duty of educators to instill the importance of "going back" among African American students by dispelling myths concerning volunteering in low-income neighborhoods through education. Through a mentoring opportunity at Florida State University, students were able to reflect on their ability to make a difference while experiencing the tangible benefits from the children they mentor and were empowered to get engaged in positive activities conducive to future life goals.

Finally, in chapter 4, "Prejudice, Pitfalls, and Promise: Experiences in Community Service in a Historically Black University," Jeff Brooks uses an ethnographic approach to focus on the importance of building relationships in order to prevent individual departments or individual faculty members from repeatedly "reinventing the wheel." Brooks argues that there is also a need for diversity sensitivity among historically black colleges and universities' students who enter the community to help empower the community stakeholders. In essence, there should be no assumption that African American students entering the field are aware of the intricacies of diversity. This ethnographic assessment found little evidence that our students directly experience prejudice and discrimination. The research identifies two major areas of improvement, including training and closer ties with the agencies that give the community a voice as interns enter their communities.

This section addressing community service offers a series of engaging chapters that provide practical suggestions to parishioners, administrators, faculty, and students as they launch and sustain community service, volunteer, and involve themselves in civic engagement projects in African American communities to address a variety of social ills.

Each community in which we work has a unique culture and history; taking time to learn about these variables is essential. For those interested in partnering with disenfranchised populations, work in communities of color that does not build on the rich history of African American scholar-activists will inevitably fall short of the goal of sustained community relations and town/gown transformation. In each case, as Martin Luther King Jr. declared, we are all in the same boat because, in service relationships, "gown" needs as much transformation as "town."

Notes

1. Kerry Strand et al., *Community-Based Research and Higher Education: Principles and Practice* (San Francisco, CA: Jossey-Bass, 2003).

2. "Foundations of Experiential Education," *National Society for Experiential Education*, 1997, http://www.nsee.org/found.htm (accessed March 1, 2004).

3. Charles Lemert and Esme Bhan, eds., *The Voice of Anna Julia Cooper* (Lanham, MD: Rowman and Littlefield, 1998), 52, 62, 75–77; Audrey McCluskey and Elaine Smith, eds., *Mary McLeod Bethune: Building a Better World* (Bloomington: Indiana University Press, 2002), 52, 85.

I

◈ ◈ ◈

The Community Folk Art Center

A University and Community Creative Collaboration

KHELI R. WILLETTS

Collaborations, at their core, create a space for those involved to bring their particular areas of expertise and insights to the relationship; however, university and community collaborations are often challenging and difficult to maintain. Those partnerships that do not privilege academia, nor relegate the community partner to the status of "other," have been able to be transformed into true collaborations. These relationships are successful because both entities value each other's knowledge and experience and they work together to develop and implement a strategy to articulate the mission and identify the goals that they have determined together. When the collaborations are successful they can create sustainable change for both partners.

As the executive director of the Community Folk Art Center (CFAC), I have found that our most successful programming occurs when we collaborate. The CFAC is a multidisciplinary art center and we partner in a number of different areas including exhibitions, dance classes, workshops, and art camps and in our after-school program. I have used some of these collaborations as a model of best practices and they inform our daily operations. In the following chapter I have outlined the creation of the CFAC, including some of our most successful collaborations. I have also provided an example of a university–community relationship that illustrates how not to collaborate. Last, I have detailed and explained the principles that the CFAC uses to govern all of our collaborative relationships.

Community Folk Art Center and Community Service

One of the lasting artistic legacies of political activism during the Black Power Movement in central New York is the CFAC. The CFAC was founded in 1972 as a result of collaboration by the faculty in the Program (now Department) of African American Studies, Syracuse University students, and members of the Black community in the city of Syracuse. Although the CFAC has always been located off campus, it is a community service–based unit of the Department of African American Studies.

The CFAC is often identified as an example of best practices in terms of its service to the community. That commitment springs from the knowledge that, as an African American cultural institution, it is a fundamental imperative to stay connected with our community and be a place where Black people can literally find themselves through art and engagement. Our hope is that we can reinsert African American people and our culture into the conversation about community service to bring an African American perspective to the forefront.

Institutions that operate from an identifiable and articulated African American perspective often get overlooked and overshadowed by community-based arts programs and projects that are created and often implemented from a more mainstream social service model. As a result of approaching community-based arts programs and projects from this social service perspective, the community members find that there is little room for collaboration; the needs of the community are based on perception instead of conversation, and ultimately there is a lack of cultural connection, which makes the community not feel invested.

Southwest Community Center Collaboration

In 2003 the CFAC collaborated with the Southwest Community Center (Southwest), a local community-based nonprofit organization located in Syracuse's Black community. We learned about a community center photography program operating for high school students. We initially reached out to the program coordinator, Kimber Gunn, to learn more about how the CFAC could play a role in the creative development of the participants. Given that we already had more than thirty years of experience working with teens in our Annual Teenage Exhibition Competition, Ms. Gunn welcomed the collaboration.[1] After a series of meetings with Ms. Gunn, we decided to host an exhibition of the program participants and offer a workshop for the community. Our only request to Ms. Gunn was that she let her students know that we were approaching this project with the same intensity and level of expectation that we would for any exhibition.

After Ms. Gunn met with the students, they decided on a project to document their world and worked throughout the summer to prepare for the show. In the fall, I met with the students to discuss in more detail the process of mounting an exhibition, the role of the artist, and how we execute our openings, and I reaffirmed that we would all work on this together. The most interesting feedback I received from these young people was that they did not believe that they were artists.

Through our discussions, I learned that this disconnect was inextricably connected to the reality that the concept of being an artist was never presented to them prior to engaging in this work. More importantly, many of them felt that they were too young to be considered artists and that what they were engaging in was just another "art project." The thought of actually selling their work (which a few of them did during the show) was beyond their comprehension. I decided that I would use the legacy of African American artists to illustrate the possibilities and let them know that they were becoming part of a tradition. I ended the conversation with a discussion about artist statements and challenged each one of them to write their own in their voice, because that statement would accompany their photographs.

The result of that collaboration was the exhibition Our Vision: Southwest Community Center Creative Photography Program.[2] Our next step was to ensure that the reception was also a collaborative venture. The CFAC curator, Gina Stankivitz, Ms. Gunn, and I asked each student to provide us with the contact information of people they wanted us to invite so we could mail them an invitation and follow up with a phone call to encourage them to come to the reception. Finally, our last step was to make sure that we secured transportation to pick up those students and their families who needed it.

The exhibition was impressive, the subsequent turnout for the reception was incredible, and the students were proud to see their work displayed and being enjoyed. Just as important, the families were amazed at the polished substantive work that was done by their children and took pride in how these young artists were being treated by the CFAC staff and the audience at the reception. One moment that I will never forget was when a parent remarked about how when someone from the CFAC called she thought her son was in trouble because that was the only time anyone called about her child.

The impact of no or low expectations of the families, and initially of the students themselves, is indicative of larger issues experienced by African Americans in the Syracuse community. However, contrary to standard museum practice,[3] by including these students from the beginning of the project and valuing their input, it became clear that all parties benefit from the interaction when one engages in truly collaborative relationships. Since 1972, the CFAC has endeavored to ensure that we include and value the role of the community residents because without them we could not exist.

History of the Community Folk Art Center

The idea for the CFAC was inspired by Syracuse University students in the early 1970s. The late Herbert T. Williams, an African American Studies professor who created and taught a course entitled Art of the Black World, found that his students wanted to do more than look at images of African American art; they wanted to meet Black artists and interact with their work firsthand.[4] Williams took their request seriously and began working with John Johnson, program chair of African American Studies, and it was at that point the larger community was brought into the discussion. The inclusion of the community was critical to the creation of the CFAC because a core philosophy of the African American Studies Program—both then and now—is the study of Black people.[5]

The CFAC, then known as the Community Folk Art Gallery (CFAG), was opened in a small storefront in the heart of Syracuse's Black community. The primary objective was to "serve people who usually do not have access to art or art instruction. It provides expertise, critiques, lectures, workshops, exhibition space, and other support to artists as well as a most important and special commitment to the residents of urban Syracuse and central New York."[6] The CFAG was the host of exhibitions featuring work that ranged from internationally known artists such as Palmer Hayden to developing artists from the area high schools who participated in the CFAG's Annual Teenage Exhibition Competition.[7] There were also educational programs that ranged from artist gallery talks and workshops to art camps that provided classes in visual arts for the youngest members of the Syracuse community at no cost.

The popularity of the CFAG grew, and within 10 years its site became too small to accommodate the artists, students, and community residents who frequented the space. With the help of Syracuse University, the CFAG moved across town but not out of the community. Over the course of 22 years, the CFAG continued to provide programs and educational opportunities in the visual and performing arts to the residents of Syracuse and the greater central New York region.

It is important to point out that the faculty in African American Studies, African American artists, and the Black community found a way to keep the institution thriving while other culturally specific arts institutions that emerged out of the activism of Black Liberation in the 1960s and 1970s began to close down. The result of that activism and vigilance has facilitated the transformation of the CFAG into the CFAC.

The Community Folk Art Center Today

What began in a small storefront and moved into a converted auditorium with a small classroom attached, now finds itself located in a new building that allows it to function as a multidisciplinary community art center. That transformation is directly related to the relationship between Syracuse University's Department of African American Studies and the various communities that consider the CFAC a vital facet of the Syracuse community.

Since its inception, the CFAC has considered community collaboration a pivotal aspect of its function. In our previous locations, we learned that our potential was only limited by our space. We moved from the storefront that allowed us to install small exhibitions and operate modest programs to a location that allowed us to expand both the exhibition and educational programming, but the community still wanted more.

In 2000, the Department of African American Studies, under the direction of chair Linda Carty, began mobilizing to get the university to find a larger space to meet the demands of the growing center. In 2005, after thirty-three years of serving the public in spaces that we had to fit into, the CFAC moved to a new building, centrally located bordering downtown Syracuse, Syracuse University, a diverse community of lifelong residents, recent immigrants, and a Black neighborhood.[8] The CFAC now houses two galleries, The Herbert T. Williams Gallery and The Community Gallery, and facilities for visual and performing arts courses in the studio and performing arts to ensure that individuals interested in the arts have a forum and setting for discussing and enjoying the world of art, regardless of age, income, or place of residence.

Blueprint for Collaboration

As a community service–based unit of the Department of African American Studies, the CFAC has an obligation to create exhibitions and programs that respond to the needs of our diverse communities while simultaneously engaging in work that dismantles the barriers, visible and invisible, that exist between the community and Syracuse University, or as it is often referred to as "the hill." The legacy of the CFAC's creation has provided an excellent foundation on which much creative collaboration has been built. What we have learned is that there are some critical and principled positions we must take for our university–community union to be truly collaborative. There are four guiding principles that the CFAC observes to continue its successful track record of partnerships.

Principle 1: Honor All Forms of Knowledge

It is important for the CFAC, as a cultural liaison between a university entity and a community, to honor all forms of knowledge. Community members have often expressed that faculty and university administrators "on the hill" only come down into their neighborhoods to impart their knowledge, and they fail to engage the people in meaningful dialogues. During the creation phase of the CFAC, the organized and engaged members of the community made sure to ask them what they thought and demonstrated that they had been heard. It is because of our "listening ear" that the CFAC has maintained its long-standing support in the community.

The programming that we have offered represents this core principle. What began as a simple request by the Black community to see and interact with the works of Black artists evolved into exhibitions that explored the African Diaspora and other cultures whose histories were often devalued and dismissed by the larger society. That allowed us to expand our focus and begin celebrating the diversity within the Black community as well as welcome other communities into the CFAC family. To date, as a direct result of community feedback or inspiration, in addition to African American culture, we have also exhibited and explored the art and culture of First Nations, Hmong, Mexican, West African, Caribbean, and Muslim people, as well as women, children, elders, and people living with different abilities from underrepresented communities.

In addition to the exhibitions, our cultural programming includes artist workshops, guest lectures, film screenings and film festivals, and tours. All of these elements are coordinated collaboratively with the CFAC staff and a guest curator from the community or via community representatives. We operate with the understanding that knowledge in all forms must be honored and that we must create spaces of opportunity for that knowledge to be valued and explored. The CFAC does not make requests for particular types of workshops, guest lectures, or films to be screened. Instead, we ask the artist or scholar conducting the program what they would like to do and how they see it working. At no point do we enter that relationship believing that our position as a university-based institution privileges our knowledge. That is why it is critical to engage a guest curator or community representatives. By doing so, we continue to adhere to these guiding principles.

Principle 2: Involve Community Members

When creating cultural programs it is vital to have members of that community at the table at all stages from inspiration through creation to installation. Whenever the CFAC installs exhibitions or implements programming representative of cultures from non-African American communities, we consider it critical to collaborate with community members. The CFAC employs artists, educators, and elders (basically anyone identified as a "knowledge bearer") to work with us through all phases of an exhibition as the guest curator or we set up a series of meetings with a collective of community representatives to honor the work and the people whose culture we are going to display. This principle is perhaps the most challenging one because it demands that as an institution we modify how we develop and implement our programming to ensure that participants from the very community that we are exploring have full membership in the process.

For example, in the fall of 2004 the CFAC exhibited Visions of Mexico/ Visiones de México featuring Mexican folk art and photographs from the collection of Dr. Alejandro Garcia.[9] We wanted to develop programming around this exhibition and relaunch our film program after a fifteen-year absence. Six months prior to the opening of the exhibit, we asked Dr. Garcia to assist us in formulating an advisory board with a broad representation of the Latino community in Syracuse. Through the diligence and hard work of Dr. Garcia as our guest curator, he organized a committee whose diversity crossed all boundaries, including country of origin, gender, occupation, affiliation, and socioeconomic status.

The committee's tasks were to suggest additional programming, assist us with the creation of bilingual labels and wall text, articulate the best ways to inform the Latino community about our upcoming exhibition and programs, and ensure that cultural accuracy was maintained. Collectively, we also decided that this exhibition provided the opportunity to explore the diversity within Latino culture through our film program and, in particular, to challenge ourselves and our communities to learn more about an often silenced membership within Latino culture, AfriLatinos. The resulting festival was entitled Voices/Voces: Colonial Experiences from the Diaspora.[10]

After several meetings, a series of programming was developed, including film screenings, a film festival, guest lectures, artist workshops, and performing arts presentations. The opening reception featured the Syracuse University dance troupe Raices, classical guitarist Victor Lopez, and food catered by a local Mexican restaurant. The advisory committee was instrumental in bringing the Latino community in Syracuse and central New York to visit our exhibition, participate in our events, and assist us in expanding our constituency.

Principle 3: Experience and Expertise Is Far More Valuable Than Money

Cultural capital can get you much further in creating responsible programming than any amount of funding. Like most small nonprofit organizations, the CFAC finds itself in constant pursuit of sustainable funding. Although we are a unit of a university department, we are given a small amount of programming support, about one-seventh of our overall need. As a result, we are often in the same financial situation as our community partners, but we are able to move forward because we use volunteers from the community, barter services with artists and organizations, and set up a series of programs that take turns sharing the financial burden. We also work with artists and scholars who reduce their fees because they believe in the work that is being done.

The experience, expertise, and commitment from our constituents and collaborators are the major reasons why we are able to provide the caliber of artistic and cultural programming we do at low or no cost for our diverse communities. For example, artist workshops are a part of nearly every exhibition. For the members of our communities to attend these workshops, we try to make them low or no cost. All the artists who agree to conduct workshops do so with the understanding that it is about exposure and education, not the bottom line. As a result, they usually slash their fees or donate their fees to the cost of supplies. When workshop fees must be charged, we try to keep them reasonable. It is the expertise of the artist and the experience that they offer our audiences that further cements everyone's commitment to what we do.

Occasionally, we enter relationships with nontraditional nonprofit organizations looking to welcome new audiences but they do not have an outlet to do so. One of our most recent collaborations was with an area radio station that was looking for ways to diversify their audience. Although they have a long history of supporting the arts, they have had little success in the African American community. A series of meetings provided the opportunity to learn more about them and what they were trying to do as well as the chance for them to learn about us, and a partnership was formed. They agreed to sponsor different exhibitions and programming receptions throughout our season in addition to interviewing our artists and advertising our events. In return, we agreed to place their call letters on publicity materials from the shows and events that they sponsor.

Sometimes the relationships come down to simple bartering. Similar to many nonprofit organizations, our small staff is often not enough to implement all aspects of the services we provide. Because we also do not have money to secure additional labor, we often use our volunteers and barter with members of our community. Volunteers who assist us with our publicity (from labeling envelopes to dropping off flyers) are a critical part of the CFAC. Their presence ensures that our information is getting into the communities we serve and they help us meet deadlines.

Bartering is often how we exchange goods and services with members of the community and other nonprofit organizations who serve our constituency. For example, when the local chapter of a national Black mother's organization wanted to use our facilities to hold meetings and workshops in, we understood that room rental fees would become cost prohibitive over time and counterproductive to what they were trying to do. In lieu of paying the rental fees, they agreed to assist us in bringing their constituency to the CFAC through volunteering, directly advertising to their members, or planning organized trips. We also agreed to continue to explore future collaborative opportunities.

Principle 4: The Young and the Wise Can Sometimes Outdo Academia

Youthful insight combined with the experience of elders can often outthink any academic. This principle is particularly true when it comes to programming for young people. The bottom line is that children know what they want, the elders know what they need, and no amount of research can match the results when you listen to both communities, combine their thoughts, and have them critique it. This technique is particularly successful with our Illuminate the Arts Project, an arts experience program that seeks to enrich the lives of children of all ages by offering state-of-the-art workshops in the visual, performing, and literary arts.

The overall objective of the Illuminate the Arts Project is "to introduce the disciplines of theater, poetry, dance, and the visual arts to young people, giving them the basic concepts and fundamentals of elocution, movement, written expression and studio arts,"[11] The children experience these art forms in a manner that allows them room to work at their own pace and abilities. By exposing students to these disciplines and providing the setting for them to find their own creative voices, the children become more confident in their abilities and it raises their self-esteem.

The teachers and artists who work at our camp reflect the racial and cultural backgrounds of the children who attend the camp. We are deliberate in this endeavor because we have found over the years that the children respond better to people who look like them; more importantly, we are told by their parents, grandparents, and guardians that this is what they need. They need to be able to see their face reflected in the teachers and artists and to experience culturally specific interpretations of the various disciplines they are learning. This type of feedback carries significantly more weight in terms of its practical applications, far more than any research studies.

Our program seeks to promote artistic exploration, inspire individual creativity, and nurture understanding, skills, and knowledge of art and culture of the African Diaspora and other underrepresented communities. Activities are designed to illuminate each child's inner artist. The environment encourages and inspires self-expression, self-esteem, and elevated academic achievement. The classes that we offer are also a direct result of the feedback from the children, most often determined by their enthusiasm and the light in their faces, but if you ask them directly, they will definitely be clear about what they and their parents think via impromptu conversations and a postcamp questionnaire.

Ultimately, we find that continuing the dialogue with the children and the elders offers far more insight and allows us to grow with and learn from our young creative artists instead of directing them in how they should learn and grow.

How Not to Collaborate

In 2006, a private university formed a partnership with a local elementary school, whose cultural population was largely African American,[12] to have university students in a photography course mentor fourth- and fifth-grade students. The goal of this partnership was to teach the elementary students about photography, have them photograph their world through their eyes or imaginations, and their work would be mounted in an exhibition at the conclusion of the project. In addition to mentoring, the university students had to photograph the project in process.

Although the photographer selected to work with the elementary students was African American, those who ultimately determined the scope of the project were not. In addition, the students' parents and guardians were not involved in this collaboration.[13] The absence of community input in the formulation and implementation of this project led to a number of problems, the largest being the resulting cultural disconnect. Another sobering reality was that this university-based program privileged the academic outcome of the university students over the enrichment of the neighborhood children, supposedly the foundation of the project, and seemed to serve the university students who went into the community rather than serving the members of the community itself.

Ultimately, this project was not about exploring how African American children in an urban environment experience their world because no one involved the custodians of their world—the parents, grandparents, and guardians. They were denied the opportunity to offer their perspectives regarding the lives of their children, which would have informed the organizers about the best way to work with the students and the African American community. That lack of involvement prevented a true investment in this project by the families and their communities. The manner in which this project was implemented also failed to address the racial and cultural location of the students involved. The discourse around this work failed to acknowledge that what we had been invited to view was the work of African American children offering us a snapshot of their world, a world experienced at or below the poverty line and effected by the social services and criminal justice system.

Race and culture as critical elements of arts participation and attendance were virtually ignored.[14] The denial of these factors in the development and implementation of this project speaks to why when Kenneth Clark's Doll Test[15] was recreated by Urban Academy student Kiri Davis, a high school senior from Harlem, the results were virtually the same:[15] Black children still equate being White as positive and being Black as negative.[16] It can be argued that part of the reason for this response is that they do not see themselves mirrored in the outside world in many positive and productive ways. However, it is also because when the opportunity presents itself for them to see who they are as Black children they are often not provided the outlet to explore what that means in a deliberate way.

An example of this disconnect was illustrated at the opening reception, which was held on campus. The campus is largely comprised of pay lots, private parking, and meters, which at the time were being used by university students because the reception occurred just prior to the beginning of exams. Families were left with the option of taking the bus, which has its own series of challenges, or walking. The lack of an organized transportation system to bring parents and guardians to the opening reception resulted in virtually no families or children involved in the project being present at the reception with a room full of university and elementary school personnel lauding its success. It was apparent that the university did not feel invested enough to make sure that community members were present.

Conclusion

These principles inform our exhibitions and programming objectives. Today and throughout our thirty-five year existence, the CFAC has been a unique force in the Syracuse community, manifested through our collaborative work and open dialogue. The CFAC centers the African Diaspora in our work and we recognize that the African American community is critical to our success. The research states and our experience has determined that acknowledgment and celebration of the cultural heritage of our community is key to our success.[17]

We value our role as a place where the community and university can meet, exchange ideas, and pursue creative collaborations in a manner that recognizes and respects our cultural heritages and traditions. Our first priority is and will always be a space where the visual and expressive arts are reflected in the culture of our communities. As a proud unit of the African American Studies Department at Syracuse University, the Community Folk Art Center strives to be a place where cultural expression is explored through engaging the Syracuse community, the region, the nation, and the world.

Notes

1. Community Folk Art Center, *Community Folk Art Center* [exhibition history from 1972–2005] (Syracuse, NY: Community Folk Art Center, 2005).

2. The exhibition was on view from September 13 to October 25, 2003.

3. B. Soren, "Audience Research Informs Strategic Planning in Two Art Museums," *Curator* 43, no. 4 (October 2000): 324–42, http://vnweb.hwwilson web.com (accessed February 19, 2007).

4. Some of those students included Mary Schmidt Campbell, George Campbell, and Bashir Alim.

5. See http://www.aas.syr.edu.

6. Community Folk Art Gallery, *Community Folk Art Gallery* [brochure] (Syracuse, NY: Community Folk Art Gallery, 1980), 1.

7. Community Folk Art Center, *Community Folk Art Center*.

8. CFAC moved to its new space on February 4, 2005. This space also houses the Paul Robeson Performing Arts Company, which is another community service–based unit of the Department of African American Studies.

9. Visions of Mexico/Visiones de México was on view from October 9 to November 20, 2004.

10. The film festival was from October 14–16, 2004. Films included *Every Child Is Born a Poet: The Life and Work of Piri Thomas* (2002), *Susana Baca: Memoria Viva* (2003), *Candombe* (1993), *Resistencia: Hip Hop in Columbia* (2002), *Palenque: un Canto* (1992), and *The Garifuna Journey* (1998).

11. Community Folk Art Center, *Illuminate the Arts Program* [brochure] (Syracuse, NY: Community Folk Art Center, 2006), 1.

12. For professional purposes, the university name is withheld. Artist Wendy Ewald's Literacy through Photography Program inspired this project. Ewald is currently the creative director of the program at Duke University's Center for Documentary Studies. This exhibition was on view from May 9 to December 31, 2006.

13. This was explained to me on January 26, 2007, by the artist involved with the project.

14. J. H. Falk, "Factors Influencing African American Leisure Time Utilization of Museums," *Journal of Leisure Research* 27, no. 1 (1995): 41-60, http://vnweb.hwwilsonweb.com (accessed February 19, 2007); Soren, "Audience Research," 329-30.

15. Clark's study was conducted during the 1940s and the results were presented at the Midcentury White House Conference on Children and Youth, December 3–7, 1950.

16. K. Davis and Reel Works Teen Filmmaking, *Girl Like Me* [film], 2005. Available from Reel Works Teen Filmmaking, 357 Ninth Street, Brooklyn, NY 11215.

17. P. DiMaggio and F. Ostrower, "Participation in the Arts by Black and White Americans," *Social Forces* 68, no. 3 (March 1990): 753–78, http//: www.jstor.org (accessed February 19, 2007); Falk, "Factors Influencing African American Leisure Time Utilization of Museums," 54; Soren, "Audience Research," 333.

2

◆◆◆

An African American
Health Care Experience

An Academic Medical Center and
Its Interdisciplinary Practice

KENDALL M. CAMPBELL

Academic medical centers serve as teaching sites for physicians, research scientists, and other health care professionals. There are students from all disciplines, including the basic sciences such as physiology and pharmacology. There are nursing, dental, medical, and physician assistant students, all with a desire to serve others through providing health care. Education is but one mission of an academic medical center, with research and patient care being two other areas of emphasis. Cutting-edge research aimed at curing chronic diseases and improving quality of life are held in high regard and are well supported. Providing excellent clinical care to hospitalized patients as well as patients in the outpatient setting is also a priority. Academic medical centers are affiliated with large hospital systems that provide a training ground for students. In addition to onsite training within the medical center, satellite clinics and hospital experiences outside of the core facility exist. These experiences allow students to experience health care in a variety of settings to broaden their exposure and strengthen their training.

Academic medical centers have been known to reach out into the communities in which they dwell.[1] Understanding the importance of such activities is paramount to the growing success of both medical center and community goals. There is literature to document relationships of this kind that exist throughout many communities.[2] Within this body of evidence, data suggest that partnerships with other organizations serving the same goal have been difficult to develop.[3] Public organizations, as well as private ones, must work with academic centers to make the shared goal a reality. University-driven community service partnerships are more likely to thrive when there is passion toward the shared goal and when that goal is designed around the patient and not the provider.

It is clearly understandable why academic centers may be less interested in forming community partnerships. Of the three-part mission, clinical services is a main revenue-generating enterprise of the institution. The mission that is the foundation of the academic center is the one that oftentimes garners the most support. Caring for an underserved patient population does not generate the revenue that caring for a predominantly well-resourced, insured patient population provides. In some respects, the thought of an underserved clinic functioning to make a profit is a paradox. Because of an underinsured or uninsured status, it is very challenging to refer these patients for subspecialty care. This leaves many medical problems that could be cared for more appropriately in the subspecialist arena in the hands of the primary care physician. Fortunately, programs do exist to help the uninsured, and those programs are great assets to patient and health provider alike. It is important to recognize that most academic centers probably do realize the financial impact of caring for underserved patients with regard to decreasing emergency department visits and hospital admissions. There are data to show that when communities receive good primary care, many emergency department visits and hospital admissions can be avoided.[4] The suggestion that communities in which primary care providers serve tend to be healthier than those communities that are served by subspecialty providers seems apparent.

There is an ongoing commitment between the university's medical academic center and the local underserved community. This commitment is realized through an interdisciplinary practice designed to provide high-quality, comprehensive care to a patient population that lacks resources. I am a family practice physician employed by a flagship, Research I, land-grant university who sees patients at this practice. I work in minority affairs to promote the recruitment and retention of minority students to the college of medicine. The African American population of the local city is about 20 percent according to 2005 Census data.[5] Approximately 70 percent of this population receives health care in this underserved clinic, and many are uninsured or underinsured. I commonly see patients who have not had routine health care and have had disease slowly destroy their bodies until there is little chance left for recovery. The impact of this problem is quite substantial given the population of African American patients we see and the growing concern for health disparities. Health disparities represent a failure in the health care system to provide equal, high-quality health care to all individuals regardless of race or ethnicity.

Specifically, there are several areas in which African Americans suffer. African Americans aged sixty-five and older were less likely than non-Hispanic Whites to report having received influenza and pneumococcal vaccines.[6] These vaccines help prevent influenza infection and community-acquired pneumonia, which can be severe, life-threatening lung infections in older populations. Compared with White counterparts, middle-aged African Americans are at greater risk of developing type 2 diabetes and have higher blood pressure prior to development of diabetes mellitus.[7] I believe that this is not only because of genetic factors but also because of a lack of preventative care with regard to nutrition education, importance of exercise, and weight management. This is even further evident in cancer screening, particularly cervical and breast cancers. Cervical cancer is a preventable disease if women receive annual gynecological care. African American women are more than twice as likely to die of cervical cancer as White women and are more likely to die of breast cancer than are women of any other racial or ethnic group.[8] My personal experiences show that health disparities exist because of decreased access to care, diminished quality care, and diminished resources availability for African American patients. This further underscores the need for preventative care and health education in the African American community.

The university–community commitment began several years ago, with the realization of a physical structure about eleven years ago. The interdisciplinary model for the practice was created by leaders within the community and the academic center. The partnership employs a multipronged approach to reaching a common goal—improving the health of the patients in the target population. The practice area was noted to be traditionally underserved by local health providers. A goal of 25 percent of the clinic's services were designed for patients who were likely to postpone preventative and regular primary care. The goal for students who rotate through the practice was to promote interdisciplinary learning and community involvement.

Within the partnership are three separate entities, all with connections to the university and designed to provide certain key elements to the practice. These groups include the university's college of medicine, the large local hospital system, and a service organization designed to help provide care and resources for disadvantaged groups. These entities have separate interests within this framework, but the overall goal is community service through improving the care of the underserved patient population in the community. The factors related to the success of similarly designed collaborations range from developing and sustaining mutual trust to shared power and decision making.[9] This partnership has been successful, and this opportunity has been beneficial to patients, providers, and students alike. This chapter will focus on the university–community commitment to this predominantly African American target population from three perspectives: the patient, the medical student, and the physician.

Let me begin with more explanation of the structure of the practice. The practice is located in northern Florida and is a college town with about 224,000 residents.[10] The city is within close proximity to major cities of Florida and has a median income of about $34,000 annually according to 2003 data.[11] The east side of the city houses the majority of the African American community, which is why it was the chosen location for the interdisciplinary practice setting. The interdisciplinary approach to patient care, which I have briefly mentioned, allows this practice to provide comprehensive care to a patient population whose medical care is often heavily dependent on how well social issues are managed. Within this group of providers are a social worker, a pharmacist, physicians, nurse practitioners, and a mental health provider. Student representation in each discipline is also a component.

Each discipline has a specific role within the context of the practice. Pharmacists provide diabetic teaching and consultations regarding medicines in addition to other services. The nurse practitioners are invaluable assets providing care to both pediatric and adult patients. The social worker coordinates programs designed for uninsured patients, which make up a little less than one-quarter of the patient population. Without social work support, resources would be limited if not unavailable. Often, a patient will be scheduled with social work before an initial evaluation by a provider. The medical providers serve as the coordinators of care, facilitating communication among the various members of the patient care team. The administrative and nursing support staff function under the direction of an executive director whose job is to manage internal affairs of the practice as well as promote community involvement and awareness.

There is an ongoing community lecture series for the target community for which providers and community professionals lecture. The lecture series is coordinated by one of the community leaders who has prioritized health issues for the underserved. The majority of the recipients of the lectures are African American, and lectures are commonly held in churches within the target community.

Educating African American Medical Students

In serving the community, health education and patient care are not the only areas of concentration. Medical education is one-third of the mission of the typical academic center, and it is important because providers-in-training need exposure to underserved populations. As a part of my responsibilities as a faculty member, medical school students see patients with me at the practice. This arrangement teaches cultural competence as well as creativity in caring for patients who have minimal resources. There is a partnership among faculty, students, and the community that provides a unique and enthusiastic learning experience. Data exist to show how effective collaborations such as this work well in medical education.[12]

There are low numbers of African American faculty and students in medical education. Medical education is traditionally organized into two years of basic sciences followed by two years of patient care experiences. My teaching role is exclusive to those medical students who have completed the basic science portion of their training. The majority of African American medical students rotate through my community practice, and I know they are attracted to the practice because of our cultural similarities and the unique learning environment. Student evaluations of the experience have been positive, and the desire to have exposure to minority faculty and community involvement expanded to include the first two years of training has been voiced.

There are data to show that minority medical students who learn cultural competence during their preclinical education may have increased cultural sensitivity as practitioners.[13] This has been evidenced through my personal experiences, as students who have rotated with me comment on their ability to connect with patients and be sensitive to issues that pertain to patient culture—from diet and religious beliefs to family traditions and perspectives. Students learn basics with regard to family medicine, receive teaching in caring for the underserved, and learn the importance of outreach to the community and the role of interdisciplinary care. This is important because physicians will serve as part of a health care team and will have to work with other providers in caring for patients. It is especially important in this central Florida community because the climate of the local medical center is not structured around primary care and service to the underserved. The medical center is located in a tertiary care hospital, which means that common conditions are not so commonly seen. More complex cases, which come from all over the state, serve as the foundation for medical education. I believe students should be encouraged to pursue careers in primary care. Attitudes toward primary care have an impact on student career choices and will certainly affect the future of primary care and quality care for African American patients. Within my practice, students learn how to interact with and treat African American patients and the importance of this education as it relates to their service in the medical field. Primary care is the most basic and comprehensive care a patient can receive, and it is the primary care provider who governs access to subspecialty providers. Routine health screening for breast, cervical, and colon cancers come through the office of the primary care physician. Screening of weight, blood sugar, and blood pressure also come through this office, and African Americans tend to be more adversely affected by these conditions and have historically received inadequate or substandard care. These experiences provide students with exposure to primary care and service to the underserved. Students have provided feedback indicating that their experience caused them to take a closer look at service to the underserved. The students and their rotation through the practice are vital components of the community service generated through this partnership between the university and the community.

African American Physicians

African American physicians tend to provide care for African American patients, and we are more likely to work with underserved or low-income patients.

This has been noted in my personal experiences and is documented in the literature as noted from a study of medical students. After graduation, the African American medical students, in large percentages, chose primary care specialties and served minority patients, low-income populations, or rural areas.[14] My personal interests in serving patients comes from a motivation to improve health and education of a people who have gone without and suffered from disinterested providers and poor access to care. The patients I care for look like my family members and share similar problems and experiences. They are oftentimes overlooked, undervalued, disrespected, and thought less of. A recurring theme that I encounter is a sheer absence of preventative care and the ravages of disease in a body that could have been salvaged if treated earlier. It saddens me when I care for patients whose lives are broken when they could have been flourishing with appropriate health education and quality care.

African American physician faculty make up a very small percentage of medical school faculty, with a larger percentage noted to be at historically Black colleges and universities.[15] The numbers are quite low at predominantly White medical schools; about 4 percent. The number does reach about 20 percent at historically Black medical colleges. From reviewing the literature, reasons for the dismally low numbers include minority faculty being undersupported and inadequately mentored.[16] Many leave academia after only four to five years due to lack of support.[17] I receive outstanding mentorship as a junior faculty member because my mentor and I share similar interests in medical education. This relationship thrives as well because my mentor was once my teacher, and I respected him highly while studying medicine at the institution where I serve. The administration has been very supportive of my efforts within the college. I am the only African American male in my department of around forty faculty members and the only African American male in the administration of the college of medicine involved in medical education. African American male students commonly seek me for mentorship and advice, and non–African American faculty gain an appreciation for my abilities and interests.

There is published data to show that minority faculty are encouraged to do more community service activities.[18] This is true regarding my personal experience, as part of my work requirement is based on my involvement within the target community. I view this opportunity as a chance to educate and share health information and would volunteer to serve even if it was not a part of my job description. My involvement ranges from participation in health fairs to performing seminars for local church groups. Some of the topics I cover include hypertension, diabetes mellitus, and weight management. Topics are usually chosen by the group that requests me to speak. One of the most recent topics requested is on faith and healing. I have noted from personal experience that faith plays a large part in how African Americans view health and disease. Community service and outreach have been increasingly recognized as important parts of academic health centers, particularly within the local academic center.

African American Patients

As an African American physician serving African American patients, I have found trust to be important in the doctor–patient relationship. From countless patient encounters, a common theme is the desire of patients to be treated with respect. A study examining the perceptions of cultural competency mirror the same experience.[19] If patients are appreciated and heard, they subsequently develop trust and confidence in their provider. Data establishes the need for being culturally competent when caring for African American patients.[20] Observing and appreciating cultures of different patient populations is the definition of cultural competence. A patient's culture impacts his or her perceptions of medicines, doctor visits, dietary practices, and hospitalizations. Patient history must include an appreciation of how ethnicity, language, tradition, and diet factor into care. This must be addressed for proper patient education, effective clinic visits, and development of trust between patient and provider. From my personal experiences, I have been able to provide better care when all factors affecting care are addressed. For example, my understanding of the traditional African American dinner—which commonly consists of collard greens, corn bread, rice and gravy, and fried chicken—helps shape dietary changes I recommend for patients. I understand salt overuse and how that affects blood pressure and how high blood pressure in African Americans should be approached differently than high blood pressure in White patients. African Americans respond better to salt restriction and to diuretic therapy than some other populations.[21] I know that being African American causes me to be more sensitive and aggressive toward health concerns specific to African Americans. If a physician looks for and appreciates differences in patients, more complete health care can be provided.

I have noted increased compliance in my established patient population when there is increased trust. Based on race alone, I have had African Americans desire to become my patients. Data seem to suggest that trust is easier to establish when the physician and patient are from the same cultural background. I perform routine skin surgeries and other minor procedures in my practice. On many occasions, African American as well as White patients sign the consent form before I have had an opportunity to explain the procedure. Upon asking them why they do this, the reply is usually, "I trust you." There have also been cases in which patients have had other procedures performed with less than satisfactory outcomes. Many times, these patients will want me to do a revision of the previous procedure or a second procedure at the same site because they "feel" that I can do more good than the previous provider. I have established a relationship with these patients and clearly engender trust. Data shows that interpersonal and technical skills of the physician then build on that foundation of trust.[22]

There is concern that African Americans are untrusting of the health care system.[23] This is certainly understandable, as we as a race have been discriminated against and mistreated in all contexts; and health care is no exception. I believe part of this mistrust comes from historical experiences of African Americans with the health care system as well as deceit from public health, specifically in the form of the Tuskegee Experiment. The experiment began in the 1930s and involved about four hundred African American men who signed up with the United States Public Health Service for free medical care. The free medical care turned out to be a study on the effects of syphilis, a sexually transmitted disease, on the human body. Participants were informed that they had bad blood and were not treated for syphilis for years after the treatment came into use. Older-generation African Americans remember this experiment,[24] and I have experienced their general distrust of the medical community. I have had patients tell me stories of how a family member died in the hospital after receiving a blood transfusion and, as a result, refuse all blood products. There have been situations where patients have had negative outcomes in the clinic or hospital setting, and those outcomes have caused them to be suspect of the health care system and refuse care. Mistrust trickles down to subsequent generations, creating a community that harbors distrust for the medical community. This partnership, as it serves African American patients, is instrumental in addressing problems of distrust of the health care system. At our clinic, the patients interact and build a relationship with an African American doctor as well as with a host of other providers and services designed to help them receive the best care possible.

I believe distrust is further alleviated when social issues that complicate medical care are addressed. Social services are one of the most beneficial aspects of our team. Patients want help with social problems, and from my personal experience, the race of the social worker has little to no effect on the services provided or received. Our practice is quite unique because few practices have social resources for patients within the practice setting in our local town. Our social worker has helped patients find resources for monthly bills and medications as well as helping with eye and dental referrals. Monetary resources are especially important, as concern for basic necessities understandably supersede purchasing medications. In addition, having insurance is helpful but may not be as helpful as one would think. I have several patients taking so many medicines that they cannot afford their medicine copays even with an insurance plan.

Patients also receive assistance with completion of insurance and other medically related paperwork. I have a large percentage of patients who are unable to read and find great difficulty with completing clinic forms. This problem seems to be a universal one and transcends race. Because of problems like this, nurses and office staff spend time assisting patients above and beyond their job requirements. The partnership assists in patient referral and provides medical supplies such as dressings for wounds and wheelchairs. Homebound patients receive home visits through clinic outreach. Patient resources through this partnership help us provide comprehensive care to our patients, and the patients are greatly appreciative.

Conclusions

There are many avenues through which further outreach to the community can be achieved. African American patients need to have initiatives developed that will educate them and empower them to be advocates for health issues. In order to further educate and provide need-specific solutions, we must conduct research targeting problems within our own population. For example, the "no show" rate is historically high within our practice. Medication noncompliance is an even broader problem, and the reason is mostly ignorance. I believe this ignorance comes from two places: (1) physicians who do not take the time to educate their patients and (2) patients who do not take the time to receive adequately provided education. As a member of the admissions committee for the college of medicine and an advisor for students who desire to attend medical school, I see too frequently the applicant who thinks medicine is all about the physician. Medicine is about caring for patients, and when physicians as a whole have full appreciation for this, African American patients and patients of all races receive better care.

The importance of the university–community commitment has broad impacts, from medical student education and patient care to faculty enrichment and beyond. One of the most important is the health of the largely African American patient base we serve. There are several areas of specific interest to African American health we are able to combat through our practice. We promote health through emphasizing the importance of routine health screening for prostate, breast, and colon cancers. We educate on reducing risks for cardiovascular disease and obesity. We give lessons on blood pressure and blood sugar control and emphasize the benefits of smoking cessation. The tools that are provided to these patients give them power to take charge of their health. By serving such a large African American patient base, we impact on a larger scale the health disparities that exist among races. The interdisciplinary structure of the practice benefits the students and faculty involved, and most importantly, it benefits the patient population served.

Notes

1. S. Bowen and P. J. Martens, "A Model for Collaborative Evaluation of University-Community Partnerships," *Epidemiology and Community Health* 60, no. 10 (2006): 902–7; F. Brancati et al., "Incident Type 2 Diabetes Mellitus in African American and White Adults," *Journal of the American Medical Association* 283, no. 17 (2000): 2253–59.

2. M. S. Hubbell and M. Burman, "Factors Related to Successful Collaboration in Community-Campus Partnerships," *Research Briefs* 45, no. 12 (2006): 519–22.

3. T. A. Albritton and P. J. Wagner, "Linking Cultural Competency and Community Service: A Partnership between Students, Faculty, and the Community," *Academic Medicine* 77 (2002): 738–39.

4. D. M. Levine et al., "Community-Academic Health Center Partnerships for Underserved Minority Populations: One Solution to a National Crisis," *Journal of the American Medical Association* 272 (1994): 309–11.

5. "State and County Quickfacts, Alachua County Quickfacts," *United States Census Bureau,* January 12, 2007, http://quickfacts.census.gov/qfd/states/12/12001.html.

6. Centers for Disease Control and Prevention, "Health, United States 2002: Hyattsville, MD," *Morbidity and Mortality Weekly Report* 51, no. 45 (2002): 1019–24.

7. National Heart, Lung, and Blood Institute, "Seventh Report of the Joint National Committee on Prevention, Detection, Evaluation and Treatment of High Blood Pressure (JNC 7) Express," *Journal of the American Medical Association* 289 (2003): 2560–71.

8. Centers for Disease Control and Prevention, *Health, United States, 2002* (Hyattsville, MD: National Center for Health Statistics, 2002).

9. Hubbell and Burman, "Successful Collaboration."

10. "State and County Quickfacts."

11. "State and County Quickfacts."

12. Arbritton and Wagner, "Linking Cultural Competency."

13. M. Lee and J. L. Coulehan, "Medical Students' Perceptions of Racial Diversity and Gender Equality," *Medical Education* 40, no. 7 (2006): 691–96.

14. "The Health Care Challenge: Acknowledging Diversity, Confronting Discrimination, and Ensuring Equality," United States Commission on Civil Rights, September, 1999.

15. S. Daley, D. Wingard, and V. Reznik, "Improving the Retention of Underrepresented Minority Faculty in Academic Medicine," *Journal of the National Medical Association* 98, no. 9 (2006): 1435–40.

16. Daley, Wingard, and Reznik, "Improving the Retention."

17. Daley, Wingard, and Reznik, "Improving the Retention."

18. Daley, Wingard, and Reznik, "Improving the Retention."

19. J. Johnson et al., "Perceptions of Cultural Competency among Elderly African Americans," *Ethnicity and Disease* 16 (Autumn 2006): 778–79.

20. R. Benkert et al., "Effects of Perceived Racism, Cultural Mistrust and Trust in Providers on Satisfaction with Care," *Journal of the National Medical Association* 98, no. 9 (2006): 1532–40.

21. National Heart, Lung, and Blood Institute, "Seventh Report."

22. F. M. Chen et al., "Patients' Beliefs about Racism, Preferences for Physician Race, and Satisfaction with Care," *Annals of Family Medicine* 3, no. 2 (2005): 138–43; E. A. Jacobs et al., "Understanding African Americans' Views

of the Trustworthiness of Physicians," *Journal of General Internal Medicine* 21, no. 6 (2006): 642–47.

23. C. H. Halbert et al., "Racial Differences in Trust in Health Care Providers," *Archives of Internal Medicine* 166, no. 8 (2006): 896–901.

24. "Sour Legacy of Tuskegee Syphilis Study Lingers," *CNN Interactive*, May 16, 1997, http://www.cnn.com/health/9705/16/nfm.tuskegee/index.html.

3

◆ ◆ ◆

African American College Students and Volunteerism

Attitudes toward Mentoring at a Title I School

JOI NATHAN

In an era where hip-hop rules the world, where the state of black leadership is in question, and it seems that the hip-hop generation has regarded the Civil Rights Movement as a thing of the past with little currency for today, one has to wonder "What is going on?" Is it really that the hip-hop generation is out of touch with reality or is it that we view activism and community involvement differently than our parents? This chapter will explore the issues surrounding the involvement of African American college students in volunteerism in communities that primarily look like them, at least racially if not economically, as Title I public schools.[1] Although it is important that our children see positive images of themselves in college students, what happens if the college student is not able to relate to the child? We are seeing an increasing number of African American college students who are growing up in the same areas, and in many cases have the same concerns and mind-sets, as their White counterparts and thus are disconnected from the communities served by our program.

Our generation has evolved in ways that no one could have imagined. Has our progression impeded our desire to help our neediest communities? Some would argue that our generation functions in society as if we have "made it." There seems to be no sense of urgency or concern for the plight and forward movement of the community. When all someone knows is a world filled with increasing opportunities and is not taught or sees firsthand the injustices that face the poor of our community, can students really be blamed for thinking that they have arrived? Although it is a false sense of security, it is difficult for anyone to feel obligated to a cause they know nothing about or that they feel does not directly affect them.

"Blacks were seen as having 'made it' when they had a high level of consumption, or when they became as assimilated as possible into White society."[2] Because the hip-hop generation is "the first generation of African Americans to enjoy the fruits of the civil rights and Black power movements,"[3] many members of the Civil Rights generation see us as taking for granted the fruits of their hard work and not being grateful enough to continue the fight for the progression of the Black community. But our world has become increasingly complicated and our culture more diverse since the Civil Rights and Black Power Movements. Many argue how our parents as "young African Americans . . . played an instrumental role in the Black Social Movement. They were the initiators and primary participants in the extension of the Black Social Movement; namely, the Black Student Movement."[4] Because of this, we have been expected to take on the same role of creating (or continuing) a nationwide movement to fight the same injustices in the same way they did. But what has to be noted are the changes the world has endured over the past forty-plus years.

When raising us with these changes, our parents were charged with the task of giving us the skills that would be needed to continue the struggle for equality for African Americans. Because the Civil Rights generation has the experience and knowledge about how to create and mobilize mass movements, it was assumed that at least some of that knowledge would be passed on. But instead of passing on the torch, it has been replaced with bitterness and finger pointing. There are some who argue that the Civil Rights generation did not fulfill their obligation to us and others who blame hip-hop for our downfall, but regardless of how either side feels it is important that we are able to instill in African American college students from all socioeconomic levels the importance of helping our neediest communities. The only way we can encourage them to "give back" is by educating them on the importance of and dispelling the myths associated with volunteering in low-income neighborhoods.

This chapter is based on my experience working with African American students through Youth Programs at Florida State University (FSU). The first section of the chapter provides a general look at Title I schools and more in-depth information about Youth Programs. I then discuss the changing view African American college students have in working in poor neighborhoods. Not all African American college students are eager to volunteer in poor communities as soon as they set foot on campus. This chapter will then explore the increasing importance of individual status and power. Although individuals have always looked out for their own interests and success, it seems that many students today may be more concerned with building their own status in an effort to live the lives of the rich and famous. The chapter then explores ways to inspire African American students to take ownership of low-income communities through community service. The last part of the chapter covers issues that will arise if students are not able to see the bigger picture.

Title I Schools

At the Center for Leadership and Civic Education at FSU, I serve as the coordinator of Youth Programs. Youth Programs places hundreds of college students as mentors at several Title I schools and after-school programs in Tallahassee, Florida. Title I schools are funded under part A of the Elementary and Secondary Education Act.[5]

Title I programs provide:

> financial assistance through State Educational Agencies (SEAs) to Local Educational Agencies (LEAs) and schools with high numbers or high percentages of poor children to help ensure that all children meet challenging state academic standards. LEAs target the Title I funds they receive to schools with the highest percentages of children from low-income families. Unless a participating school is operating a schoolwide program, the school must focus Title I services on children who are failing, or most at risk of failing, to meet state academic standards. Schools in which poor children make up at least 40 percent of enrollment are eligible to use Title I funds for schoolwide programs that serve all children in the school.[6]

An indicator that is used to determine the percentage of low-income families in a community is the percentage of students on free or reduced-price lunch. Currently, the schools we serve, of which between 73 percent and 98 percent of the school populations are African American, have between 78 percent and 98 percent of students who receive free or reduced-price lunch.[7]

Each year, we place hundreds of college students in Title I schools to work with children in the areas of reading, writing, math, and science. Each of our students attends a mentor training session and receives a thorough sexual predator and criminal background check (required and paid for by the Leon County School District) before being allowed to volunteer in the schools. During mentor trainings, students are provided with information about what it means to be a mentor, they are educated on the communities and schools they will be working in, and they receive curriculum training. We cover a range of issues, from how to deal with children when they do not want to do their work to understanding multiculturalism.

Youth Programs began at FSU during the 1997–1998 school year as the America Reads Mentoring Program. The program has since evolved to include the following programs: four America Reads schools, two Governor's Mentoring Initiative schools,[8] and three 21st Century After School Programs. Our programs are open to FSU, Florida A&M University, and Tallahassee Community College students, and our mentors range from first-year students to graduate school students to student athletes. We have been fortunate to have the support of the Leon County Title I/21st Century After School Program, the Leon County School Volunteer Program, and FSU and Tallahasee Community College professors.

This year will mark my fifth year working with the program. For the first two years, I worked as a graduate assistant for our program for several schools and in May 2006 I took over as the program coordinator. I am responsible for the complete oversight of the program. That ranges from working with school district personnel to school principals and university professors. During my time with this program, I have noticed that many of our students have the same concerns regardless of race. Oftentimes, it is not uncommon to hear an African American student react negatively when he or she hears that a White student is apprehensive about volunteering at one of our sites because of its location, but I hear many of those same concerns coming from African American students. Many students view poor communities as places where there is a continuing flow of violence—robbery, gang activity, shootings, and stolen cars, to name a few. Some of our students also have issues with "fitting in." For many of our students, volunteering in a low-income neighborhood is completely out of their element. So being able to feel comfortable and fit in to a new environment is a big concern. Working with an increasing number of African American students with similar concerns as their White counterparts does not mean that they are "sellouts" or "Uncle Toms." But what it should show us is that we have to be as diligent in educating African American students about our communities as we are in educating White students.

Volunteering in Low-Income Communities: The Concerns

"I have to go where? To the projects? Seriously, I have to go to the ghetto?" That was the reaction I received from an African American male that I was trying to convince to mentor some of the young boys in one of our after-school programs located in a public housing community. He had mentored with me the previous semester at Oak Ridge Elementary (about twenty minutes away from FSU) and was great with his student, so I was excited that he decided to return but found myself spending ten minutes trying to convince him that he would be okay mentoring at Griffin Heights (Griffin Heights Apartments is five minutes from campus and is a subsidized housing complex). I thought that I did a great job convincing him of the impact he would be able to make in the lives of the children there but was disappointed when he decided not to continue with the program. There could have been many reasons why he chose to not continue, but based on our conversation, some part of his decision was based on the fact that he would be mentoring in a housing complex located in an area that is notorious for gangs and drug dealers.

Is he wrong for having concerns? Of course not. Students want to feel comfortable and safe when they volunteer. And it is part of my responsibility to not only make volunteers aware of where they will be mentoring and challenge their preconceived thoughts on low-income communities, but also to ensure (as much as I can) their safety (there is a site coordinator at each place we serve, so our volunteers have complete supervision while they are there).

Part of the changing view of low-income communities by some African American college students is partly due to our changing culture. Today's generation of African American college students is composed of members from all levels of the socioeconomic ladder. "In the 1940s, 1950s, and as late as the 1960s . . . communities featured a vertical integration of different segments of the urban black population. Lower-class, working-class, and middle-class black families all lived more or less in the same communities (albeit in different neighborhoods), sent their children to the same schools, availed themselves of the same recreational facilities, and shopped at the same stores."[9] Once African Americans were afforded the opportunity to move to "better" communities, those who could afford to move did.[10] In doing so, the children who moved were no longer attending schools in their old communities and were beginning to be provided access to certain things because of their newfound status (certainly, even African Americans who moved into White neighborhoods still had to deal with racism and many other issues, but the desire was that parents wanted to provide their children access to the same opportunities the White children had). But an issue that continues to surface is that once this status change has occurred there is no attempt by the "select few" to pull others up with them.

The term *Talented Tenth*, coined by W. E. B. Du Bois more than one hundred years ago, still applies to many African Americans today (although Du Bois would later renounce the notion of the Talented Tenth and "Black elites," it is still a term that some use today to describe the "leaders" of Black America[11]). "The Talented Tenth; it is the problem of developing the Best of this race that they may guide the Mass away from the contamination and death of the Worst, in their own and other races."[12] Working to ensure the success of the entire community is not a new concept to African Americans. For hundreds of years, the African American community has been in the business of working to help everyone succeed because all we had was each other, but today it seems that the Talented Tenth "unlike their predecessors . . . may not seem very effective or overly ambitious in their political challenges and confrontations on behalf of nonelite blacks. In our more pessimistic and individualistic age, another spirit of race leadership prevails among elites."[13]

With these issues coupled with rampant media stereotyping of what a poor community is and the same stereotyping going on in schools it is no wonder why some of our college students are afraid to go into these communities. The saying goes that we fear the unknown, and that is the case for many of our students. Many of our mentors have no knowledge and have never had to deal with living or working in poor communities, so they fear what may happen to them if they venture outside of their comfort zone. Mentoring in these communities is a shock to many of our college students. It is hard for them to imagine being unable to buy anything at any moment and they take for granted being able to have their own vehicle or not having to work three jobs to pay bills. Many of the children have endured more in their short lives than many of our mentors have ever had to deal with in their eighteen or twenty years and that is intimidating to the college students. Because they have not had to deal with many, if any, of these issues, they feel that they will not fit in or be able to make a difference because they cannot relate to the children and their circumstance.

Because many of our mentors come to us with these issues and concerns, we make a concerted effort to address these issues with them during their training. By addressing these issues before they begin mentoring, engaging in reflection activities with them, and encouraging open conversations with their coordinators and other mentors, we are able to show them that just because they see a box Chevy on twenty-eight-inch rims riding through a neighborhood does not make it "the projects." Or that just because there are a group of young Black men outside talking does not mean that they are plotting on the best way to rob you. There is hope in that the views of many of our college students are changed once they start mentoring and see how smart and friendly the children are and that the residents of the neighborhoods and housing communities are not focused on harassing them. My hope is that their experience in our program will allow them to become advocates for children from low-income communities and show them that you cannot always believe everything people tell you; some things you have to experience to understand.

It's All About Me

According to Dyson, if you ask some older African Americans there is a

> belief that young blacks are very different from any other black generation. Among esteemed black intellectuals and persons on the street, there is a consensus that something has gone terribly wrong with black youth. They are disrespectful to their elders. They are obsessed with sex. They are materialistic. They are pathological. They are violent. They are nihilistic. They are ethically depraved. They are lazy. They are menaces to society. Right away we must admit that some of these complaints form the rhetorical divide that grows between all generations. Some of these cants and carps are no more than predecessor blues. They are laments of those who come Before judging those who come After.[14]

From the Montgomery Bus Boycott to the Black Panther Party for Self-Defense, their desire was analogous: to promote equal rights for all African Americans. But as with each generation, we are different. In today's culture, hip-hop has taken over the world. The most popular fashions and trends are dictated by rappers, hip-hop moguls (e.g., Sean Combs and Russell Simmons), and "urban youth." Young people from "the streets" are making millions and becoming successful entrepreneurs (starting their own businesses, creating independent record labels, etc). In this "I'm gonna get mine" era, individualism has become a way of life. Of course, one may help close friends and relatives "get on" but as one student told me "society isn't going to do anything for me, so why do I have to do something for them?"

"A person's patterns and norms of behavior tend to be shaped by those with which he or she has had the most frequent or sustained contact and interaction."[15] When we are inundated with images of thirty-two-inch rims and rappers bragging about one hundred carat diamond rings and designer clothes, some desire of wanting what these symbolize is going to arise. And of course, everyone wants to fit in; no one wants to be left out or made fun of, so obtaining these items becomes increasingly important for reputation and self-esteem. According to Johnson:

> Some Blacks associate being *somebody* with having or possessing *something*. So the more they spend, the more they possess, and with the greater monetary value of their goods, the better persons they are. Thus a person's self-worth may be defined in very materialistic terms. If one has no or few lavish, expensive material possessions, then that person is a nobody. Since this society places an extreme amount of emphasis on material acquisitions, and Blacks have historically been denied access to many of these material "goodies," some Blacks may feel denied and left out. Thus, they may attempt to compensate for these feelings by outward appearances and material goods such as fancy clothes, luxury-model cars, lavish homes, expensive jewelry, and the like.[16]

When so much of the focus is on materialism, we should expect nothing less then what we are getting. It is the responsibility of parents and communities to be diligent in educating students on why worldly things should not be tied to their self-worth. In that same breath, our communities must be taught that self-worth should be tied to community involvement and empowerment.

One afternoon, I had a conversation with an African American male about Black history. I started talking about Malcolm X and he had no idea who he was, so I proceeded to ask him a few questions and the only people he could tell me about were Reverend Dr. Martin Luther King Jr. and Rosa Parks. I was amazed that he did not know more but had to realize that not everyone is taught the same things while growing up. Much of the desire in some of the members of our generation is to be seen and accepted in the same way Whites are, so many times learning about (much less volunteering in) poor black communities is not a concern.

Steps to Increase Involvement

Just as "1965 marked an important turning point for the Black liberation movement,"[17] 2007 also served as that turning point. And it is now time that there is an open and honest dialogue about the role the hip-hop generation plays in the current state of Black America. It is not enough to simply degrade or talk down to our generation. The hip-hop generation is intelligent and has a lot to offer to the forward movement of Black people in this country. The challenge is working to find innovative ways to use those talents.

"Although most groups don't have to pay the heavy identity tax that blacks do for negative information circulating in the culture, it is still a gesture of racial maturity to embrace our complexity."[18] One way to embrace this complexity is by listening to our generation. Not dismissing every idea as degrading to the culture because it is not what has been done in the past will allow our generation to feel more empowered and motivated to help the community.

> I've heard enough of [our youth] to know that we ought to be holding them up and sharing with them what we know instead of standing on top of them telling them what they're not doing right. They're doing a lot right and some things wrong. We continue to fail these brilliant, very talented, very creative and courageous young people because they're not saying what our message was. But for Christ's sake . . . we're about to enter the 21st century. Something should be different. And they may be right about some things.[19]

It is amazing the great work that African American college students do when they feel they have support and are provided with the right tools and motivation to get a task done (one such great work was the formation of the Student Coalition for Justice created by and composed of FSU, Florida A&M University, and Tallahassee Community College students to fight for justice for the late Martin Lee Anderson[20]). Unfortunately, college students are often lumped into one group viewed as being lazy and always wanting to party and get drunk, but they shine when given the opportunity. I have had conversations with community leaders who have blatantly dismissed the thousands of hours (fall 2006 mentors volunteered 2,719 hours through Youth Programs) college students have volunteered in schools because they assume that they are being paid or that they only come once a month. I have had to vigorously defend the incredible work our mentors do to help "poor-performing" students (poor performing is defined as students identified by their school as being academically in the bottom 25 percent of their class) catch up to their classmates. Each year, more than three hundred college students will have given thousands of hours to help children become better readers and writers and improve their understanding of math and science. During the fall 2006 semester, we had a total of 191 college students mentoring in schools through our program. Of that 191, only 45 students (or 23.56 percent) identified themselves as African American. Caucasian students comprised 63 percent of that mentoring group. Hispanic students comprised 6 percent, and Asian students comprised 1 percent of our population.

For the spring 2007 semester, out of 153 college students (these are new, not returning, mentors to our program), 35 students (or 22.87 percent) identified themselves as African American. Caucasian students comprised 60 percent of that mentoring group, with Hispanic students comprising 11 percent, and Asian students comprising 2 percent.

One step toward encouraging African American college students to become more engaged in service in poor communities is to show them how volunteering can help create building blocks for future endeavors (e.g., jobs, organizational and campus involvement, fraternity and sorority involvement, and leadership training). Volunteering allows students to spend time in potential future careers, which can help them decide whether a certain career path is for them. And, of course, while doing this, serving allows them to make a needed and lasting impression on their community.

Another step is showing African American students that they are needed in their community. The usual mantra held by some community members and business leaders that "college students are not reliable" and dismissing them as people who really do not matter in the grand scheme of things because they will be gone in a few years is not a great way to get students excited and motivated to volunteer. It is somewhat naïve to expect that students will automatically find the campus volunteer center and immediately start serving in the community once they arrive on campus. As campus administrators, we have to do our part to convey to students that service should be a part of their college experience and not something that is an afterthought once sorority or fraternity interest meetings come around.

African American college students do great work on campus everyday and we must do our part to help them continue to work in the community. Our students have the motivation, desire, and talent to change the world in a major way if only given the opportunity. Part of giving them that opportunity is making them aware of all of the opportunities that are available to them. Encouraging them to mentor and volunteer enables them to use their skills and knowledge in a positive way to help others. I have had many conversations with students who do not volunteer and when I ask them about what would make them get involved in the community, they always focus on being able to do activities related to their major. This shows me that there is an interest and that we need to be more flexible in creating opportunities for them and helping them understand that service is what they make it and that it does not have to only include doing road clean-ups or feeding the homeless.

The Challenge Ahead

"Change occurs only in times of systemic crisis or when sufficient pressure is brought to bear" so that the crisis can no longer be neglected.[21] With the increasing push of high-stakes testing and the end of social promotion, it is becoming increasingly imperative that the children in our communities are provided positive role models and a good education. During my time as a coordinator, it was always great to see the development of the mentor–mentee relationship. I have always been thrilled at how excited each child was to have a college student visit them every week. The children were not just happy to get out of class for an hour but were excited to have a person who was dedicated to them and only them. It made them feel special to have someone spend an hour or two out of the week just to see them. My first year, I did a project with the children focused around dreams and what they wanted to be when they were older. I had children who at the beginning of the year when I asked that question wanted to be princesses, basketball players, and football players, but at the end of the year wanted to be like their mentor or wanted to go to college (I even had a few boys who wanted to be first-grade teachers). Allowing the children to see themselves in college students is an amazing thing and provides them with a different viewpoint in life. It shows them that there is nothing wrong with being smart and that college is a possibility for them.

If we do not prepare our college students to lead our community in the next few decades, our interests and voices will become increasingly diminished. I have watched student leaders work with freshman and groom them into the next campus leaders. They would take that particular student or group of students under their wing and make sure that they made the right connections. The leaders would lobby on their behalf to obtain positions within the most important campus organizations. They would start them at the bottom and work with them to ensure that they gained the skills needed to move up the ladder. Before you knew it, three years later that freshman was student body president. Just as I have seen members of student organizations groom new members to take on certain leadership roles on campus, we must take on that same mentality.

"Inasmuch as the survival of African Americans is dependent upon each generation's ability to challenge and correct social injustices, methods and vehicles must be devised to ensure that young African Americans are culturally informed."[22] It is the responsibility of the Civil Rights generation and the hip-hop generation to make sure that we are passing on the culture of Black America to this new generation. And that means teaching them everything from the roots and essence of hip-hop to inspiring them with stories of the great African nations—

Ghana, Mali, and Songhay. We are the only ones who can guarantee our survival and ensure that our culture and history are preserved in the hearts and minds of generations to come; if we are too selfish to see the impact that we can have in the world and in our community, we will continue to fight one another and forget about our poor communities in the same way America has.

Notes

1. The purpose of Title I is "to ensure that all children have a fair, equal, and significant opportunity to obtain a high-quality education and reach, at a minimum, proficiency on challenging state academic achievement standards and state academic assessments." Information regarding the purpose, appropriation, school improvement and the state administration of Title I can be viewed on the U.S. Department of Education's Web page: http://www.ed.gov/programs/titleiparta/legislation.html.

2. H. P. McAdoo, "Upward Mobility and Parenting in Middle-Income Black Families," *Journal of Black Psychology* 8, no. 1 (August 1981): 1-22.

3. B. Kitwana, *The Hip Hop Generation: Young Blacks and the Crisis in African American Culture* (New York: Basic Civitas Books, 2002).

4. K. S. Jewell, "Will the Real Black, Afro-American, Mixed, Colored, Negro Please Stand Up?: Impact of the Black Social Movement, Twenty Years Later," *Journal of Black Studies* 16, no. 1 (September 1985): 57-75.

5. Improving basic programs operated by local education agencies (Title I, Part A). U.S. Department of Education, http://www.ed.gov/programs/titleiparta/index.html (accessed December 10, 2006).

6. Title I, Part A.

7. GreatSchools: The Parents Guide to K–12 Success (1998-2007), http://www.greatschools.net/search/search.page?state=FL&q=Tallahassee&type (accessed December 10, 2006).

8. The Governor's Mentoring Initiative, also known as the President's Focus on Achievement Mentoring Program, was established in "January 2006 as a part of former Governor Jeb Bush's Access and Diversity Initiative. This program was created as a way to provide incentives to traditionally underrepresented students. The curriculum used in this program encourages middle school students to attend college and emphasizes that higher education is attainable." For more information on this program visit Florida Campus Compact at http://www.floridacompact.org or visit the Volunteer Florida Foundation at http://www.flamentoring.org.

9. W. J. Wilson, *The Truly Disadvantaged: The Inner City, the Underclass, and Public Policy* (Chicago: University of Chicago Press, 1987).

10. Wilson, *The Truly Disadvantaged.*

11. J. James, *Transcending the Talented Tenth: Black Leaders and American Intellectuals* (New York: Routledge, 1997).

12. W. E. B. Du Bois, "The Talented Tenth," in *The Negro Problem: A Series of Articles by Representative Negroes of To-Day.* http://teachingamerican-history.org/library (accessed January 19, 2007).

13. James, *Transcending the Talented Tenth.*

14. M. E. Dyson, *Race Rules: Navigating the Color Line* (Reading, MA: Addison-Wesley, 1996).

15. Wilson, *The Truly Disadvantaged.*

16. R. C. Johnson, "The Black Family and Black Community Development," *Journal of Black Psychology* 8, no. 1 (August 1981): 35-52.

17. A. Shawki, *Black Liberation and Socialism* (Chicago: Haymarket Books, 2006).

18. M. E. Dyson, *Is Bill Cosby Right? Or Has the Black Middle Class Lost Its Mind?* (New York: Basic Civitas Books, 2005).

19. Quote from Afeni Shakur, mother of Tupac Shakur in Kitwana, *The Hip Hop Generation.*

20. Fourteen-year-old Martin Lee Anderson died in January 2006 in a Bay County, Florida, boot camp. Anderson died after a severe beating by several boot camp guards. The Student Coalition for Justice was formed to help see that justice is served and that all persons involved in Anderson's death are held accountable. Since its formation, the coalition has hosted several marches and sit-ins and most recently has urged all students to not spend their spring break in Panama City, Florida. You can find more information on the fight for justice for Martin Lee Anderson at http://justiceformartin.tripod.com.

21. R. C. Smith, *We Have No Leaders: African Americans in the Post-Civil Rights Era* (Albany: State University of New York Press, 1996).

22. Jewell, "Will the Real Black?"

4

◈ ◈ ◈

Prejudice, Pitfalls, and Promise

Experiences in Community Service in a Historically Black University

JEFF BROOKS

Sociologists place issues of race and ethnic relationships and social stratification as primary concerns for their discipline. While service-learning only recently started at Fayetteville State University, our school has a long history of engaging students in a wide variety of community services programs so that they can improve their location in the stratification hierarchy. Hence, I am in a good position to share some insights on race and community service. A key issue in this chapter discusses whether minority (African American) students encounter prejudice or discrimination when they are sent to do community service work or service-learning activities. Whereas a considerable body of literature is available on the value of community engagement to educational outcomes, there is not much information focusing on the situation of African American students. For this reason, the issue of race and community service merits more attention. With this task in mind, this chapter presents an initial step that aims to shed some light on neglected topics and hopefully to stimulate research and program changes.

This chapter presents an ethnographic assessment of approximately two decades of sending students from Fayetteville State University, an institution of the historically Black colleges and universities (HBCU), to serve their community. Ethnographic studies provide qualitative details of events and statements made by the people being studied.[1] A classic ethnographic study, *Fun City: An Ethnographic Study of a Retirement Community*,[2] serves as a model for the study presented in this chapter. The qualitative approach used following is also

53

called "grounded theory."[3] Ethnographic and qualitative approaches often precede the use of more rigorous methodologies and are extremely useful to developing theory, policy, and building better practices. These research philosophies provide the framework for this project to examine if race discrimination against Fayetteville State University students occurs. This method also allows an evaluation of current practices and problems. The goal is to present a model to help university programs and agencies in the community work more closely together, educate a larger number of students, and help prepare those students to join the workforce with the skills needed. Results of qualitative interviews about racial prejudice provided by both faculty and students will be presented as support. An additional topic considers if this minority institution and others like it encounter a prejudice of prestige or racism. The chapter also includes a brief discussion of some problems and pitfalls in our university's practices and proposes a "best-practice" conceptual model for assessing where community representatives would be better integrated as stakeholders.

Most individuals probably already hold favorable attitudes about community service activities by students and are familiar with the general topic(s). Some of the various terms that apply to the following study include service-learning, internships, field education, and community service. Simply stated, there are many benefits for students who engage in community service activities as well as additional benefits for the university, agencies hosting the students, and the larger community. The goal here is to augment the available literature focusing on the experiences of African American students, because it remains sparse, and to encourage others to challenge arguments that community service activities by minority students and institutions have been dormant for two decades.[4]

Issues that motivate some of the research about African American students, such as student retention,[5] civic orientation,[6] and identity theory,[7] are helpful background for this study. However, my research focuses on discussions with faculty and students about racism encountered by students while doing community service. Results of these discussions provide reason to be optimistic, as there appear to be few risks of exposing students to racism when engaged in community services. These interviews also provide a suggestion as to why racism has rarely been encountered. In addition, comments from both the faculty and representatives from the community service agencies provide some valuable information about problems or pitfalls. Finally, the chapter concludes with some suggestions for pulling together all the stakeholders and adding school administration to these practices in order to engage more students in community service.

A Sociological Assessment of Minority Students in a Southern City

Langton and Kammerer provide a useful guide for sociology programs to follow in establishing or revising programs.[8] Social justice is the topic of their book;

therefore, it is also relevant to discussions of race relations and social stratification. I mention it here as social justice is the mission of the HBCU. Social justice also opens the door to the need for cultural competence.

This qualitative report is based on collegial discussions with eight faculty and seven students from what we call the Upper Cape Fear River Region of North Carolina. Faculty members sharing information make up a very diverse group of Africans, Whites, African Americans, and an Asian person. Students' responses come from a sample of convenience, targeting only African American students in the form of exit interviews/discussions. All of the students interviewed are female. They are upper-level students, but three are nontraditional age. They volunteered to talk about race relations during their community service experiences upon completing the service. This African American female group overrepresents females but our student body is predominantly Black females with many nontraditional-aged students included in the upper division. Documents and qualitative data from the individuals representing the community agencies include those of both White and Black races. The matching of student race with agency supervisor race is a point to be considered.[9] A limitation of the information from students is that all seven students report a match for race and gender.

Because this is an ethnographic study, it is appropriate to include a brief discussion of a profile of the community.[10] Fayetteville State University is a member of the sixteen-campus system in the University of North Carolina including about six thousand students. The university's charter requires schools to keep tuition low. The socioeconomic background of Fayetteville State University students is that they are predominantly first-generation college students, and more than four out of five rely on financial aid (typically student loans) to pay tuition. Unlike the larger universities of the United States, most students reside in the nearby community and intend to stay there after graduation.

U.S. Census Bureau data reveal that the institution serves a diverse and financially disadvantaged community.[11] Most students live in or near Cumberland County. About three hundred thousand people now reside in the county, with the adjoining counties being predominantly rural and less densely populated. Cumberland County and Fayetteville serve as the region's economic center. The area has government agencies, numerous medical facilities, and one of the state's highest-density shopping and service regions. A devitalized downtown with pockets of poverty is a candid description of the city. Because many jobs are in sales services and restaurant services, the Census data on income is predictably low and poverty rates are high. In 2005, the median income for the county was $39,019, with 19 percent of the residents living in poverty. Poverty rates for children under eighteen is 27 percent, and the rate for female householder families is 41 percent. Census data reveals the community is about 36 percent African American, which is about three times the national rate. The data indicate that Hispanic persons make up about 8 percent of the population, which is much lower than the rate in the state or nationally.

As expected from the income and poverty rates, educational attainment statistics for the region are lower than the state or the national statistics. Only 8 percent hold advanced degrees, with another 14 percent holding bachelor's degrees. Local crime rates are high, and recreational facilities are inadequate. Finally, racial tension is clearly evident in local politics. The city did recently elect the first African American mayor, but a White mayor replaced him in the last election. This candid description of the community setting should help explain why social justice is important to Fayetteville State University. There is an urgent need to examine social justice for minorities, which was made abundantly clear by what happened in New Orleans when Katrina hit our coastline. Helping minority students train for professional careers is one way to address these problems. It is the reason this school was founded over a century ago.

There can be no doubt that racism is difficult to study. My approach utilizes Goffman's work to gain insights about race relations.[12] Goffman developed a concept he calls "stigma," and it appears to explain the report of low rates of service activities on HBCU campuses mentioned previously.[13] It seems reasonable to suggest that there is a stigma or negative connotation attached to the phrase "community service." Several brief surveys of Fayetteville classes support this contention. The stigma apparently occurs because individuals convicted of crimes often receive sentences for community service. A second example is that the school's policy on student misconduct states that students must do community service as a form of punishment. Another example is a faculty member who says that he will be "off campus doing community services, not because I have been convicted of a crime, but because all university professors are expected to engage in community service activities." The point is that if the term community service is associated with crimes and punishment, community service may be something young Black individuals avoid doing. Many African American students feel the criminal justice system discriminates against their race and are aware of how frequently a social science textbook contains predictions saying one in three Black males born today can expect to go to prison in his lifetime.[14] Research on stigmas is clearly needed, or adopting the phrase "service-learning" may be a worthwhile strategy.

Method

Methods include an ethnographic approach and the use of qualitative interviews with faculty and students. Another source of information is our master's degree in sociology because it allows students to select an optional practicum requiring 150 hours of community service. Community staff members could not be interviewed for this report, but this source reveals that more agencies express interest in having students than are available. Interviews with faculty from other departments and their documents from the agencies also reveal there is a shortage of students willing to do community service, as voiced by agency members. Interviews with faculty and students asked about their experiences with prejudice or racism. The interviews with faculty also offer more information in order to identify problems and pitfalls in our current practices.

Seven undergraduate students shared their perceptions about racism, which came from exit interviews after completing a new internship elective in sociology. Because this report is a pilot project, I could not contact students from other programs or any alumni for the study. Fortunately, I serve on a university committee around student engagement that requires me to evaluate programs. In addition, I have an established rapport with virtually every faculty member supervising community service activities in other departments in our liberal art program. Fifteen people in total were willing to have candid discussions about experiences with prejudice or discrimination.

Interviews with faculty serve as an indirect source for exploring whether students experienced racism during community service projects. Faculty interviews were qualitative with a specific goal of asking about having heard any reports or written records of prejudice or discrimination during the time they supervised internships. Then, they were asked if contacts with agency representatives provided any indications or reasons to be concerned about racism, sexism, or any other problems. The interviews also included a discussion about whether there were any problems generally, and then the faculty discussed any pitfalls in their programs. These discussions provided information needed to achieve the second goal of this project: to identify better practices.

Interviews with faculty include five tenured faculty members who have years of experience with internships, field education, or community service courses in sociology, social work, and criminal justice programs. An additional three new faculty also participated. Students seeking training in social work are required to do a semester of fieldwork, and students in criminal justice can enroll in an elective internship course. This gave eight faculty members sharing their perceptions about problems of racism and other issues that they observed while supervising community service courses. Collectively, we have supervised several hundred students. These discussions offer insights that expand what Maike called "a practitioners tale," to include more than one person's experience.[15]

Existing documents and information from the agencies supervising the students collected by the different departments provide some insights about the community voice and, thereby, help complete this ethnographic assessment. These documents show both agencies and students express being satisfied. As stated previously, the voice of the community is loud and can be clearly heard by most of the faculty in that many agencies want more students than we provide. The largest obstacle is that agencies are only open during hours that conflict with students' class schedules. Many students have both jobs and classes, so they want paid internships, which are rare in our community.

To explore experiences about encountering racism, each of the students was asked directly about race relationships during their internship. Questions included if they directly experienced racism or could recall observing it occurring between other parties at the agency. Questions covered race and gender of supervisors and the ethnic background of the clients and staff. These interviews included typical exit interview questions such as overall satisfaction and endorsement of the agency. In all seven of the student interviews, I asked the students if they felt gender and race problems were more common on campus or at the agency. They all responded that they saw or heard more of these problems on the campus than in the agency.

My protocol in recruiting students to have an exit interview was that they were informed it was optional or voluntary and would include questions about racism. Based solely on my observations, the fact that race and prejudice were central in my discussions with students did not appear to bother the students in any way. One point to clarify is they had taken the internship course from another instructor, and grades had already been submitted. I have established a degree of rapport with these seven sociology majors (four with social work minors), and the fact that I have a Master of Social Work degree may explain why students were willing to be interviewed and showed no distress with the subject matter. I used open-ended questions for the interviews. Individual interviews took place in the privacy of my faculty office. Students were informed of the confidentiality of the information and privileges of not answering. I disclosed the dual purpose of the interview as being for my committee work and for this chapter. Overall, students appeared to be genuinely interested in the topic and comfortable discussing it.

What is interesting and surprising is that no direct experience of prejudice was reported by any students during these discussions. They also could not recall or did not tell me about observing other problems. They did not report seeing any racism or sexism in the agency. Sadly, they said both were more common on the campus than at the agency. Readers may question the validity and reliability of this kind of interview technique, so I encourage others to explore these issues using more rigorous methods.

During these discussions I uncovered what may explain the lack of any findings in these interviews. Simply stated, they had what one study of service-learning labels as matched race supervisors.[16] When asked to describe the clients served in the agency, the students reported that they were predominantly African Americans from the local community. Overall, in our discussions of internships, students expressed satisfaction with the agency supervisor and were visibly excited that they would be using the supervisors for job references or had been told to apply at the agency after graduation. Clearly, in the eyes of the student, engaging in community service is a valuable activity.

Students in all programs were required to ask for a written review from the agency to receive a grade. These reviews are verified by the instructors with the agency. They are generally favorable reports about our students. Faculty reports and documents on interns reveal the agencies voiced desires to have another student assigned, and sometimes several students are requested. During my interviews with sociology majors, answers to questions about the internships revealed the community agencies were willing to help students to find jobs. In several cases, students report their agency expressed willingness to hire them, and others obtained job recommendation letters or promises to provide one. Unfortunately, as will be discussed shortly, a few irresponsible students and some negative reports do occur, and it is important to address this potentially serious problem. It is an open question how widespread this kind of problem is in the service-learning programs of other schools.

My overall assessment of the quality of the responses when asked about having experienced or observing racism while doing community service is that the students were candid and thoughtful. They would answer my questions about having experienced prejudice, without hesitation, and with body language that revealed no signs of discomfort. Furthermore, I believe the slight hesitation and body language I noticed when I asked about having ever observed race problems at the agency is related to thinking back over the weeks and months to provide accurate information. Admittedly, the nature of recall could make these reports unreliable and social desirability may also be a factor. One point to acknowledge is that the author/interviewer is "minority faculty" (i.e., White at an HBCU), and this raises the issue of mismatched or cross-race interaction effects in our discussions. Nonetheless, I am reasonably confident that these informal interviews generated data about the subjective component of the students' experience and these results are both valid and reliable.

Faculty discussions took place as informal face-to-face interviews in the office of the faculty member being interviewed, with one taking place over the phone. Faculty members were asked if they could recall during all of the time they had been supervising students if there were any students who reported experiencing racial prejudice while in the agency. Not one faculty member reported students raising this issue. In fact, only one problem was reported, and it was sexism. Given the absence of any reports about racial prejudice being mentioned by our students discussed previously, I contend the congruence of these findings shows a strong finding that overt prejudice is not a widespread problem for our students.

Another question asked of faculty was if they had asked students to report experiencing any prejudice toward them or included these questions in forms they used. None had done either. I hasten to add that a search of available information about service-learning and student internships did not produce any instruments that tap this issue. Calls for cultural competence are increasing and are clearly more common than calls for inquiries about racism, sexism, or other prejudices.

We should not overlook the possibility that students' fears may prevent reporting something that could result in an unsatisfactory grade and/or no credits being earned. An unsatisfactory grade could postpone graduation. It is unfortunate, but I am personally aware of many minority students who justifiably felt they were the target of racial prejudice and did nothing to report it. The same is true of sexism. It would be naïve to accept the findings reported in this chapter as indicators that racial problems do not exist in community service activities. However, findings from this research help alleviate fear that sending minority students to work with minority staff in agencies that serve minority clients causes them to experience racism.

Pitfalls and Other Problems

It should come as no surprise to teachers who have experience supervising community service and service-learning courses that virtually all of our faculty could tell many stories about students failing to do the internship requirements and complaints from agencies about negative experiences with students. Body language and vocal cues exhibited during these parts of the discussions can be described as animated. There is no way to be certain if these complaints about students are race-based issues or whether they are truly about being unmotivated and/or underperforming students. However, we have no good reason to believe they are based on racism. When faculty members finished telling the stories, I asked if they felt the agency complaints could have been influenced by racism; without any hesitation, they responded that racism was not a factor.

We need to examine these complaints more closely. One specific point is to start keeping data on the complaints that includes the race of the agency supervisor and the student. Having this data may reveal the kind of overrepresentation of Blacks that is seen in data about our criminal justice system. Given racial tensions are clearly evident in local politics, it seems logical that racism could be encountered by students.

Points mentioned about faculty members not asking about racism or sexism made earlier are not meant to be a harsh evaluation, as research of available literature on racial discrimination, prejudice, or sexism was not successful. A search for questionnaires on service-learning experience that are published or in the public domain lead to the conclusion that students as a whole are not being asked about these issues. However, the fact I did see several recent dissertations holds some promise for the future. Racial problems, sexism, and the issue of cultural diversity experiences all appear to be overlooked in service-learning literature and practices. The literature search found one book that called the need for cultural diversity "an educational imperative."[17]

While this investigation provides reasons to feel better about the issue of racism, it reveals that our students are not being exposed to enough training in classes or training off campus about cultural diversity issues and experiences. With this point in mind, I would give our school a passing grade but say it needs to improve dramatically in the area of teaching cultural diversity. Hogan provides a useful guide for developing competence on cultural diversity.[18]

It is important to provide some additional theoretical background about Erving Goffman's dramaturgical approach to analyzing human interaction to explain what is discussed next.[19] Goffman's approach recognizes that people may act differently in public arenas (front stage) than they do in more private settings (backstage behavior). According to Goffman, people seek to present themselves in a favorable light to others by conducting themselves in socially acceptable performances. His theory helps explain how a professional hides personal beliefs. As context for this idea, consider three recent examples in the media. One is the controversy surrounding Michael Richards (television actor most noted for his role as Kramer on *Seinfeld*) who engaged racial slurs during a stand-up comedy routine. Another was Mel Gibson (movie actor and director) allegedly expressing anti-Semitic sentiments. A third is the Isaiah Washington (television actor formerly on *Grey's Anatomy*) controversy about using an antigay epitaph about a coworker. While only the first example was about race, each reveals the nature of people being able to project a front-stage performance that does not reveal private thoughts (backstage behavior) for long periods. These private thoughts only become troublesome for the individual when they become public such that other people become aware of these hidden and socially unacceptable beliefs.

Some contacts between faculty and agency staff are mentioned next using the dramaturgical approach.[20] The stories may be anecdotal, and I cannot unequivocally say they are race problems. The point is merely that these qualitative reports make it obvious that there are problems we need to address, as they have an impact on opportunities for service placements and social justice. Interviews with faculty brought out several comments from faculty members about details of a few experiences with agencies that gave negative evaluations of a student or students. One public agency manager made negative statements to the program director about a student, the program, and the whole university. Another problem was an agency staff person made negative comments to one faculty member about another faculty member and the students. In both cases the complaints came from a White person about an African American person.

One faculty member noticed what might be racism when he said it appears White persons in the community frequently contact the White college in town first, and then are referred to our school by his colleagues at the other school. This may reveal the hidden quality of racism. For lack of a better term, I call this a kind of institutional racism where an institution is the object of prejudice and discrimination. The point is we need to examine if racism occurs toward the institution such that the school and the students/alumni suffer from prejudice and discrimination. School prestige is clearly something that needs to be studied. An openly discussed issue on our campus is that there is a double standard for minority students and minority institutions. The perception is that our institution is substandard and has only weak students. It is much lower in prestige than private schools such as Duke and other public schools such as the University of North Carolina at Chapel Hill or North Carolina State University. These perceptions are widespread, and they damage our gifted students who are as good as students from the other schools but are being prejudged as inferior to those going to White colleges. An example of the problem is reported by a White faculty member who attended a national conference and asked an African American professor staffing an exhibit recruiting students to new a Ph.D. program for information; this person was told that no students from our school should even waste their time applying.

My contention is that research should be conducted to investigate the pervasiveness of these prestige perceptions and if they are indicators of racism. A solution to biases inherent in prestige and status evaluations of universities must be brought into public discourse. This prestige problem is universal, as it applies to every state. Every report about the best colleges unjustly perpetuates perceptions that only elite colleges can produce a well-trained workforce.

One truly sad point in this ethnographic study is the story of one faculty member who broke down in tears as he told me about an incident with a high-status public official from a large city agency. The official (White) told the faculty member (White) that the student (Black) was terminated, and no other students from the department or the entire school would be accepted at the agency. We do not know what was said directly to the student. This point brings out what is possibly the single biggest problem or pitfall. It should be obvious that whatever happened, the reputation of the faculty member, his department, and the school had been damaged. Lest we forget, the student was probably stigmatized. The collateral damage here is one negative experience with a student prevents future training and employment for all other (gifted) students in this agency and possibly in other agencies of that official's social network.

Another "horror story" involved a student who fabricated or falsified her internship completely. Imagine you work at an agency, and a school inquires about a student who never came to the agency and forged documents about serving in the agency! Various forms of student misconduct were reported by virtually all the faculty members, and this reveals that a lot of agencies have negative experiences with our students. This recurring finding is perhaps the biggest pitfall of our community service/service-learning programs. Clearly, we need to study the consequences of placing a poor-performing student for any and all kinds of collateral damage they may do. Some kind of screening of students and better supervision by the faculty members is badly needed. My colleagues at other schools assure me that these problems are not specific to our school, but I fear we need to be extra vigilant in protecting the reputation of the school and preventing the collateral damage to the hundreds of good students graduating every semester.

Thinking back over my twelve years supervising students and some discussions with faculty members in past years, some of the complaints we heard from agencies were across same race or mismatched race between students and supervisors. The only complaint I heard about a fellow faculty member was in a case of mismatched race between the faculty member and the agency representative. This completes what we can contribute to the issue of race.

Before I conclude this report, there are a few more points within one general topic that deserves attention. We must improve the connections between the different programs and the community. It has become obvious to me that little communication takes place across the disciplinary and department boundaries; there is a need for a centralized university office that can serve as the entry point for agencies. I hasten to add that there are some cases where there are no direct contacts between the faculty and the agency. Agencies and teachers should collaborate more often than they currently do. With these points in mind, I will introduce a service and service-learning model for improving university–community relationships.

A Grounded Theory Model for Service and Service-Learning

By applying a grounded approach to the development of school and agency learning partnerships, it becomes apparent that a university-wide community integrated model needs to be created. Glasser and Strauss argue that a grounded theory approach can identify observable events, adds perspective, is understood by all participants, and thus should produce a foundation for action. Hence, the fact that community agencies are not well integrated with what is taught, individual departments are not cooperating, and a central administrative office does not exist, the grounded approach tells us what we need to do if we are to develop the best practice model of service and service-learning where all stakeholders actively participate in the entire process:

1. Increase communication between university faculty and community staff.
2. Include a more prominent position for participating community agencies in classrooms and learning objectives.
3. Encourage student participation in the entire process of forming university–community relationships.
4. Modify the traditional method of establishing agency contacts through individual academic departments by adding a centralized office. Make this central office a place for community agency contact and for students to find information.
5. Make this teamwork approach dynamic and fully recursive or interactive.[21]

Consequently, a grounded theory model of service and service-learning could be self-correcting and self-perpetuating because it incorporates multidirectional paths of communication among all participants. Agencies, faculty (especially new faculty), and students could all use the centralized office where students could search for agencies, and agencies could post announcements for students. Data collection on students and agencies could also be more systematic.

Discussion

Results revealed virtually no racial tension is being experienced by our students. Just the same, I urge others to give this issue more attention than we have in the past. Students and faculty gave no reports of prejudice or discrimination, which helps alleviate fears about sending students out to do community service. However, several concerns remain. One is that widely held perceptions about prestige and status exist for different schools. Another is that there is collateral damage being done by irresponsible students that hurts responsible students/alumni. These points are not unique to our HBCU, but they take on added significance if our students must add them to any racism they confront in the battle to find jobs.

There is a need for more training in cultural diversity because a self-segregation of local community may be occurring. This point needs to be examined more closely. My fear is that a lack of cultural diversity experience results from this self-segregation and possibly prevents our alumni from competing for the best jobs available. As is typical of most research, this project generated more questions than we could answer. Do students pick an HBCU because of proximity and price? Or, is it a race-based self-segregation or another reason?

One of the more practical findings from this project is the need for a central office on the campus. The office should be created so community agencies can easily contact the school when they are interested in recruiting student interns. Liability issues must be overseen by this office. There is currently a highly disjointed pattern of individual departments or individual faculty repeatedly reinventing the wheel. A better model would include having faculty and administrative offices establish closer ties. An institutional memory for information would be an asset, and a centralized database of agencies with "intern" job descriptions is badly needed. Data collection procedures could also be centralized. All research must go through an Internal Review Board process, but much of the service in the community is essentially laissez-faire.

The main issues for faculty are that ties between faculty members and community agencies appear weak, and irresponsible students put the entire school at risk of negative labeling and informal sanctioning. Perhaps the most vital issue here is already within the power of the faculty because they could establish ways to screen out the poor performers that may harm the prestige of the school and provide fuel for racial stereotypes.

Conclusion

Qualitative data reported here tentatively tells us we need not fear that students face racism when we send them out to the community in race-matching agencies. Our hearts tell us there is still much to be done in the realm of race relationships and social justice. This HBCU has been successful in helping educate minority students for participation in the workforce, and some of those workers are alumni who are happy to help educate more workers. However, students and agency staff reported serving a predominantly Black population such that our ethnographic approach yielded a pattern of self-segregation. This forces us to raise questions about cultural diversity training. Are we truly training our students to compete for jobs in the larger society?

Other conclusions from this ethnographic assessment are that candidly reported constructive criticisms reveal there are places to improve the training of our students. In addition, closer ties with the agencies and community are badly needed as the voice of the community is strong but, on coordinated campus efforts, is muffled at best.

Notes

1. J. B. Williamson et al., *The Research Craft: An Introduction to Research Methods* (Reading, MA: Addison-Wesley, 1982).

2. J. Jacobs, *Fun City: An Ethnographic Study of a Retirement Community* (Prospect Heights, IL: Waveland Press, 1974).

3. B. G. Glasser and A. L. Strauss, *The Discovery of Grounded Theory: Strategies for Qualitative Research* (Chicago: Aldine, 1967).

4. R. T. Schaefer, *Racial and Ethnic Groups* (Upper Saddle River, NJ: Pearson Prentice Hall, 2006).

5. Schaefer, *Racial and Ethnic Groups.*

6. J. Lott, "Civic Orientation Predictors of Black Students: An Exploratory Study," *Dissertation Abstracts International* 66, no. 7 (2006): 2510A. (UMI No. 3184079)

7. M. C. Pickron-Davis, "Black Students in Community Service-Learning: Critical Reflections about Self and Identity," *Dissertation Abstracts International* 60, no. 7 (1999): 2406A. (UMI No. 9937775)

8. P. A. Langton and D. A. Kammerer, *Practicing Sociology in the Community: A Student's Guide* (Upper Saddle River, NJ: Prentice Hall, 2005).

9. L. Jucovy, *Same Race and Cross Race Matching (P/PV Rep.)* (Washington, DC: U.S. Government Printing Office, 2002).

10. Jacobs, *Fun City.*

11. U.S. Census Bureau, http://factfinder.census.gov (accessed January 22, 2007).

12. E. Goffman, *Presentation of Self in Everyday Life* (New York: Doubleday, 1959); E. Goffman, *Stigma: Notes on the Management of Spoiled Identity* (New York: Simon and Schuster, 1963).

13. Goffman, *Presentation of Self.*

14. H. Allen et al., *Corrections in America: An Introduction* (Upper Saddle River, NJ: Prentice Hall, 2007).

15. I. P. Maike, "Race, the College Classroom, and Service Learning: A Practitioners' Tale," *Journal of Negro Education* 7 (2003): 230–40.

16. Jucovy, *Same Race.*

17. J. A. Galura, P. A. Pasque, D. Schoem, and J. Howard, eds., *Engaging the Whole of Service-Learning, Diversity, and Learning Communities*(Ann Arbor, MI: OCSL Press, 2004).

18. M. Hogan, *Four Skills of Cultural Diversity Competence* (Belmont, CA: Thompson Brooks/Cole, 2007).

19. Goffman, *Presentation of Self.*

20. Goffman, *Presentation of Self.*

21. Glasser and Strauss, *The Discovery of Grounded Theory.*

Part 2

Community Service-Learning

Michelle R. Dunlap

When I read an early version of Don Blake's final word, about how his parents made him return the weekly twenty-five cents that would have provided milk and bread for his family in favor of his sharing his labor as a matter of Christian service, I found myself gushing with tears. I was reminded of that same expectation in my own family. My grandparents and many members of their communities had migrated from West Virginia and Georgia in the 1930s and 1940s in hopes of working in the automobile factories in Detroit, Michigan. Anyone migrating from the same community, whether blood-related or not, had to look out for one another. By the time I was born in the 1960s, I had aunts, uncles, and cousins—many of whom I had not realized were not blood relatives until after I was grown. We were all just family, and looking out for one another was as natural as breathing. Then I was reminded of myself as a single parent rearing an African American man-child in the 1990s and in the new millennium in an overarching culture that seemed dangerous to our Black children. My oldest son, whom I adopted when he was three, is now a grown, tall, strong, stately, and intelligent young man who puts me in remembrance of what Don Blake might have been like at the age of twenty-one. I can recall years ago sending my own son back to return money that an elder neighbor had given him for moving boxes or for shoveling snow. I can see my baby looking up at me with bright but curious eyes, with money held tightly in his hand asking, "But why can't I keep this money? I *earned* it."

As I read Don Blake's final word, I was reminded of having to go back to history, to legacy, to duty, to debt, to family, to Christ, and then all the way to heaven and "reaping later the treasures that we sow now" to explain to my eldest child that the bigger reward is in returning the money. There must be almost a half-century between Don Blake's experiences and my own son's. But the tradition of service must be like the blood—or perhaps even the DNA—that flows within cultures that have depended on one another for their very survival from one century to the next, from one day to the next, and from one moment to the next.

As Stephanie Evans so powerfully detailed earlier in her preface regarding the lasting legacy of Septima Clark and her colleagues, we are all the beneficiaries of the sacrifices and the service and justice-minded orientations of traditionally disenfranchised peoples and allies like her. And generations later, our sons and daughters have the opportunity to be inheritors or beneficiaries of these same traditions and sacrifices.

Nonetheless, the collectivistic sharing and service that occurs within the Black community often go unnoticed by the media and by others from outside the Black community who interface with us. Perceiving, understanding, and appreciating this kind of informal service orientation is something that I and the other editors and authors work at constantly, in order to help our students of all backgrounds better embrace and appreciate its significance.

For the past fifteen years, like many of the authors already presented as well as those in the chapters ahead, I have worked extensively with service-learning students engaged in urban, primarily African American, Caribbean, and Latina, communities. For all of those fifteen years, I have been the only African American professor in my department, and the only African American tenured female in the college—a status that is common in academia in general, and difficult, if not impossible, for me to celebrate despite how much I appreciate and enjoy my students, fellow colleagues, and career. Like the other editors and authors of this book, I know a little something about trailblazing. Like many of us, I am a person of color—a woman—sending, for the most part, predominantly White students into a community of color that sometimes they know little about except the stereotypes they have seen on television. I applaud myself for having survived it, especially in my early years as a faculty member, for I knew not the significance of what I was doing until years later. I guess I was young and determined enough. God and the spirit of the ancestors, along with many supporters and allies, girded me up enough to make it work.

Initially I was astounded by the degree of trepidation and anxiety that my students—and to the greatest extent, my White students—had about engaging in inner-city environments. I learned quickly that it wasn't just my students or my colleagues that were challenged by going into the inner city. Having grown up in Detroit in a multiracial family, I would be taken aback at times by some of the faculty and staff I encountered across the country who reported fears, anxieties, and even negative and inaccurate stereotypes as they pondered sending their students to engage in predominantly Black and Latina environments that were different from those with which they were familiar. Their anxieties may have stemmed from their worry that they would not have enough experience to appropriately address or answer their students' needs, questions, and issues that could—and should—arise as they engage in unfamiliar environments. Our edited volume hopefully will assist in the intellectual and emotional preparation of this kind of important community engagement.

Like the challenges outlined in Colette Taylor's introduction, my experiences facilitating service-learning have revealed similar challenges. I have found the challenge of providing effective engagement in African American and other communities of color to involve the following issues: (1) service-learning partners (including students, faculty, staff, and other facilitators of the service-learning process) coming into the community with either very little, negative, or inaccurate knowledge or stereotypes concerning the history, oppression, communication styles, and so on, of African American people and communities; (2) service-learning partners failing to gather an appropriate understanding of the past, current, future, and cumulative systemic and contextual barriers that hinder African American progress in any given community, so that the systemic oppression can be worked on while individuals also are being engaged; (3) service-learning partners not appropriately inviting the community into equal-status partnerships and effectively nurturing those partnerships; (4) service-learning partners taking a heroic posture with respect to community partners; (5) service-learning partners trying to rush the rapport and trust-building process; and (6) service-learning partners taking personally the cautious worldview of African Americans who themselves, their ancestors, and/or their communities were (or still are) exploited by people from the same racial or socioeconomic backgrounds as the partners trying to engage with them now.

I drafted this list of challenges prior to receiving and reading the five chapters that I will now introduce. Having drafted our chapters independently, I found confirmation in the resonance between the challenges I identified and the authors of these five chapters' tendency to present and address these specific challenges. The authors of the following chapters provide insight both into the African American community and effective engagement methods, approaches, and strategies for partnering and engaging with the African American community through service-learning.

Lucy Mule, in chapter 5, shares experiences and methods that work with predominantly White preparatory teachers who engage in service-learning as part of their education certification training. She reveals the importance of assisting these teachers-in-training by providing in-depth knowledge and experience concerning the history and cautious worldview of African American cultures, as well as methods for developing trust through the slow and sometimes painstaking relationship-building process.

In chapter 6, August Hoffman, Julie Wallach, Eduardo Sanchez, and Richard Carifo share their research on predominantly African American college students in Compton, California, who engage in service-learning as they develop and maintain a phenomenal gardening program in the community. They reveal that students who garden with role models and mentors feel more in control of their educations and futures than students who do not engage in these service-learning experiences.

In chapter 7, Troy Harden discusses the flaws and pitfalls of service-learning, especially the kind that "comes in a 'split the scene'" manner that provides only a superficial relationship at best. He discusses his own unique experiences, paradoxes, and ironies as a Black male facilitator of the service-learning process, as well as the ambivalence that many students of color bring to the service-learning process itself.

In chapter 8, Annemarie Vaccaro philosophically questions the ethics of service-learning, not to discourage us from service-learning itself, but to challenge us to think more critically about why and how we build trust and engage with the community.

Meta Mendel-Reyes and Dwayne Mack, in chapter 9, share their experiences taking their students into post-Katrina and post-Rita Louisiana to work with families. Mendel-Reyes, a Jewish White woman, and Mack, an African American man, bring two different yet complimentary perspectives to the experience. They provide a three-pronged, multidimensional model and examine relationships and tensions between themselves and their students, between their students and the community, and among the students themselves while also providing recommendations for others engaging with devastated communities.

I find it an honor and privilege to introduce these nine extremely powerful authors and their chapters. I have thoroughly enjoyed reading, editorially commenting on, and now introducing these five chapters. I believe that our understanding of service-learning and community engagement and our commitment and work within them will never be the same after considering the wisdom within these chapters.

5

◈◈◈

Can the Village Educate the Prospective Teacher?

Reflections on Multicultural Service-Learning in African American Communities

LUCY MULE

Service-learning, as a way of connecting academic learning and relevant community service, has gained prominence in the American higher education landscape since the 1980s.[1] In many departments of education, however, "community" has come to mean mainly K–12 schools within the immediate vicinity of the university or college. Teacher educators in these institutions of higher learning form partnerships with K–12 schools that provide opportunities for service-learning and internship experiences for their students. The professional development school model has been particularly successful at establishing university–school partnerships and involving higher education faculty and students in the education of K–12 students.[2] Few educators, however, have reached out to the community for similar partnerships, despite a growing body of literature suggesting that college students accrue academic benefits as well as a self-awareness of values such as multiculturalism, civic responsibility, and social justice from engaging in community-based programs (CBPs) with ethnic and racial minorities.[3] In encouraging what is now known as multicultural service-learning (MSL), teacher educators are urging their colleagues to engage, especially the preservice teachers preparing to teach African American students in communities through CBPs.[4]

71

This chapter supports the call to engage preservice teachers in CBPs serving African American communities. I argue that CBPs serving African American children are more than responses to perceived shortcomings in the mainstream school system. Community-based programs also function as alternative sites for educational activity[5] and promising sites for teachers preparing to teach African American students. The CBPs that I focus on are education oriented, located in African American communities, and staffed mainly by African Americans. Education here is understood as defined by Murrell as "a total process of promoting the intellectual, spiritual, ethical, and social development of young people . . . stewarding them into capable, caring, and character-rich adulthood."[6] Education-focused CBPs in African American communities exist in a variety of formal and informal, voluntary, and nonprofit groups and organizations that engage in several activities in various settings. These can include religious institutions, after-school programs, grassroots organizations, community centers, local libraries, social clubs, sports clubs, and local chapters of national groups (e.g., Boys & Girls Clubs). Some popular CBPs offered within these structures include Saturday schools, a variety of literacy programs, the rites of passage programs[7] or African American male- or female-oriented programs,[8] and homework and tutoring programs, some operated in partnerships with schools.[9]

The chapter also emphasizes that CBPs are important educational sites that have not been optimally used by teacher educators for teacher preparation and community engagement. If this claim is to be taken seriously, we must ask several related questions. Why is there such little interest among teacher educators to reach out to African American CBPs as sites for community engagement and preparation of future teachers? Why should teacher educators pay attention to CBPs among African American communities? What are the possibilities and challenges involved in using African American communities as sites for community engagement and teacher preparation? How can campus–community relationships involving African American CBPs be strengthened? Answers to these questions are important because they suggest that learning about African American children and effective pedagogy for them can be enhanced if teacher education programs strengthen partnerships with African American communities. In this chapter, I reflect on these questions and review a cross section of literature on the role of CBPs in the education of African American children and youth. I also reflect on MSL in African American CBPs and share insights drawn from my experience as faculty in education involving students in MSL.

Community-Based Programs as Alternative Sites for Educational Activity

In this section, I examine the notion of CBPs in African American communities and present examples of what I refer to in this chapter as "education-focused

CBPs." In many African American communities, CBPs act as bridges between the home and service-providing institutions such as the school. Heath and McLaughlin describe them as "resources that extend beyond family and schools."[10] In African American communities facing challenges such as poverty, urban violence, drugs, dysfunctional homes, and so on, CBPs are critical in supporting the growth and development of young people.[11] Community-based programs also serve as purveyors of African American culture and sites for community building.[12] More importantly, they serve as sites where students experience deeply educational activities in culturally affirming contexts, with the goal of individual and community empowerment. Ball summed up the multifaceted function of CBPs in African American communities:

> Historically, community-based organizations have served as social, cultural, and political spaces in which African Americans have been able to assert their right and their responsibility not only to read, write, and understand, but also to gain new literacy skills needed for them to transform their life experiences. Community-based organizations have also served as spaces where African Americans have been able to contribute their voices to wider projects of possibility and community empowerment.[13]

The fact that CBPs play a variety of roles makes them one of the most influential factors in the education of many African Americans.[14] In highlighting the educational role played by CBPs, it is important to examine some of the educational activities that take place in literacy programs, Saturday school, and other programs mentioned previously. Literature on the subject reveals three unique features, which evoke the popular African adage, "It takes a village to raise a child," and tend to characterize these programs: (1) a holistic view of the learner that advocates a pursuit of intellectual development while also paying attention to social, affective, moral, and political dimensions of development of children and youth; (2) the understanding that race and identity play a significant role in the education of African American children and youth. In other words, race continues to matter in education just as it does in society at large and, as a result, it can be argued that educators of, and educational programs for, African American students must see color in order to be effective;[15] and (3) a pedagogy grounded in culturally responsive practices[16] or what Boykin et al. called the "Afro-cultural ethos,"[17] one that is historically and racially grounded. As the following examples show, these three areas of emphasis are likely to be present in varying degrees in many education-focused CBPs serving African American students.

Ball and Lardner discuss three education-focused CBPs serving African American communities.[18] One specific example is relevant here. The program called Ujima (a Swahili word meaning "collective work and responsibility") meets on two to three Saturdays each month in a church to provide urban African American girls, ages six to eighteen, with language, literacy, and life skills learning activities. The program, with an average weekly attendance of sixty to seventy-five girls, uses the rites of passage model in which African American adult instructors engage the participating youth in several learning activities, including impromptu oral performances, memorized recitations, reading, writing, literature, drama, art, music, dance, and so forth. According to Ball and Lardner, CBPs like Ujima provide African American youth with numerous opportunities to access "adult role models that support them with opportunities to experiment with language and literacy interaction models that not only reflect standards of the dominant society but also standards of the students' cultures."[19] A deeper look at the philosophy, goals, and activities of the Ujima program shows clearly how it reflects the three characteristics of African American CBPs outlined above.

Warfield-Coppock provided further examples of the rites of passage CBPs in African American communities.[20] These programs probably present the best example of instruction for social, affective, and moral development steeped in cultural relevance and empowerment at both individual and community levels. Rites of passage programs are based on traditional African systems of socialization through which youth are mentored into adult roles and responsibilities. These programs can be school and/or community based. Harvey wrote of an after-school manhood development program in Washington, DC, in which "[t]he emphasis is on youths interacting with youths to develop constructive lifestyles and positive solutions to life problems, as well as to recognize their personal and cultural strengths and abilities."[21] In these programs, participating youth are provided with a structure that values and respects them while demanding that they step up to their roles as productive members of the community. These programs are likely to appeal to African American youth who do not always feel validated or valued in a racist system.

The legendary Algebra Project remains an enduring illustration of both the intellectual development emphasis and connectedness to community building and empowerment elements. The project "was born out of one parent's concern with the mathematics education of his children,"[22] but "first took root in Boston at Freedom House, a community-based organization."[23] Bob Moses, the founder of the Algebra Project, "considers higher math to be key to economic equality."[24] The acclaim for the Algebra Project among African American communities is in no small part due to its grassroots nature and its goal of empowering African American students to be successful in mathematics, and hence all schooling. Math success and school success are almost synonymous because of the gatekeeping role that math, especially algebra, is understood to play in the school system. Academic success is of course considered a means of social and economic advancement in many African American communities.

Many education-focused CBPs in the African American communities are like the Algebra Project in the sense that they are sparked by the vision of an individual or a group committed to the intellectual, social, economic, and political empowerment of African Americans. The Books of Hope project in Somerville, Massachusetts, is another good example of a community-based literacy program with humble beginnings.

> In March 1999, Anika Nailah, [an African American] writer . . . walked over to the Mystic Housing Development in Somerville, and proposed an idea. She believed in the passionate intelligence of young people . . . she wanted to work with them to liberate the hopes that lived in their hearts . . . she believed that she could help the youth in Mystic write, publish, and sell their own books.[25]

Doug Holder, reporting on an interview with Nailah, observes that, since 1999, "the program has trained kids from the projects and elsewhere in four key areas: writing, publishing, performing, marketing and outreach. The youth are involved in many aspects of producing a book, and their development is advanced through a writer-in-residence, guest artists and mentors, as well as field trips."[26] The youth, most of whom are of color and come from economically challenged backgrounds, get to keep the proceeds from the sale of their books.[27] Especially notable is the work Busch and Ball document that is being done by groups such as Streetside Stories, Youth Speaks, and WritersCorps, which offer literacy instruction to youth in culturally affirming contexts within their communities. Busch and Ball's investigation of community-based writing programs reveals that these programs use culturally responsive pedagogical approaches to help young people become effective, enthusiastic writers within their communities.

A final example that I am familiar with as a participant–observer is the Academic and Other Initiatives program that meets on Saturday in the college town of Amherst, Massachusetts. The program supports academic and cultural awareness, as well as personal and community-building goals for Black students attending the local public schools. Founded in 2004 by a grassroots parent group concerned with the academic success of African American children and youth in Amherst public schools, the program uses community- and college-based volunteers to provide academic support. The program also engages participants in culturally enriching activities, including lectures, sports and games, movie discussions, field trips, and potluck socials. This wide range of activities reflects the three-pronged focus of the program: providing instruction to African American children to enhance their academic success, especially in math, literacy, and science; using the human and material resources residing in the African American communities to build culturally affirming contexts to support the holistic education of these children and youth; and drawing on the image of the village, providing a culturally affirming and supportive community for them through family and community-building social activities. Since its inception, the organization has seen increased participation by families and students in all its activities, and appears to have taken root in the Black community in Amherst.

The preceding discussion demonstrates that CBPs in African American communities serve as more than just alternative sites for educational activity. The distinguishing element of many African American CBPs, compared to mainstream programs, is their vision of what a good education for African American students might entail. It is also significant to note that in many cases key individuals involved in CBPs are well-educated persons of color who have made deliberate efforts to connect their work in institutions of higher learning with civic engagement work. Evans (in the preface to this volume) speaks to this distinguishing characteristic and its long history among African American educators. I now turn to a central question posed earlier in this chapter: Why should teacher educators pay attention to CBPs among African American communities?

Culturally Responsive Education for Preservice Teachers Preparing to Teach African American Students

The demographic challenge and manifest shortcomings of current teacher education in preparing effective teachers of African American students underscore the need to pay attention to CBPs. The demographic challenge is widely discussed in literature, and is summarized by Cooper when she noted that over 40 percent of school-age children are students of color.[28] "Of these, 17.25 percent of students enrolled in public schools are Black. . . . Black teachers represent only 7.3 percent of public school teachers, whereas more than 90 percent are [W]hite."[29] It would seem necessary that preservice teachers with limited familiarity and skills to engage with students of color and their communities receive this education in the course of their teacher preparation. The reality in a typical program does not reflect this concern. Often, preservice teachers are likely to be exposed to course work and a series of field experiences that leave them inadequately prepared to teach students of other racial, ethnic, cultural, and class backgrounds. Examining the gaps in the preparation of teachers of African American students, Ladson-Billings noted:

> With very few exceptions, the literature does not expressly address the preparation of teachers to teach African American learners effectively. . . . Instead, references to the educational needs of African American students are folded into a discourse of deprivation. Searches of the literature base indicate that when one uses the descriptor, "Black education," one is directed to see, "culturally deprived" and "culturally disadvantaged." Thus the educational research literature, when it considers African American learners at all, has constructed all African American children, regardless of economic or social circumstance, within the deficit paradigm.[30]

Few field experiences in teacher education programs explicitly seek to expose preservice teachers to other views of the African American child beyond the deficit perspective that Ladson-Billings refers to here (see exceptions in Hamm, Dowell, and Houck; Seidl and Friend; and Sleeter[31]). It may be that many preservice teachers are receiving an education that could potentially harm African American students. I emphasize in this chapter that CBPs in many African American communities, especially those with an educational focus, may present alternative views of African American students and their communities and potentially counter some of the harmful education to which Ladson-Billings alluded. The available literature suggests that while CBPs with an educational focus undoubtedly serve mainstream education objectives by offering supplementary schooling, they also engender spaces of contestation to the racialized and often deficit notions of African American students and their communities that frame mainstream education thought and practice. This is more often the case for grassroots CBPs. For these reasons and others, education faculty should seriously consider using CBPs as sites for teacher preparation.

Challenging the Myths: Preparing Culturally Responsive Teachers for African American Students

Undoubtedly, one of the most prominently expressed goals in many teacher education programs is the preparation of teachers who can teach every child effectively. However, the kind of training such a teacher would need to receive is often vaguely articulated. Teacher educator, Ladson-Billings, argues that an effective teacher of African American students must exhibit three characteristics she associates with culturally responsive pedagogy: emphasis on academic achievement, cultural competence, and sociopolitical consciousness.[32] Teachers who emphasize academic rigor among African American students operate in the belief that all students can learn. Their cultural competency allows them to be confident, at ease, no-nonsense teachers who "take care of business" and have positive relationships with their students in and out of school. Culturally responsive teachers also seek to connect, rather than alienate, students from their cultural spaces by engaging in meaningful pedagogy imbued with sociopolitical consciousness. A culturally responsive pedagogy suggests that teachers need to be thoroughly conversant with their students' lives, not just in the context of the classroom or school, but also in their communities. Using CBPs as a gateway to the African American communities is a viable way to develop in preservice teachers the consciousness suggested by the culturally responsive pedagogical model. More importantly, CBPs provide education programs and departments in institutions of higher learning with opportunities to develop initiatives in African American communities that are aligned with the notion of the engaged campus.[33] Healthy engagement can lead to the fracturing of myths often associated with the cultural Other.

Myths shared by both university- and school-based educators that may explain the exclusion of African American CBPs as sites for community engagement and teacher education can be divided into two categories. The first category includes explanations that defend cultural neutrality in the practice of schooling and a belief in "best-practice" models that are abstracted from the knowledge of students' sociocultural, political, and historical realities. This perspective may include beliefs that educators know the child well, based solely on the interaction in the classrooms;[34] that educators engage in culturally neutral practices and there is no need to understand communities to which they do not belong;[35] and that educators can engage in culturally responsive pedagogy by simply adding information they deem true about other cultures without a deep knowledge of the target community of color.[36] The claim to value and cultural neutrality of schooling is problematic at best. Giroux urges educators to view schooling and knowledge as "neither neutral nor objective and, instead, to view it as a social construction embodying particular interests and assumptions."[37] Educators who understand that competing values are enacted every day in schooling practices are more likely to engage in culturally responsive pedagogy.

The second category of myths includes beliefs based on the deficit theory of culture and pathological perspectives about African American communities. Within these perspectives, educators' beliefs may include the views that CBPs are peripheral to the education of African American students;[38] that African American families and communities are not involved in the education of their children;[39] that interacting with African American communities is uncomfortable and should evoke fear among educators;[40] that African American communities are complex and relationships with them often get loud, complicated, messy, or political;[41] and that African American communities lack cultural funds of knowledge.[42] In contrast to these sentiments, many African American educators underscore the important role played by community-based initiatives in the education of African American students, both in the past and currently.

A look at Black education in the United States reveals that these myths are hardly supported by historical evidence. Education through self-help community initiatives, as well as culturally responsive pedagogy, are not new in African American communities. James Comer observed that "there has been a long-standing self-help tradition in the African American community," and that a strong desire to provide better conditions for their children has historically driven social change in African American communities.[43] Realizing the need to rally community efforts to promote the educational welfare of their children amid a majority culture that seems to care little for their success, African American communities have a track record of educational initiatives by and for African Americans dating back to slavery. Williams's study of the history of African American education in slavery and freedom examined the clandestine places and ways in which slaves organized their education, and how acquiring education became a symbol of resistance.[44] Royster described the Sabbath Schools, common soon after slavery, that were run predominantly by African Americans for African Americans.[45] These schools offered free instruction long before the advent of "public" or "free" education and were operated on weekends; they reached thousands of students who could not attend the weekday schools.[46] Freedom Schools, popular during the Civil Rights era, would continue the self-help educational charge among African American communities.[47] Hoover chronicled the African American independent schools during this era, including The Nairobi Day School in Palo Alto, California; the Center for Black Education in Washington, DC; the African Free School in Newark, New Jersey; Uhuru Sasa in New York City; and Malcolm X University in Durham, North Carolina.[48] More recently, Afrocentric and African-centered schools continue to offer models for education targeting the African American child within public, independent, and charter school contexts.[49]

African American educational initiatives, whether in the context of CBPs or in more formalized contexts such as those outlined above, have common threads weaving through them that are relevant here. One is the belief among African American communities that African American children are often not well served by the prevailing educational system. Another thread suggests that African American communities are an alternative site in which educational activity takes place. The third points to the need for educational reformers to take community-based educational initiatives seriously in their efforts toward equitable education and culturally responsive teacher education. Looking at what CBPs already do, institutions of higher learning should find ways of building on these strengths rather than treating African American communities as "pockets of needs, laboratories of experimentation, or passive recipients of expertise."[50]

MSL in Teacher Education: Possibilities and Challenges

Teacher educators have decried the scarcity of opportunities and programs that prepare teachers to teach African American students. Ladson-Billings and Seidl and Friend spoke to this scarcity in detail.[51] Although I am not suggesting that immersion experiences in African American communities, as presented in the MSL approach, are in and of themselves sufficient to prepare teachers of African American students, I want to emphasize that they are an important step. As a concept and a practice, MSL has steadily gained popularity since the 1980s.[52] It can be argued that MSL currently stands as a substitute in the absence of significant efforts to educate, support, and sustain teachers committed to the education of African American students. Its appeal among teacher educators concerned with developing teachers capable of and willing to engage in culturally responsive pedagogy for African American students is that it seeks to embrace the "assets model" and avoids engaging in the voyeuristic, sensationalized, and "tourist" approach that is characteristic of many service-learning experiences in communities of color.[53] MSL also emphasizes the goals of multicultural understanding, community building, and social critique.[54] Most important, MSL emphasizes that race and ethnicity must be placed front and center in teacher education.

Seidl and Friend described the efforts of their teacher education graduate program at Ohio State University to partner with Mt. Olivet Baptist Community, which is predominantly African American.[55] The program requires preservice teachers to engage in a community-based internship, which involves "working for two to three hours a week across the entire academic year with adults from the Mt. Olivet community in planning and implementing a number of different programs for children within the community."[56] Preservice teachers offer after-school homework help as well as reading and math tutorials. They also work with Sunday school classes, and participate in a community unity circle, in which community members discuss political, spiritual, and social concerns. Seidl and Friend reported that through this yearlong service-learning experience, participating preservice teachers have gained deeper understandings regarding cultural and the sociopolitical viewpoints of the African American communities they have interacted with.[57] They have also gained a more nuanced understanding of racism. The course also helped build more trusting relationships between the campus and the surrounding community—two communities that have traditionally been divided.

Boyle-Baise described a one-credit-hour service-learning experience for preservice teachers that was linked to a three-credit-hour multicultural education course.[58] Preservice teachers, who were predominantly White, were required to spend twenty hours service-learning in churches and community organizations serving low-income communities of color, including African American communities. The college instructor facilitating the service-learning had collaborated with leaders of the various community organizations to develop a service-learning program that was based on mutuality, shared control, and respect for communities. She noted, "Our partnership included two pastors, one for a racially mixed congregation, the other for a predominantly Black church; a director of university program for students of color and education director for the Black church; the program director for the Boys & Girls Club; the director of a community center; the parent coordinator for Head Start; and a teacher education professor."[59] The service-learning component afforded preservice teachers opportunities to become acquainted with culturally and economically diverse communities. It also allowed preservice teachers to situate children within family and community life, and to identify assets and resources within the communities. Boyle-Baise noted that despite the immersion experience and the reduction of stereotypes that resulted, the preservice teachers' understanding and social and institutionalized inequalities remained elusive.[60]

In her education courses for preservice teachers, Sleeter engages her preservice teachers in service-learning in several community centers, churches, and the Boys & Girls Club.[61] She chooses community centers that are staffed by people from the community. After their interaction with students, parents, and community members in the community centers, Sleeter reported that her students who were predominantly White gained a deeper understanding in key areas that will most likely impact their future teaching of African America students. For instance, they compared the conversational and interaction patterns present in community sites to patterns often privileged in mainstream classrooms. They also interacted with African American parents from low-income backgrounds and learned of the parents' educational aspirations for their children. Additionally, they observed the skills and abilities that African American children use in church or community centers that "suggest a higher level of responsibility, as well as cognitive knowledge and/or linguistic skills, than the children display in classrooms."[62]

What these examples highlight are some key tenets of MSL. Multicultural service-learning demands that prospective teachers participate in carefully designed community-based service-learning experiences that allow them to interact with communities of color and engage in community-building activities in their service-learning sites. Most important, however, is the reflection and learning that results from purposeful engagement with these communities. The benefits of this Freirean notion of praxis for both prospective teachers and communities are wide ranging. Purposeful engagement provides opportunities for prospective teachers to reconsider deficit or supremacy views,[63] fracture the essentialist positions that define African Americans in simplistic and stereotypical terms,[64] gain an appreciation for sociopolitical complexities that face African Americans in their contexts and limit their engagement in school tasks,[65] learn to appreciate the community wisdom, strengths, and resources,[66] and gain a deeper understanding of sociopolitical critique and action.[67]

The obvious challenge that MSL faces as a new field is that it has yet to develop a supporting, comprehensive research base that shows its impact among preservice teachers. More research is needed to show ways in which MSL can develop the skills, knowledge, and dispositions needed to become effective teachers of African American students. Perhaps the biggest challenge facing MSL in teacher education programs is a lack of institutionalization. Multicultural service-learning is largely regarded as an "add-on" experience, even in programs that encourage a series of field experiences for their teacher candidates. In addition, many teacher educators—even those who do not subscribe to the myths outlined earlier—find that establishing sustainable relationships with CBPs is a daunting task.

Enhancing Multicultural Service-Learning through Developing Purposeful Campus–Community-Based Program Partnerships

I have argued in this chapter that MSL experiences should be encouraged in teacher education programs that seek to prepare culturally responsive teachers of African American students. This would involve changes on two fronts: a broadened definition of community partnerships and relationship building with African American CBPs. Education faculty in institutions of higher learning must broaden the definition of community partnerships to include both K–12 schools and CBPs. In this broadened sense of partnerships, MSL, as described in this chapter, would become a core rather than peripheral field experience alongside the traditional practicum. Such a move is both political and pedagogical, and it forces departments of education to examine institutionalized mechanisms that have served to validate some knowledges and cultures and exclude others. It also demands that faculty members form working, if not collaborative, relationships with other offices and programs on campus that would not normally have strong links with education departments. Since adding MSL to my courses, I have found myself working closely not only with faculty in other academic disciplines, but also with campus offices that offer the logistical support needed to establish sustainable relationships with communities. Last, institutionalizing MSL would need to be accompanied by an alignment with the reward systems. Multicultural service-learning, like other community service-learning experiences, require a great deal of work from faculty to organize and operate.[68]

Building healthy relationships with CBPs is vital to the institutionalization of MSL. Literature emphasizes that good relationships with community are based on (1) common goals, (2) mutual trust and collaboration, and (3) being mindful of history and power differentials. Langseth explores literature and stresses that three myths must be addressed in order to preserve campus–community collaboration: (1) there exists superior and deficient cultures; (2) there is superior knowledge and experience in higher education as compared to the communities; and (3) there is a hierarchy of wisdom, with faculty wiser than students and students wiser than community.[69] These myths, among others, prevent a healthy engagement between education faculty and CBPs. A paradigm shift must occur to allow for the development of a mutually beneficial relationship. At the core of this paradigm shift must be the willingness to share the "expert" role with community members who know their children best. The conviction that communities are committed and knowledgeable only happens when education faculty gain deep, rather than superficial, knowledge of the community. Such knowledge leads to the embracing of the "assets model"[70] that suggests an orientation of "doing with" rather than "doing for."[71] Taken together, the broad-based programmatic change in departments of education suggested here would go a long way toward institutionalizing MSL.

Conclusion

Educating America's diverse K–12 students demands that institutions of higher learning prepare teachers who are deeply knowledgeable and skilled in teaching all students. For effective teaching to occur, teachers must gain experience in cultures other than their own. Multicultural service-learning, with its emphasis on learning in community-based contexts involving communities of color, offers the opportunity for prospective teachers to gain this vital experience. As a teacher educator who spends considerable time working with CBPs in both African American and Latino contexts in Amherst, Northampton, and Springfield, Massachusetts, I have come to appreciate the potential that lies in engaging with community sites for teacher education. In this chapter, I have explained why MSL in African American communities makes sense. However, I must acknowledge that embracing MSL with African American or other ethnic or racially based CBPs is not consistent with the typical teacher education program. Teacher educators do see value in their students' service-learning and interning in schools. Few, however, see the need to extend beyond the school into the larger community. Yet, available research tells us that teachers' perceptions of students' culture and communities influences the way they teach, particularly with African American communities. Multicultural service-learning essentially demands that to produce proficient teachers in the twenty-first century, education faculty must undertake programmatic initiatives and changes on their campuses and commit to the development of healthy partnerships with communities.

Notes

1. D. Butin, ed., *Service-Learning in Higher Education: Critical Issues and Directions* (New York: Palgrave Macmillan, 2005); E. Daigre, "Toward a Critical Service-Learning Pedagogy: A Freirean Approach to Civic Literacy," *Academic Exchange Quarterly* 4, no. 4 (2000): 6; R. A. Rhodes and J. P. F. Howard, eds., *Academic Service-Learning: A Pedagogy of Action and Reflection* (San Francisco, CA: Jossey-Bass, 1998); B. Speck and S. Hoppe, introduction to *Service-Learning: History, Theory, and Issues*, eds. B. Speck and S. Hoppe (Westport, CT: Praeger, 2004), vii–xi.

2. L. Darling-Hammond, *Professional Development Schools: Schools for Developing a Profession* (New York: Teachers College Press, 1994); M. Langseth, "Maximizing Impact, Minimizing Harm: Why Service-Learning Must More Fully Integrate Multicultural Education," in *Integrating Service-Learning and Multicultural Education in Colleges and Universities*, ed. R. O'Brien (Mahwah, NJ: Erlbaum, 2000), 45–71; L. Mule, "Preservice Teachers' Inquiry in a Professional Development School Context: Implications for the Practicum," *Teaching and Teacher Education* 22 (2006): 205–18.

3. M. Boyle-Baise, *Multicultural Service-Learning: Educating Teachers in Diverse Communities* (New York: Teachers College Press, 2002); R. O'Grady, ed., *Integrating Service-Learning and Multicultural Education in Colleges and Universities* (Mahwah, NJ: Erlbaum, 2000); Speck and Hoppe, introduction to *Service-Learning*.

4. Boyle-Baise, *Multicultural Service-Learning*; M. Boyle-Baise et al., "Shared Control: Community Voices in Multicultural Service-Learning," *Educational Forum* 65, no. 4 (2001): 344–53; C. Sleeter, "Strengthening Multicultural Education With Community-Based Learning," in *Integrating Service-Learning and Multicultural Education in Colleges and Universities*, ed. C. R. O'Grady (Mahwah, NJ: Erlbaum, 2000), 263–76; G. Ladson-Billings, "Fighting for Our Lives: Preparing Teachers to Teach African American Students," *Journal of Teacher Education* 51, no. 3 (2000): 206–14.

5. A. F. Ball, "Empowering Pedagogies That Enhance Multicultural Students," *Teachers College Record* 102, no. 6 (2000): 1006–34.

6. P. C. Murrell Jr., *African American Pedagogy: Developing Schools of Achievement for African American Children* (New York: State University of New York, 2002), xxxviii.

7. N. Warfield-Coppock, "The Rites of Passage Movement: A Resurgence of African-Centered Practices for Socializing African American Youth," *Journal of Negro Education* 61, no. 4 (1992): 471–82.

8. J. Berrien, "A Civil Liberties Imperative: Promoting Quality Education for all African American Children," *Teachers College Record* 94, no. 4 (1993): 790–99.

9. C. T. Adger, "School-Community-Based Organization Partnership for Language Minority Students' School Success," *Journal of Education for Students Placed at Risk* 6, no. 1, 2 (2001): 7–25.

10. S. B. Heath and M. W. McLaughlin, "Community Organizations as Family: Endeavors That Engage and Support Adolescents," *Phi Delta Kappan* 72, no. 8 (1992): 623–27.

11. J. Comer, "The Potential Effects of Community Organizations on The Future of our Youth," *Teachers College Record* 94, no. 3 (1993): 658–61.

12. Ladson-Billings, "Fighting for Our Lives."

13. Ball, "Empowering Pedagogies," 1008.

14. Murrell, *African-American Pedagogy*.

15. Ladson-Billings, "Fighting for Our Lives;" G. Gay, *Culturally Responsive Teaching. Theory, Research and Practice* (New York: Teachers College Press, 2000); G. Gay, "Preparing for Culturally Responsive Teaching," *Journal of Teacher Education* 53, no. 2 (2002): 106–17.

16. Ladson-Billings, "Fighting for Our Lives."

17. A. W. Boykin et al., "Communalism: Conceptualization and Measurement of an Afrocultural Social Orientation," Journal of Black Studies 27, no. 3 (1997): 409–18.

18. A. F. Ball and T. Lander, *African American Literacies Unleashed: Vernacular English and the Composition Class* (Carbondale: Southern Illinois University Press, 2005).

19. Ball and Lander, *African American Literacies Unleashed*.

20. Warfield-Coppock, "The Rites of Passage Movement."

21. A. R. Harvey, "An After-School Manhood Development Program," in *Educating Our Black Children: New Directions and Radical Approaches*, ed. R. Majors (New York: Routledge Falmer, 2001), 161.

22. C. M. Silva, R. P. Moses, and P. Johnson, "The Algebra Project: Making School Mathematics Count," *Journal of Negro Education* 59, no. 3 (1990): 378.

23. Silva, Moses, and Johnson, "the Algebra Project," 385.

24. J. Cass (2002), *The Moses Factor 2002*, http://www.motherjones.com/news/feature/2002/05/moses.html (accessed January 31, 2007).

25. R. J. LaMothe, *Uncharted Territories: Past, Present & Future* (Somerville, MA: Books of Hope, 2001).

26. D. Holder (2008), "Books of Hope Brings the Writer Out in Somerville Youth," http://www.somervillenews.typepad.com/the_somerville_news/2008/08/books-of-hope-b.html.

27. A. E. Busch and A. F. Ball, "Lifting Voices in the City," *Educational Leadership* 62, no. 2 (2004): 64–67; Ball, "Empowering Pedagogies."28. P. M. Cooper, "Effective White Teachers of Black Children: Teaching within a Community," *Journal of Teacher Education* 54, no. 95 (2003): 413–27.

29. Cooper, "Effective White Teachers," 414.

30. Ladson-Billings, "Fighting for Our Lives," 206.

31. D. Hamm, D. Dowell, and J. W. Houck. "Service-Learning as a Strategy to Prepare Teacher Candidates for Contemporary Diverse Classrooms," *Education* 119, no. 2 (1998): 196–204; B. Seidl and G. Friend, "The Unification of Church and State: Working Together to Prepare Teachers for Diverse Classrooms," *Journal of Teacher Education* 53, no. 2 (2002): 142–52; C. Sleeter, "Preparing Teachers for Culturally Diverse Schools: Research and the Overwhelming Presence of Whiteness," *Journal of Education* 52, no. 2 (2001): 94–106.

32. Ladson-Billings, "Fighting for Our Lives," 206.

33. Taylor (introduction to this volume); B. Jacoby and Associates, *Building Partnerships for Service-Learning* (San Francisco, CA: Jossey-Bass, 2003); E.L. Boyer, "The Scholarship of Engagement," *Journal of Public Service and Outreach* 1, no.1 (1996): 11–20.

34. Boyle-Baise, *Multicultural Service-Learning*.

35. Sleeter, "Strengthening Multicultural Education."

36. Boyle-Baise, *Multicultural Service-Learning*.

37. H. Giroux, *Teachers as Intellectuals: Toward a Critical Pedagogy of Learning* (Westport, CT: Bergin and Garvey, _____), 7.

38. Busch and Ball, "Lifting Voices in the City."

39. G. Thompson, *What African American Parents Want Educators to Know* (Westport, CT: Praeger, 2003).

40. Seidl and Friend, "The Unification of Church and State."

41. G. Thompson, *Through Ebony Eyes* (San Francisco, CA: Jossey-Bass, 2004).

42. C. D. Lee, "The State of Knowledge about the Education of African Americans," in *Black Education: A Transformative Research and Action Agenda for the New Century*, ed. J. E. King (Mahwah, NJ: Erlbaum, 2005), 45–71.

43. J. Comer, *Waiting for a Miracle: Why Schools Can't Solve Our Problems—and How We Can* (New York: Plume 1998), 141.

44. H. A. Williams, *Self-Taught: African American Education in Slavery and Freedom* (Chapel Hill: University of North Carolina Press, 2005), 11.

45. J. J. Royster, *Traces of a Stream: Literacy and Social Change among African American Women* (Pittsburgh, PA: University of Pittsburgh Press, 2000).

46. J. D. Anderson, *The Education of Blacks in the South, 1860–1935* (Chapel Hill: University of North Carolina Press, 1988).

47. J. E. King and S. Parker, "A Detroit Conversation," in *Black Education: A Transformative Research and Action Agenda for the New Century*, ed. J. E. King (Mahwah, NJ: Erlbaum, 2005), 243–60.

48. M. E. R. Hoover, "The Nairobi Day School: An American Independent School, 1966-1984," *Journal of Negro Education* 61, no. 2 (1992): 201–10.

49. For information on Afrocentric schools, see M. K. Asante, *The Afrocentric Idea* (Philadelphia, PA: Temple University Press, 1987). For information on African-centered schools, see D. S. Pollard and C. S. Ajirotutu, *African-Centered Schooling in Theory and Practice* (Westport, CT: Bergin and Garvey, 2000), and Murell, *African-American Pedagogy*.

50. R. G. Bringle, R. Games, and E. A. Malloy, *Colleges and Universities as Citizens* (Boston, MA: Allyn and Bacon, 1999), 9.

51. G. Ladson-Billings, "Culturally Relevant Pedagogy in African-Centered Schools: Possibilities for Progressive Educational Reform," in *African-Centered Schooling in Theory and Practice*, ed. D. S. Pollard and C. S. Ajirotutu (Westport, CT: Bergin and Garvey, 2000), 187–98; Seidl and Friend, "The Unification of Church and State."

52. Boyle-Baise, *Multicultural Service-Learning*; O'Grady, *Integrating Service-Learning*.

53. Boyle-Baise, *Multicultural Service-Learning*; Sleeter, "Strengthening Multicultural Education"; K. Ward and L. Wolf-Wendel, "Community-Centered Service-Learning: Moving From Doing for to Doing With," *American Behavioral Scientist* 43, no. 5 (2000): 767–80.

54. Boyle-Baise, *Multicultural Service-Learning*; M. Dunlap, "Voices of Students in Multicultural Service-Learning Settings," *Michigan Journal of Community Service Learning* (fall 1998): 58–67.

55. Seidl and Friend, "The Unification of Church and State."

56. Seidl and Friend, "The Unification of Church and State," 149.

57. Seidl and Friend, "The Unification of Church and State."

58. Boyle-Baise, *Multicultural Service-Learning*.

59. Boyle-Baise, *Multicultural Service-Learning*, 78.

60. Boyle-Baise, *Multicultural Service-Learning*.

61. Sleeter, "Strengthening Multicultural Education."

62. Sleeter, "Strengthening Multicultural Education," 270.

63. M. Boyle-Baise and P. Efiom, "The Construction of Meaning: Learning from Service-Learning," in *Integrating Service-Learning and Multicultural Education in Colleges and Universities*, ed. R. O'Grady (Mahwah, NJ: Erlbaum, 2000), 209–26.

64. Ladson-Billings, "Culturally Relevant Pedagogy"; S. B. Heath, "Island by Island We Must Cross: Challenges from Language and Culture Among African Americans," in *African-Centered Schooling in Theory and Practice*, ed. D. S. Pollard and C. S. Ajirotutu (Westport, CT: Bergin and Garvey, 2000), 163–86.

65. Ladson-Billings, "Culturally Relevant Pedagogy."

66. Sleeter, "Strengthening Multicultural Education"; Ladson-Billings, "Fighting for Our Lives"; Boyle-Baise et al., "Shared Control."

67. Ladson-Billings, "Fighting for Our Lives"; Sleeter, "Strengthening Multicultural Education."

68. Boyle-Baise et al., "Shared Control"; K. O'Meara, "Reframing Incentives and Rewards for Community Service-Learning and Academic Outreach," *Journal of Higher Education Outreach and Engagement* 8, no. 2 (2003): 201–20; Sleeter, "Preparing Teachers."

69. Langseth, "Maximizing Impact, Minimizing Harm."

70. Sleeter, "Strengthening Multicultural Education."

71. Ward and Wold-Wendel, "Community-Centered Service-Learning."

6

❖ ❖ ❖

Sowing Seeds of Success

Gardening as a Method of Increasing Academic Self-Efficacy and Retention among African American Students

AUGUST HOFFMAN, JULIE WALLACH,
EDUARDO SANCHEZ, AND RICHARD CARIFO

Community service work has been shown to play an important role in not only how individuals feel about themselves in terms of self-efficacy and self-esteem, but in helping individuals "rediscover" their sense of civic and community pride. Service-learning, as defined by Taylor and colleagues, involves students using what they learn in their formal study to work with others to make a beneficial difference in the world.[1]

In our previous research that explored the relationship between community service programs and self-perception, we identified several characteristics that may promote one's level of ability and performance relative to a variety of outdoor horticultural tasks (planting flowers and vegetables).[2] Our results indicated that when students are afforded opportunities to work cooperatively in a community college garden, self-perceptions of aptitudes and self-efficacy increase significantly.

While significant amounts of research have been addressed exploring the benefits and value of community service work in general, little research has been made available that explores the benefits of a community service-learning program (i.e., a campus gardening program) with academic improvement among the African American community college student population.[3]

Research shows the complications of service-learning in an underrepresented, mainly African American neighborhood.[4] We created the Compton College service-learning program with the specific objective of showing the benefits of collaborative group work on race relations and academic retention and transfer. In order to specifically determine key benefits of our service-learning program, we defined the construct "academic self-efficacy." A key concept central to this chapter, academic self-efficacy is defined as an inherent belief system in the ability to control the outcome of the individual's academic performance (see the appendix). Thus, students with strong academic self-efficacy believe that they have control over the content of what they learn as well as the ability to improve their overall academic standing (i.e., higher grade point average).

In just one of his several innovative concepts throughout his illustrious career, Albert Bandura originally coined the generic term *self-efficacy* as a particular belief system in one's ability to accomplish specific tasks, such as improving one's academic skills in a particular course, improving one's physical health, and so on.[5] We have created a more specific concept relative to self-efficacy addressing one's belief system in mastering and controlling their academic performance. Academic self-efficacy is critical to all students and individuals who are concerned about learning and academic performance. However, we feel that academic self-efficacy is critical to historically disadvantaged African American students who have often faced numerous economic and educational challenges.

The community college in the city of Compton, California, serves as one of the few remaining resources still readily available for predominantly African American students to excel and to help transition to higher education. Academic self-efficacy is clearly a critical concept to them as academic success and educational achievement is often the only escape route out of poverty and economic and social repression. Without offering academic resources and higher educational opportunities to these students, their ability to transfer out of the economically repressed areas would be greatly reduced. A significant scope of this chapter is therefore dedicated to identifying effective strategies in improving academic performance and self-efficacy at the community college level among the African American student population. Understanding one's capacity for successful learning and overcoming educational challenges through the discovery of academic self-efficacy therefore is critical to ethnic minority students who often face these challenges daily.

The purpose of this chapter is to identify the positive components (improving academic performance and academic self-efficacy) and characteristics of a community service-learning program that has served several thousands of African American community college students. Important issues that we will explore are how African American students can improve their academic self-efficacy in educational achievement and how this concept is unique among African Americans. Most importantly, we wish to identify and explore the overall African American experiences of working collaboratively in the community garden and how these subjective experiences helped establish a stronger sense of academic self-efficacy.

We will also provide empirical evidence addressing the numerous benefits of community service work through a variety of gardening projects and activities with students who are currently enrolled both as community college students and the mentors that have worked with them at the university level. The members of the community in Compton, as well as the registered students who participated in the gardening project, are the actual beneficiaries of the cooperative garden. The participants worked in the garden by planting vegetables and flowers and continued maintenance throughout the growing season.

Within the last five consecutive years of research addressing the effects of an outdoor gardening program on community college students and four-year state university students, we have compiled considerable data that suggests involvement in community service programs such as gardening work and community service work have had a significant positive influence on student academic performance, self-esteem and self-efficacy, connection to campus and community, and civic responsibility as well as reductions in self-entitlement.[6] In this chapter we will briefly address the numerous positive effects of our community service gardening program and provide suggestions for future research.

The History of El Camino College–Compton Center

El Camino College–Compton Center has historically served underrepresented students (predominantly African Americans) for the past eighty years and has recently experienced changes among the ethnic diversity of the student population. There have been two dominant changes or shifts among the student population within the past sixty years. During the early history of the campus (i.e., from approximately the early 1930s to the late 1950s) the student ethnicity was predominantly Caucasian. However, during the early 1960s the ethnicity of the student population of the campus changed dramatically, where over 75 percent of the students were of African American descent. African Americans still remain the dominant ethnicity at the college, although the student population is almost equally Hispanic (2006 U.S. Census data). California Community Colleges demographic data for fall 2005 show an almost equal African American and Hispanic student population, with 2,509 African Americans and 2,254 Hispanics. Given the fact that El Camino College–Compton Center serves primarily underrepresented students, the faculty are committed to helping students prepare for transferring to higher education by remedial skills training (i.e., basic reading comprehension skills and writing skills).

The student-to-faculty ratio has historically been very low (ten to twelve students per faculty member), which adds to the appeal of the campus, where students may typically receive individual attention and remedial training for courses by faculty. The campus itself is a vital component to an economically repressed area, and has historically served students who have been interested in successfully transferring to higher education. The campus covers over eighty-five acres in southeast Los Angeles and is very popular among students. This commitment has improved the morale among ethnically diverse students who face challenges every day, from taking three or four different buses to school to raising children on a limited income. It is precisely this warm and supportive culture provided by the faculty that remains popular among students today.

Gardening Activities and Academic Performance

Recent research shows that when instructors are capable of showing how their courses relate to current themes in the "real world," students take more interest.[7] In an interesting study that illustrates the need for instructors to take a more proactive position in community-based projects that will create effective learning environments, Fusco demonstrated how a community garden stimulated interest and improved performance in science education.[8] When students can see that what they are learning in the classroom has relevance and a direct relationship with events in the outside world, they are significantly more likely to take interest in the classroom projects.

The benefits of garden work also include how the students communicate and relate to each other while working outside. For example, in earlier research at Compton Community College we explored the effects of a gardening program on the levels of self-esteem among community college students.[9] The results were very encouraging, as we discovered that when students find that they are successful in planting and maintaining a simple campus garden, this positive sense of self-esteem becomes generalized and transferred to the classroom in terms of academic performance. Additionally, through anecdotal observations while the students worked, we discovered that the students (they were enrolled in the same course) were able to review and question each other while performing the physical labor of weeding, planting, and watering in the campus garden. An additional benefit of working in a campus garden is that of assimilation and interaction among ethnically diverse student groups. In an interesting study that explored the interracial interaction among diverse student groups, Langhout and colleagues discovered a broad range of positive effects when student groups work together in a community garden and other community-based activities.[10]

Given the inherent and dynamic problems that face ethnically diverse student populations, a major focus of our research was in discovering a variety of methods that are practical and useful in helping students improve not only their academic levels of performance but, perhaps more importantly, provide a method of self-empowerment among diverse students that will facilitate their transition into higher education and increase success in the job market. Our prior research has empirical support in showing that when ethnically diverse students are afforded opportunities to volunteer and work in a community service-learning program under the supervision of a student mentor, their academic self-efficacy improves significantly. We also focus on the current problems that are now facing African American students and other underrepresented students and what are some of the things that teachers and mentors can do to help improve their success to higher education.

Current Trends in Community Service Work among African American Students

The primary focus and purpose of our research with African American students who are enrolled at the community college level is in improving their current levels of academic self-efficacy. We hypothesized that as students engaged in community service gardening work with California State University–Northridge (CSUN) mentors their academic self-efficacy would increase. Additionally, we predicted other several important factors relevant to academic performance to increase, such as increases in the desire to transfer to higher educational institutions as well as improvements in GPA.

Historically, African American students have had low rates of university transfer (i.e., less than 10 percent at Compton Community College) for a variety of reasons. The most common reasons cited by students who are successful while attending the community college level but fail to transfer to higher education is threefold:

1. *Lack of financial aid or support* (over 80 percent of the community college students who are enrolled at Compton College are on some form of financial aid). Without receiving some form of financial aid, many students reported that school "would be impossible to continue because I have a family to support";
2. *Remedial or basic skills requiring improvement* (i.e., reading comprehension, writing skills and critical thinking). Many African American students who are currently attending the community college level feel that they are underprepared to meet the academic rigor of higher education;
3. *Increased vocational interests.* Compton College has a disproportionately higher number of vocational students; therefore transfer to a four-year college or university for these students may not be necessary. For example, many community college students at Compton College are enrolled in the nursing program, welding program, or child development program. However, given the significantly lower numbers in successful transition to higher education, a primary function and purpose of our research was in improving academic performance via a community service gardening program.

Our current study involves over 21 African American students who are enrolled in a variety of introductory psychology courses (psychology: five) or developmental psychology (psychology: sixteen). The current study addresses techniques involving community service-learning principles with community college students who wish to transfer to higher educational institutions, such as the California State University or University of California level. We hypothesized that students who participated in a structured community service gardening program over six months time would show increases in their levels of academic self-efficacy as well as show significant increases in recognizing and appreciating community service work and volunteer work.

The African American community college students worked with student mentors from California State University–Northridge during the gardening experiment to provide assistance while gardening and also provided information about how to transfer to the CSU system. The mentors from the CSU system served as role models in working with the community college students and provided information and guidance throughout the course of the academic semester. Additionally, we predicted that the students who were involved in the community service program would show increases in their desire to transfer to a four-year college or state university program based on their experiences in working with the mentors and demonstrate higher academic performance in their psychology course. An important function of the mentors was through the development of positive relationships with the community college students and the emphasis in continuing higher education after graduating from Compton College. The mentors demonstrated the importance and value of continued higher education at the four-year level by discussing how a four-year degree can help them in achieving their goals relative to psychology and discussing various employment opportunities in psychology.

Students who participated in the study were enrolled in an undergraduate psychology course at El Camino College–Compton Center and volunteered to work in a community service program with CSUN student mentors who worked with students every Saturday in a gardening program for six months. The CSUN mentors were provided with instructions in working with the students from Compton College and created teams of students working together under the direction of each mentor each Saturday morning.

During this time, the CSUN mentors provided assistance and support to the community college students while working in the campus garden. The CSUN mentors were all psychology majors and offered assistance to the community college participants in terms of transferring to higher education and information about majoring in psychology. Often the community college students at Compton College would ask questions pertaining to transferring to higher educational institutions, which the mentors would answer and provide information relative to higher education and majoring in the discipline of psychology. The CSUN mentors provided academic guidance and support during this period of time and would often bring literature (i.e., applications to various colleges and universities) to the community college students. A CSUN mentor participated in a national psychology conference (Southern California Conference on Undergraduate Research) with one of the Compton Community College students who is involved in the current study. The overall experience was very rewarding and highly educational for both students and illustrated the tremendously positive experiences that are gained in a student–mentor relationship. After attending the conference, the community college student indicated that she was "confident" in her desire to transfer to higher education in psychology as a designated major.

Thus, one reason why the CSUN mentoring program is highly successful in increasing the academic self-efficacy among the community college students was in helping them realize that they in fact had the potential and ability to succeed in higher education. The CSUN mentors helped the community college students identify and clarify their goals, such as identifying potential majors in psychology and transferring to a four-year college. The CSUN mentors essentially served as positive role models and had overcome similar challenges with the community college students. This similarity served as a profound impetus in increasing the community college student's academic self-efficacy, where many had commented: "If they [CSUN mentors] could do it and succeed in college, then so can I." This study also illustrates the importance of establishing higher levels of academic self-efficacy and how a positive belief system in achieving your academic goals may become generalized to a positive belief system in achieving other types of goals.

For example, if African American students who are enrolled at the community college system have improved levels of academic self-efficacy as a result of participating in a community gardening program, then they may also have increased levels of internal attribution (feeling more in control of events in their lives). With an increased level of academic self-efficacy and internal attribution, students are more likely to engage themselves in various activities that will promote not only educational advancement, but also economic advancement.

Method

Participants

Thirty participants (ages ranging from eighteen to thirty-five) originally volunteered to participate in the study; however, ten subjects withdrew for personal reasons or scheduling conflicts, leaving a total of twenty participants to complete the study. Individuals who participated in the current study were all students who were enrolled in two psychology courses (introductory psychology and developmental psychology) at El Camino College–Compton Center (a predominantly African American community college located in a southeast urban area of Los Angeles, California).

Apparatus

Participants were administered the Academic Self-Efficacy Questionnaire (ASEQ) in pre- and posttest design. Tools that were used in the gardening program included shovels, rakes, mowers, and a variety of perennial plants and citrus trees that were planted by each subject.

Procedure

During the first week of the gardening program, participants were administered the pretest ASEQ. Participants were then instructed to report to the community college garden area each Saturday morning between the hours of 0700 and 12 noon. Each participant was then required to work a minimum of fifteen hours over the course of a fifteen-week semester. Thus, if each participant worked one hour each Saturday they would complete their required hours within a fifteen-week semester. After reporting to the campus at 0700 hours, participants were given a variety of assignments to complete during their shift and were paired with a CSUN student mentor to work with. The CSUN mentors earned independent units by volunteering in the study and were instructed to provide assistance to the community college students while working in the garden. During the process of planting flowers, weeding, and performing other typical types of gardening activities, the CSUN student mentors provided the community college students with information regarding academic skills and how to improve academic performance, such as reading skills, critical thinking, and writing skills that are required in higher education. The CSUN mentors were instructed to work with the community college participants both manually in working in the garden and also to help participants identify future goals relevant to their majors in psychology as well as transferring to higher education after graduating from community college.

Additionally, the CSUN student mentors were instructed to provide the community college students with specific information about how to transfer to a four-year state college or university and provided them with information about how they could contact the mentors for future assistance if needed. Materials facilitating this process were also provided to the community college students, such as applications to four-year colleges and universities, study guides, and contact names to provide assistance in transferring to higher education. After working several hours each Saturday, the community college students enjoyed lunch together with a barbecue at which they were able to socialize and exchange information relative to school work, study skills, and techniques in improving academic performance. At the end of the semester each participant was given a posttest questionnaire (i.e., ASEQ) to determine if any significant changes occurred during testing.

Results

An independent samples t-test was conducted and results strongly supported the hypothesis. Ten participants withdrew from the study for "personal" reasons leaving a total of twenty participants completing the study. Students who participated in a campus gardening program showed significant increases in academic self-efficacy: $M = 4.6, t = (10) = -1.40, p < .003$. These robust findings show strong significance relative to the impact of the CSUN mentoring program and increases in academic self-efficacy.

Discussion

The results of the current study suggest that when African American community college student's work in a campus garden environment under the supervision of college mentors their academic self-efficacy significantly increases. There may be several interpretations and reasons that support our robust findings. Perhaps the most important finding in the study was that when African American students are provided an environment within which to work with other students of color where they are able to share ideas, experiences, and academic skills with each other, their perceptions and their attitudes of what they are capable of learning also increases significantly. The fact that Compton Community College provided a specific community service-learning environment relative to gardening and academic self-efficacy was very appealing to each individual who participated in the study.

Students were able to not only identify with each other based on their African American ethnicity (i.e., collective self-efficacy) but they were able to share ideas and plans for their academic future in transferring to higher educational institutions. This unique form of collaboration while working in an outdoor campus garden provided an environment where African American students were able to share their ideas with each other and support each other in future academic projects. The students remained in contact with each other after the gardening experience and thus formed an alliance throughout the academic semester that provided them with increased self-confidence in future projects. The students often shared and exchanged ideas with each other relative to academic work as well as long-term future goals and their collaboration with each other appeared to inspire their future goals and academic self-efficacy. This was demonstrated by the number of anecdotal comments from the African American community college students during postexperimental interviews: "Working together [with the other community college students] in the garden makes me feel better about what I can accomplish individually, and that helps me to concentrate and study better."

The fact that the students were able to improve their perceptions of academic self-efficacy may have also been demonstrated through their overall style of working together in a highly supportive and collaborative process with each other as well as the CSUN mentors. Throughout the study, we observed students creating partnerships with the mentors that helped foster a collective sense of unity as they completed their work in the gardening program. This sense of collaboration and collectivistic philosophy helped improve their perceptions of not only what they could achieve individually, but also what was possible as a group. Thus, academic self-efficacy became a unique phenomenon among the African American community college students by achieving individual goals (i.e., improved academic performance) via group efforts in the gardening program. The students who were participating in the study were now achieving their goals through their collective efforts with other students and more importantly they felt more empowered in achieving their individual goals.

Another reason why we believe academic self-efficacy increased significantly among the participants working in the garden was their consistent exposure in working with student mentors from California State University–Northridge throughout the five-hour shift each Saturday. In many ways, the CSUN mentors also served as academic role models in helping the community college students improve their academic work and influence them into transferring to higher educational levels, such as the CSU system. There are a number of available CSU campuses that are available for the Compton community college students to transfer to (i.e., CSU Dominguez Hills, Long Beach, and Northridge). During the experimental procedure the mentors would provide the community college students with valuable information to assist them in this process.

The community college students were able to review and discuss various theories in psychology relevant to the course that they were enrolled in at El Camino College–Compton Center. The participants in the gardening program felt more confident about their own skills not only limited to the psychology course but also their overall academic progress in the future. The CSUN mentors were able to provide valuable feedback to the participants in the gardening program by encouraging them to discuss psychology theory while they were actually working outdoors.

As part of their required assignment at the end of the semester the CSUN mentors were instructed to document and summarize all of their memorable experiences (positive as well as negative) in a short report paper. Included are some excerpts of the postexperimental interviews with the Compton community college students and the CSUN mentors (initials are used here to ensure anonymity):

> MENTOR CM: The mentoring program had an impact on me as well as the students that I came in contact with on a weekly basis. . . . [The community college] students that I worked with on Saturdays told me that the experience has increased their levels of self-esteem and self-efficacy. . . . One student told me that after leaving Compton College on Saturdays that it makes him "want to get more accomplished throughout the day at work and my homework." Another student told me that as a result of the gardening program that they would like to come back and participate in the gardening program next semester. . . .

She said that the gardening program had a "therapeutic effect" and helped improve her mood which helped her to focus on her academic work. This mentoring and gardening program reminded me of working with my grandfather, and that made me feel relaxed and more capable of concentration.

MENTOR SP: After working with the [African American] students at ECC [El Camino Collge]–Compton Center, I felt better about myself and I wanted to work on my own academics. The students and I were able to discuss topics relevant to psychology theory (i.e., a psychology conference that we were presenting in November, 2006: Southern California Conference Undergraduate Research). The students that I worked with told me that they were better able to concentrate and retain information about their work in the classroom. I think the best part of the gardening program was in seeing the gradual changes in the students. They appeared more confident about themselves and their ability to succeed in future academic work. Several students told me that as a result of this [gardening experience] they now wanted to transfer to CSU Long Beach or CSUN because they think that they can succeed. It may sound funny, but seeing that you have the ability to plant something, and see it grow can also influence how you feel about yourself, your potential and how well you do in school.

COMPTON COLLEGE STUDENT AND GARDEN WORKER CP: I think of the inspiration and knowledge that I acquired while studying in your [Dr. Hoffman's] psychology class . . . in particular, I enjoyed working in the gardens with the other students and mentors. Every time I look over the yards and walk through the areas where we worked it brings back a fond memory of the times we worked together with my classmates and the mentors from CSUN. It may sound simple and foolish to say these things, but learning something of value, working together on something worthwhile [such as gardening] and meeting people with similar interests and goals, can be a gift in life. Thank you for reminding me of these wonderful things.

MENTOR JH: I had a great time working in the garden and sharing life stories and goals with other people. . . . I appreciated their efforts trying to get ahead in life and do something positive for themselves and their families. For example, one student has the goal of getting his master's degree and opening a school for kids with ADD because he has ADD he believes that he can make a difference for others.

MENTOR CP: Being able to do something for the community is a wonderful feeling that I will always remember. For me, being a part of the garden reinforced my prior feelings about doing something good for the community. . . . I have learned a lot about giving back and helping others due to this program. I really enjoyed the time I spent in working with the community college students and I believe the others felt the same way. My experiences at the garden will be with me forever. Working with the students made me feel proud of what I was doing for the community. . . . [T]here was one [community college] student in particular who I found amazing because she went back to school for her degree and then wanted to work with disadvantaged youths in her home state. The gardening program helped prepare people to succeed in their lives and that this program is going to touch many lives.

COMPTON COLLEGE STUDENT AND GARDEN WORKER TQ AND PQ: The gardening program helped us to work with our son and teach him about plants and vegetables. It was great to come out and work with people and see everyone working together. Our son was able to work in the garden with other children. . . . It was a very positive experience for everyone.

Overall Summary and Conclusions

In summary, while many students from various ethnic minority groups face challenges, there are several unique challenges that face African American students at Compton Community College. The African American students at the college typically have less support in completing their academic work and face more economic challenges than other students in the community college. Several of our students who participated in the study indicated that they were working at two or three jobs and were still enrolled in several classes. Academic self-efficacy, therefore, played a unique and critical role among our participants because at the completion of the study many of them indicated a stronger perception in their beliefs that they could accomplish their goals. These goals not only included traditional academic goals (i.e., improving academic performance), but also an increase in their belief that they could successfully complete their higher educational goals (i.e., four-year college or university) and ultimately find secure employment.

The students who comprise the African American community at Compton Community College face many obstacles to their education and they still succeed despite the challenges. Because of the numerous challenges facing students of color, an inherent belief system in achieving academic goals is critical. There are many things that are taken for granted by students in more affluent areas, such as transportation, books, work utensils (pens, pencils), clean bathrooms, and even a healthy diet. We wish to point out that these things that contribute to successful learning environments are not taken for granted among the students at Compton Community College. Our students face these risks and challenges daily, and yet they come to school to excel despite the obstacles.

Any method that is designed to help them succeed academically is critical in the overall effort to improve matriculation and transfer to higher education.

Community Service Work: More than Socializing

What makes this study and this research unique regarding academic self-efficacy is in how the African American students worked together and identified as a group and how this work improved their perceptions of what they felt they were capable of achieving in other important areas in their lives. All of the students who began working in the community garden made a commitment to complete their project, and they indicated that they took pride in their work. More than simply "socializing with friends," community service work is a serious commitment made by each participant to make a positive and significant improvement in a community college garden. Past research indicates that approximately one out of four (25 percent) of the community service participants successfully transfer to higher educational institutions. This figure is significantly higher than the general population where less than 10 percent of students transfer to institutions of higher learning.

Many of the students reported a strong sense of ethnic pride and identification with Compton Community College and how participating in the gardening program gave them a sense of educational pride and even personal ownership to the school. After our study was completed, many of our students would still come to the garden and point to the areas where they worked and indicated that this was "their school and their community."

After reviewing our research, several areas come to mind as suggestions for improving future research in related areas. Perhaps the most significant suggestion is in improving our external validity; in other words, a broader and more generalized subject population would be appropriate to determine if academic self-efficacy can be improved among different ethnic groups. While the development of academic self-efficacy was apparent among the African American students in the current study, future research may address the possibility of developing academic self-efficacy among different ethnic groups.

A second suggestion of improvement would be to address what the specific benefits of gardening are to academic self-esteem. In other words, what is it specifically about outdoor gardening that improves academic self-efficacy? In order to adequately address this question, one would need to review the anecdotal comments by the community college students as well as the CSUN mentors. The best answer to this critical question is in exploring the context of the relationship between the community college students and their mentors. As the participants increased their work experiences in the garden with their CSUN mentors, their trust with them grew as did their experiences in success in planting, composting, cutting, watering, and so on. As the community college students increased their levels of confidence while working in the garden, this increase in self-esteem and self-confidence generalized to increases in self-efficacy in the classroom.

A third suggestion for improving future research addressing community service work in a garden may be in the hours students report to the community college for their gardening work. We would suggest a more "gardener-friendly" program that would accommodate different schedules of each student. Many of the students commented that it was "difficult getting up at six or seven in the morning" and wanted to begin work at a later time in the morning or afternoon.

A fourth area of potential future research addressing the benefits of an outdoor gardening activity and community service-learning could focus on the problems of inner-city youth gangs and hate crimes. Recently the problems of gang activity in urban areas (such as those recently reported in Los Angeles) have received national attention due to the increasing frequency in which gang-related crimes are occurring. Additionally, these gang-related crimes have now become very central to how inner-city groups assimilate and interact with one another. A fourteen-year-old African American girl (Cheryl Green) was tragically murdered while playing outside in her neighborhood by rival Hispanic gang members simply because of her race (*Long Beach Press-Telegram,* January 19, 2007). All law enforcement agencies have combined their efforts (including the FBI) as a means to control this ethnic gang violence. Clearly, reducing violence that is caused by gang affiliation and prejudice will require more effort than law enforcement agencies can provide. If we assume that a predisposing need to belong to gangs is through some form of an ethnic or cultural identification process, then perhaps community service work and volunteer work that is designed to enhance and improve communities of all races may be a good place to begin. Perhaps collaborative work through community service-learning projects that encourage assimilation of all ethnic groups may be one way to reduce this serious increase in gang violence.

The current study addressed how academic self-efficacy may be fostered among African American community college students as a means to improve transition into higher education as improved academic performance. Our results were very encouraging in the sense that the majority of the African American students who were involved in the study felt more empowered academically by their participation and interdependent work with each other in the community service gardening program. The participants in the study also reported that their increases in academic self-efficacy and empowerment were attributed to working with CSUN mentors who provided assistance to them not only in working in the garden, but in providing valuable information relative to transferring to higher education. One final suggestion for future research addressing academic self-efficacy may involve a longitudinal study (i.e., one that extends beyond one academic semester) as a means of identifying and understanding the long-term effects of community service gardening work and increases in academic self-efficacy.

Appendix
Academic Self-Efficacy Questionnaire
On a scale from "1" through "5" please indicate which response
most accurate pertains to you, where a score of:

"1" = **Absolutely Disagree;**
"2" = **Disagree;**
"3" = **Unsure / I Don't Know;**
"4" = **Agree; and**
"5" = **Absolutely Agree** *(scoring scale below)

1. I feel that I can control what I learn in school and how my academic performance progresses _____;
2. Whatever grade I receive in class is primarily due to my performance and my effort _____;
3. Most of the time I feel that the grade that I have received in class is fair and represents my level of work and commitment to that class _____;
4. I believe that if I try hard enough I can excel and perform well in all of my classes _____;
5. Usually when I perform well in a class it is due to hard work and determination on my part _____;
6. I do not really believe in "chance" or "luck" when it comes to the scores I receive on an examination or the grade I get in class _____;
7. People who say that they have had "bad luck" in life haven't really applied themselves hard enough to get out of those situations _____;
8. I believe that parents are capable of teaching their children to work hard and persevere to reach their goals _____;
9. I am usually confident that I can achieve my educational goals and that I can control my academic outcome in school _____;
10. What I learned in the garden helped me to better understand myself and my beliefs in achieving my goals _____;
11. If I am experiencing problems with my academic work, I know where to go for help so I can improve my performance in class _____;
12. My family supports me in my academic achievements and my educational goals _____;
13. I have had problems in school before and have worked through them by applying myself harder _____;
14. When I begin a class I try to first find out where the tutors are to get help and review the syllabus very carefully _____;
15. I find that the discipline and determination that I have learned in school helps me with other projects and goals in my life _____.

Notes

1. M. D. Sarver, "Agritherapy: Plants as Learning Partners," *Academic Therapy* 20, no. 4 (1985): 389–96; T. D. Glover, "The Story of the Queen Anne Memorial Garden: Resisting a Dominant Cultural Narrative," *Journal of Leisure Research* 35, no. 2 (2003): 190–212; L. A. Hammond, "Building Houses, Building Lives," *Mind, Culture, and Activity* 10, no. 1 (2003): 26–41.

2. A. J. Hoffman, J. N. Wallach, and L. Morales-Knight, "Gardening Activities, Education and Self-Esteem: Learning Outside of the Classroom," *Urban Education* 42 (September 2007): 403–11; A. J. Hoffman, B. Trepagnier, A. Cruz, and D. Thompson, "Gardening Activity as an Effective Measure in Improving Self-Efficacy and Self-Esteem: Community College Students Learning Effective Living Skills," *Community College Enterprise* 9 (2004): 231–239; W. E. Roweton, "Plants as 'Children' in Introductory Child Psychology," *Psychological Reports* 45, no. 3 (1985:, 768–70; M. D. Sarver, "Agritherapy: Plants as Learning Partners," *Academic Therapy* 20, no. 4 (1985): 389–96; P. G. Taylor and C. Ballengee-Morris, "Service-Learning: A Language of 'We,'" *Art Education. Reston.* 57, no. 5 (2004): 6–12; R. J. Riordan and C. S. Williams, "Gardening Therapeutics for the Elderly," *Activities, Adaptation, and Aging* 12, no. 1–2 (1988): 103–11.

3. L. J. Sax and A. W. Astin, "The Benefits of Service: Evidence from Undergraduates," *Educational Record*, 78 (1997): 25–32; L. J. Sax, A. W. Astin, and H. S. Astin, "What Were LSAHE Impacts on Student Volunteers?" *Evaluation of Learn and Serve America, Higher Education: First Year Report* (Santa Monica, CA: RAND Corporation, 1996).

4. C. Pappas, "Lessons from Hammond Heights: Service Learning and Race in an Oklahoma Town," paper presented at the annual meeting of the APSA Teaching and Learning Conference, Washington, DC, February 2006.

5. A. Bandura, *Self-Efficacy: The Exercise of Control* (New York: Freeman, 1997).

6. Hoffman, Wallach, and Morales-Knight, "Gardening Activities, Education, and Self-Esteem."

7. D. Fusco, "Creating Relevant Science through Urban Planning and Gardening," *Journal of Research in Science Teaching* 38 (2001): 860–77.

8. D. Fusco, "Creating Relevant Science."

9. Hoffman, Wallach, and Morales-Knight, "Gardening Activities, Education, and Self-Esteem."

10. R. D. Langhout, J. Rappaport, and D. Simmons, "Integrating Community into the Classroom: Community Gardening, Community Involvement, and Project-Based Learning," *Urban Education* 37, no. 3 (2002): 323–49.

7

A Service or a Commitment?

A Black Man Teaching Service-Learning at a Predominantly White Institution

TROY HARDEN

Nameless, faceless, endangered, obsolete, and *invisible* are terms Ellison, as well as other writers, have used to describe the identity of Black men in the United States.[1] For Ellison and the others, these terms speak more to the claiming of an identity that transcends these terms, when the rest of society would have them faceless and "not seen." This desire to reclaim a "surrendered identity," as Erikson called it in reference to Blacks and development,[2] seeks to name, recover, and identify the self that is often unseen in modern America. My experiences as a service-learning instructor inform my perspective about the interaction between race and service-learning both within the classroom and the community. There are few scholarly interpretations of the Black perspective and experience within service-learning, and even fewer reflecting the views and opinions of Black men, particularly from a critical perspective. Many studies focus on research about Blacks to learn "from" diverse perspectives within academic institutions. Few studies, however, are performed from the perspective of Blacks. This chapter seeks to bring forth the voice of the Black perspective within the context of service-learning and university-community partnerships, particularly a Black man teaching a service-learning course within a predominantly White institution in Chicago at a university committed to service-learning and civic engagement within the urban environment. This weaves the relationships between professor and student, student and community, and community and professor and situates them within the institutional forces that surround them. These institutional forces include service-learning discourse, dominant culture ideology, and higher education. Understanding how these factors are always a part of the service-learning dynamic is useful for service-learning faculty, community representatives, and students seeking common places to develop meaningful interactions concerning service-learning that serve, without exploitation, the interests of all parties involved. This chapter critiques the dominant discourse concerning service-learning and offers an alternate view that seeks to inform service-learning pedagogy and community–university relationships. In unpacking these dynamics, the possibility of authentic projects and partnerships that reflect a common emphasis on social justice and education can be realized.[3]

Community-Based Service-Learning and Critical Race Theory

There are several ways to define community service-learning, with common elements including the understanding of service-learning as a teaching method rooted in formal courses that combine community service with academic learning,[4] reflection that helps develop a broader appreciation of an academic discipline,[5] and an attempt to support a positive change in individuals, organizations, neighborhoods, and larger social issues.[6] Service-learning has been offered as a way to improve cross-cultural relations, civic engagement, and personal efficacy, including interpersonal and communication skills.[7] The field of service-learning, while having grown tremendously since the early 1990s, is not without critique, and its establishment as a teaching methodology has been challenged as being unscientifically measurable, with little critique among its advocates.[8] Manley et al. stated that the nature of service-learning methodology, including the role of reflection, raises questions concerning how reciprocal service-learning is to those being served.[9] Manley et al. shared that "in the soup kitchen model of service-learning, there is little commitment to those being served, the frequency of interaction is limited, and the amount of time spent serving those in need is short term." Serving and "splitting the scene" become a part of this interaction and pedagogical approach.[10] Eby contended that service-learning often offers a simplistic understanding of service, teaches a false understanding of need and response to need, diverts attention away from social policy to volunteerism, encourages diversion of agency agendas, and, most critically, can do harm, particularly to children that students may work with "reflecting ethnocentrism and racism in ways that are harmful."[11]

While John Dewey's work concerning the importance of experiential learning the origins of service-learning has been widely discussed, *Unrecognized Roots of Service-Learning* exist within the Black community.[12] Community empowerment, social activists, women's groups, and educators used various educational procedures to encourage community service concerning social welfare initiatives that promoted racial pride and influenced social change.[13] This level of care was reflected in the beginnings of African American communities in the United States. To survive slavery's harsh conditions, Blacks were forced to look after each other and support one another's well-being. The level of activism that has existed also supported community participation reflective of service to the greater good. The Freedom Schools, the Black Panthers, and other groups were involved in community service. The Black church's history of service also reflects this emphasis.[14]

Given the importance of reflective practice, or praxis that develops in the service-learning pedagogy, creating opportunities for voices from multiple perspectives becomes a critical part of the emerging scholarship. Understanding ways to approach issues of race and pedagogy becomes relevant in discussing the role of faculty within institutions of higher education. Critical race theory (CRT) is a method to engage in service-learning pedagogy and scholarship that can ask questions concerning race, higher education, and community. Derived from critiques of critical theory in legal scholarship, CRT merges several disciplines including law, sociology, history, and ethnic and women's studies and has since been used in a number of academic disciplines, including the field of education.[15] Critical race theory offers the opportunity to understand service-learning experiences from its greatest stakeholders—the communities that students serve in. It is this "flipping the switch" that enables a critical lens on approaching community work from an academic perspective and creates the trust and dialogue for communities to enter relationships with universities in a shared space. Here, the concept of a counternarrative becomes useful. Counternarratives challenge the dominant narrative that is reflective of service-learning, including the voices of practitioners, students, and community members from the dominant cultural grouping.[16]

The basic CRT model consists of five elements: (1) the centrality of race and racism and their intersectionality with other forms of oppression, (2) the challenge to dominant ideology around societal problems, (3) the commitment to social justice, (4) the centrality of experiential knowledge, and (5) the transdisciplinary perspective.[17] Critical race theorist, Richard Delgado, claimed that "we cannot identify with or love anyone who is too different form us."[18] The strange "Other" is essentially different from the mainstream and has little concern or care for it, even if it is a vulnerable population.[19] Racially informed relations of power are often fixed in the seemingly objective social languages, especially those associated with science, popular culture, and the media that administrators, educators, and students employ to make claims about Black communities.[20] I argue here that the values and practices of service-learning normalize racism, offering in its literature the association of the community as an "Other."

Critical race theory shows up in several ways concerning educational and pedagogical practices. Taken from critical theories' approach to societal and class struggles, CRT's beginning within the law often cited case history and narrative as a key to understanding voice within the different systems. Critical race theory applies here to education, calling for race to be understood as an important dynamic within the educational system and structure. Service-learning, in its approach to developing an engaged citizenry, looks at educating its students with little understanding of the impact that it has on the community. Creating citizens who care can often backfire. Many White students, when not confronted by these dilemmas, often cite negative stereotypes being reinforced. Many professors struggle with critically assessing societal factors that contribute to problems with education. For example, many students provide tutoring services. College students can enter a tutoring relationship with preconceived notions about education and learning for children in an urban environment. Without training concerning working with children and youth, difficulties may arise in the tutoring relationship.

The Black Man and Higher Education: Oppressed, Liberated, Privileged?

A mentor of mine once told me that it is more important for me to let the community know that I have not left it, than for them to let me know that I am still accepted. While I may carry some visible markings of being a Black man in the United States such as skin color and hairstyle, I carry behind me many of the subtle nuances of the academy such as language, knowledge, position, and power. The university is literally "on my back." Having grown up in two predominantly Black communities—one in Gary, Indiana, and the other on the south side of Chicago—and later entering Morehouse College in Atlanta, Georgia, I was struck with how the perception of myself as a Black man was altered in multiple ways. The "privileging" of a college education, particularly at a prestigious institution such as Morehouse, had several meanings within the Black community.

Morehouse, in the early 1980s, along with the Atlanta University Community, was centered in the middle of a low-income Black community. Having grown up across the street from public housing in my youth, this setting was not strange to me. However, many of my peers at Morehouse often found themselves in conflicting situations with local residents. One of my freshmen classmates was shot in the stomach in "the bottom"—an area literally at the bottom of a hill situated near Clark Atlanta University—during our second month in school after an argument with a community resident. In my second year, my cousin, who was then a freshman, was shot in the head. Both young men survived these traumatic incidents and moved on to graduate and lead productive lives; yet these stories belie the tension that exists between university and community, even between members of the Black community. However, not all neighborhood encounters were problematic and filled with tension, and the majority of experiences interacting with community members were positive.

Upon returning home to Chicago for the first time during a break from school and sitting down for Thanksgiving dinner, my younger nephews and nieces stated that I was "talking White." Although I had not noticed anything different about my speech, it became obvious later that something had changed. Upon visiting familiar places in the neighborhood, although I was still "down" with many of my peers that did not attend college, an interesting tension developed. The privileged distance of being college educated, yet being Black and a man, began to emerge. For many Black males, this negotiated terrain meant sacrificing some of the privileges associated with being a part of neighborhood life. The contrary part is that many of those who opted for other ways of existence beyond the academic space viewed many of the college-educated Black men with envy, hope, and empathy. The envy related to the opportunities that higher education would afford many of us, including economic and social opportunities. Hope was associated with the inspiration of "making it" out of difficult terrains and in a world that discriminates based on race and class, and empathy related to the sense that there will always be a shared understanding of the struggles that Black men encounter both within and outside the Black community. Thus, the importance of staying connected with the Black community becomes relevant to many Black educators; yet, how can this occur without compromising integrity, and how can the existing scholarship be strengthened without co-opting to dominant ideology, particularly in relationship to the Black community and the African Diaspora? As a Black man committed to the nonexploitative development of the Black community service-learning often conflicts with my ethics and values. Black faculty members often deal with the negotiation of this "insider/outsider" status.[21] Sutton asked:

> Can I use my classes as a model for elaboration of a different map of a truly integrated, multicultural society while simultaneously promoting those "rules of the game" that will allow students to become mainstream practitioners? Is it possible to center a teaching agenda on the subject of urban redevelopment—a subject in which I have a deep personal stake—without appearing to be too radical, too Black, too feminist?[22]

Based on this questioning, I worked to develop a service-learning course that could reflect an understanding of the important history and scholarship concerning service and social justice, connect students in the spirit of service to a community and people that may be racially and ethnically different than them, and would not harm the persons within the community, the students, or my personal integrity.

The University, the Class, the Students, and the Community

DePaul University offers the largest service-learning program in Illinois, and one of the top twenty-three service-learning programs as cited by *U.S. News and World Report* on service-learning programs for three consecutive years.[23] I have a unique perspective as having developed one of the first service-learning courses at the institution, having worked to establish partnerships with over one hundred organizations within the Chicagoland community on behalf of the service-learning program, and having taught several service-learning courses since the program's inception within several cross-listed departments at the university (Sociology, Psychology, Community Service Studies). The course was developed in the Community Service Studies Department, a minor for DePaul University undergraduates, in collaboration with the Steans Center for Community-Based Service-Learning at DePaul. Students from all disciplines are encouraged to pursue courses within the minor. The main courses in the minor—Perspectives in Community Service Studies, Introduction to Nonprofit Management, and Community Internships—are taught by DePaul faculty and Steans Center staff. The Perspectives in Community Service course enables DePaul students to receive their Junior-Year Experiential Learning requirement, which is an important feature of DePaul, for every DePaul student must meet this requirement prior to graduation. Students have three options to meet the requirement: (1) an internship, (2) a study abroad course, or (3) a service-learning course with twenty-five service hours as part of its curriculum. The section that I taught of this course offered every student the opportunity to engage in service in a Black community, while learning about the history of community service nationally and abroad. I chose the North Lawndale community and the organizations within it because of my history with the area and the partnerships I had created with the organizations there. Students could have the shared experience of working within the same Chicago neighborhood while participating in diverse experiences within their respective agencies. This community, noted in William Julius Wilson's *When Work Disappears*,[24] reflected a dynamic history of some of the racial dynamics of Chicago in the past century. The predominantly Black community had one of the highest rates in Chicago of ex-felons returning to the community from state penitentiaries.[25] Students are often surprised to find out that Dr. Martin Luther King Jr. stayed in this community during his time in Chicago in the 1960s. They are also surprised when informed that the community was predominantly White and Jewish pre-1960.

Capped at twenty-five students, the demographics included all junior- or senior-level students, predomnantly White. Course readings and lectures reflected the history and models of community service; community organizing and activism within the United States and abroad, including missionary work, nonprofits, and non-governmental agencies within low-income community settings; and readings concerning historically oppressed groups, including the intersections of race, gender, and class and community service. Readings and class topics also covered White privilege, race and racism, and the North Lawndale community, particularly in regard to race and community service and justice.

University–Community

When students from the university enter a relationship with the community, the notions of power and privilege often interact. Many community organizations are vulnerable to slashed budget cuts from federal and local governments, lack of creativity with programming due to funding constraints, and the need to develop and maintain relationships with various economic and social resources. The university is often seen as a potential resource in many cases and, at best, a willing ally to the plight and development of the organization. However, institutions of higher learning have often served to exploit community interests, utilizing community participants as research subjects with little return, engaging in displacement processes based on university land grab into predominantly economically depressed areas that also happen to be communities of color, and offering service and volunteerism that impose values from outside the community, carrying perceptions that often view the community-as-deficit.

Not unlike other discourses, these practices and policies of service-learning appeal to common sense while at the same time shaping programs that serve specific interests.[26] Some believe that service-learning attempts to supplant the removal of federal dollars into urban communities. More and more organizations struggle with developing consistent streams of funding, and service-learners end up taking the place of skilled nonprofit professionals who work and offer services in low-income communities. The value of the workers becomes replaced by the value of the college student. The student, through educational commitment, becomes available to fill in gaps unable to be met with government or private funding. This relationship, based on power and privilege, can be difficult to negotiate, and community voice that declares what it needs versus what the university needs becomes difficult to hear, yet important to understand. As a Black instructor, I often ask the question, Why am I doing this? Do I really want to harm my community? Am I being a sellout by presenting White students to my community, giving them access and entry points for potential? The history of Whites in Black communities has been exploitative. Here I am, a brother from the neighborhood, with an education, walking in to sell them on the fact that we have some students who are going to come in and somehow "help." The community organizations themselves often ask university personnel to keep sending students, so I am torn. Much of these organizations' workers' actions in relationship to institutions of higher education, I judge, are based on the poor conditions of education within so many of our communities.

Faculty–Students

Black faculty have to deal with institutional racism that often manifests within a predominantly White institution, and also the student confusion, mistrust, and bias toward Black professors. Another factor in this is the expectations of students of color, particularly Black students, who have different ideas about connection to professors and educators. I am often the first Black instructor many students, including Black students, have ever encountered. With this, when discussions take place concerning notions of race, often in courses that do not emphasize multiculturalism, cultural competence, explicit race, or racism, then the opportunity and vehicle to discuss issues of race become a negotiated terrain where the Black instructor has to tread lightly on being able to bring attention into focus. It can be argued that race and ethnicity, as it is in the larger society, continue to be important to understand, discuss, and "see" in educational settings.[27] However, this contradicts the other popular notion that one has to be color-blind in order to be fair in seeing students as individuals as opposed to stereotypical members of a racial or ethnic group in higher educational pedagogical practices.[28]

As a Black man teaching classes where the majority of students are women, particularly White women, I know this terrain can be delicate. Ladson-Billings, in discussing silence within the classroom, offered:

> As an African American female, I have grown accustomed to asking myself whether or not perceived slights and discriminations have come as a result of my race, gender, or both. . . . As a college professor I try to understand why and how students interact with me and with the ideas I present in my classes. Am I accorded the same deference they show White male professors? Must I be doubly gracious and accommodating so as not to appear embittered and militant? Do they want me to wear a mask so they do not have to?[29]

Although from a Black female perspective, these negotiated terrains are similar for Black male professors as well, particularly noting the history of Black men in the United States, their relationship with White men and White women, and the different and storied ways these relationships are seen. How do notions of race play into the relationship with students? How does my own privilege of being a heterosexual, well-educated man intersect with race within the shared classroom space? Voice and power have to be recognized, as the terrain and notion of service is often dominated by women's voices, but yet, White men's scholarship still exists within the academy. So within this, do I remove a student from their site that I perceive as racist in their views and, thus, potentially unfit for working with students of color? On what grounds do we as educators have to stop a student we perceive as holding negative views about the Black community? Is a student who says something that can be considered racist simply offering dominant societal views and, thus, although privileged, a victim as well to societal notions of White supremacy and Black inferiority?

There are different roles within this that I often have to play that are not at times complementary, including the role as educator, professional, and community member. Sutton offered the concept of the "tempered radical," negotiating working within a university, understanding how the university is "on my back," and attempting to advance within it, yet understanding the university as racist, patriarchal, and hierarchical in need of change.[30] Often, when Black professors present either a cultural perspective similar to a Black or African-centered worldview in a course that is not within Black or African studies departments, students are often uncomfortable with discussions concerning race, the Black community, or the like. Students often report that the professor is focusing "too much on Black issues." The struggle is to challenge students' worldviews immediately on entering the course, in a manner and way to increase the level of relevance to course discussions and to the notions of service. How do I validate a White student's experience without losing the Black students? Does it matter?

Students–Community

Reflection becomes a part of the voices of the students and not the voices of the communities they serve. University administrators depend on faculty to challenge the students concerning their privilege and dominant group ideology. Students enter into these spaces with little challenge to dominant ideology, and often are not challenged by community-based organizational representatives. One White female student from another course taught by a White professor was challenged by a Black worker who shared with her that "I don't know if White people should be doing this work." When the White professor heard this, he immediately went to the best interest of the student, hearing what he perceived may be a slight against the student. I looked at this as a wonderful opportunity for the student: a Black person in the community being honest about thoughts and feelings that many Blacks have and often do not share.

When students and faculty enter the relationship offering service and a challenge is presented, a *differend* often occurs. A differend occurs based on a conflict between two or more parties that cannot be equitably resolved for lack of terms to which all parties can agree, causing the members of the subjugated group to continue suffering.[31] A differend occurs when "a concept such as justice acquires conflicting meanings for two groups."[32] The ability of those who are oppressed to tell their stories in their own terms, to request their needs and be heard, becomes an important part in this dialectic. Traditional service-learning does not necessarily question the status quo and seeks little to involve the voices of communities of color in its decision making, reflection, and understanding of critical societal issues. Service can take on multiple meanings and reflect subtle nuances from religious to cultural perspectives.

A student of mine was asked by a teacher at a service-learning site to read *The Frederick Douglass Story* to fifth-grade Black children. Although the student read the story, during class he shared how he was appalled that the teacher asked him to read a story about slavery and that children should not talk about slavery in educational settings. He also shared that, as a White man, he felt uncomfortable talking about the subject. Another student, a White male, confronted him, saying "It's this country's history . . . why shouldn't you?!" Here, I had created the space to have critical analysis and reflection of race and race-related issues. I did not have to challenge this student concerning his dominant ideological position, that Black history is a part of U.S. history.

White students often bring their perceptions of the Black community that are based on media and their own community perceptions of race. So what happens when a student comes from a privileged and White background, not having experience with many Blacks, and walks into a setting where the Blacks he or she encounter come from economically impoverished communities? In terms of the violence, the level of drug-related crimes, and the like, the student often looks at the Black community as "What's wrong with these people?" There appears to be a fascination about the mystique of what it means to be Black, urban, inner-city, "ghetto," and a thug, yet these experiences are often awed and vilified at the same time. The result for many of these students is an interest and fascination with Black culture, and a revulsion and disdain for the Black community. So their desire to "help" becomes clouded in White guilt, White supremacy, and moral superiority.

For students of color, oppression becomes a critical part of their lens as well. Many students of color bring ambivalent feelings about the Black community. Students want to give back, have heightened emotional levels, and often bring a level of passion, interest, and commitment that White students do not seem to bring. For many Black students, they have been involved in similar programs or have worked or had family members in similar situations. This dynamic plays itself out with the Black student and the Black professor. So it is within these tensions that Black students become torn with the need to serve while dealing with the guilt of the community conditions.

One student, serving in a community agency run by Blacks that often struggled with financial stability and professionalism in the office, stated that she was not so concerned with how the agency looked for her, but was more concerned about her peers. This student was struck with her own ambivalence and care for the Black community and, at the same time, embarrassed by the conditions of the agency. The Black students all wanted to work together, away from the White students, so as not to have to deal with the tension. The shared relationship here becomes important to meet common and divergent goals that are based on respect and mutuality. When students come back from the site experiences, they are able to discuss items they encountered with different lenses to explore notions of privilege and site challenges in problem areas that can be perceived in helpful, nonracist ways.

Conclusion

Lisa Delpit called the dynamic that can enter into a classroom between diverse constituents "the culture of power," with five major tenets: (1) issues of power are enacted within classrooms; (2) there are codes or rules for participating in power, that is, there is a culture of power; (3) the rules of the culture of power are a reflection of the culture of those who have power; (4) if you are not already a participant in the culture of power, being told explicitly the rules of that culture makes acquiring power easier; and (5) those with power are frequently least aware of—or least willing to acknowledge—its existence.[33] Those with less power are often most aware of its existence. The interest of Whites for the betterment of Black students disappears. In citing what may be important to many Black students, for example, one Black female community worker stated that she has very low expectations of academic improvement from tutoring with White students. The greater impact for her is that her children learn to interact with those who might be different from them, understanding that the children's culture may be largely different from what they may experience in a White world. For that reason, I share with many of my students that it may be more important to share experiences of travel, what it may be like to be in college or to be a child in school, and the like in order to demystify the experience of Whiteness as perceived by many students of color. However, many students struggle with this and attempt to focus more on improving literacy and math skills in the short periods that they are at the site.

Duncan wrote that

> whether or not Black teachers and cultural workers accept it, we hold positions of moral and intellectual leadership in our communities. Therefore, to uncritically teach assimilation and accommodation— to teach life as accepting life as it is—is to teach a lie and to affirm the violence that places Black children and youth at risk and beyond love.[34]

In summary, a brief story can help place closure to the intent of this writer. The chicken and the pig were walking on the farm one day. The chicken said to the pig, "Let's offer a service for the farmer." The pig replied to the chicken, "What do you have in mind?" The chicken replied, "How about cooking him some bacon and eggs?" The pig then replied, "What might be a service for you, is a commitment for me." This commitment lies at the heart of this chapter: service-learning may be a service or occasional indulgence for some faculty or students. However, it is beyond simple service for many faculty of color, particularly those whose histories have been steeped within the Black community.

Notes

This chapter is dedicated to Dr. Caleb Dube, the hardest-working faculty engaged in service-learning at DePaul University. Your scholarship, teaching, and engagement within community will surely be missed, but most of all, the absence of your soul here can never be replaced. Peace, Black man.

The author uses the term *Black* in reference to himself as an African American, as well as those considered to be a part of the African American community and the African Diaspora.

1. R. Ellison, *Invisible Man* (New York: Random House, 1947); J. T. Gibbs, "Young Black Males in America: Endangered, Embittered, and Embattled," in *Young, Black, and Male in America: An Endangered Species*, ed. J. T. Gibbs (New York: Auburn House, 1988), 1–36; H. Madhubuti, *Black Men: Obsolete, Single, Dangerous? The African American Family in Transition* (Chicago: Third World Press, 1991).

2. E. Erikson, *Identity: Youth and Crisis* (New York: Norton, 1994).

3. T. Manley et al., "Putting the Learning in Service-Learning: From Soup Kitchen Models to the Black Metropolis Model," *Education and Urban Society*, 38 no. 2 (2006): 115–41.

4. A. Furco, *Service-Learning: A Balanced Approach to Experiential Education, Expanding Boundaries: Serving and Learning* (Washington, DC: Corporation for National Service, 1996), 2–6.

5. R. G. Bringle and J. A. Hatcher, "A Service-Learning Curriculum for Faculty," *Michigan Journal of Community Service-Learning* 2 (1995): 112–22.

6. N. I. Cruz, "Where's the Community in Service-Learning Research?" *Michigan Journal of Community Service-Learning* 7 (2000): 28–34.

7. J. Eyler, D. E. Giles Jr., and C. J. Grey, "Research at a Glance: The Effects of Service-Learning on Students, Faculty, Institutions and Community, 1993–1999," in *Introduction to Service-Learning Toolkit: Readings and Resources for Faculty*, ed. Campus Compact (Providence, RI: Brown University, 1999), 21–24.

8. J. Eby, "Why Service-Learning Is Bad," unpublished manuscript, 1998.

9. Manley et al., "Putting the Learning in Service-Learning."

10. Manley et al., "Putting the Learning in Service-Learning," 117.

11. Eby, "Why Service-Learning Is Bad," 5.

12. C. E. Jones, P. Dixon, and A. O. Umoja, "Return to the Source: The Role of Service-Learning in Recapturing the Empowerment Mission of African American Studies," *Western Journal of Black Studies* 27, no. 3 (2003): 205–14; C. S. Stevens, "Unrecognized Roots of Service-Learning in African American Social Thought and Action, 1890–1930," *Michigan Journal of Community Service-Learning* 9, no. 2, (2003): 25–34; B. Jones, "Discovering Our Heritage: Community Service and the Historically Black University," *Successful Service-Learning Programs: New Models of Excellence in Higher Education* (Boston, MA: Anker, 1998), 109–23.

13. Stevens, "Unrecognized Roots."

14. Stevens, "Unrecognized Roots."

15. G. A. Duncan, "Beyond Love: A Critical Race Ethnography of the Schooling of Adolescent Black Males," *Equality and Excellence in Education* 35,

no. 2 (2002): 131–43; G. Ladson-Billings, "Silences as Weapons: Challenges of a Black Professor Teaching White Students," *Theory Into Practice* 35, no. 2 (1996): 79–82; D. Solorzano, M. Ceja, and T. Yosso, "Critical Race Theory, Racial Microaggressions, and Campus Climate: The Experiences of African American College Students," *Journal of Negro Education* 69, no. 1/2 (2000): 60–74.

16. C. A. Stanley, "When Counter Narratives Meet Master Narratives in the Journal Editorial-Review Process," *Educational Reseacher* 36, no. 1 (2007): 14–24; L. Parker and M. Lynn, "What's Race Got to Do with It? Critical Race Theory's Conflicts With and Connections to Qualitative Research Methodology and Epistemology," *Qualitative Inquiry* 8, no. 1 (2002): 7–22.

17. D. Solorzano and T. J. Yosso, "Critical Race Methodology: Counter-Storytelling as an Analytical Framework for Education Research," *Qualitative Inquiry* 8, no. 1 (2002): 23–44.

18. R. Delgado, *Critical Race Theory: The Cutting Edge* (Philadelphia: Temple University Press, 1995), 55.

19. Duncan, "Beyond Love."

20. Duncan, "Beyond Love."

21. Stanley, When Counter Narratives Meet"; S. Sutton, "Contradictory Missions of a Tempered Radical," in *Praxis I: A Faculty Casebook for Community Service-Learning,* ed. J. Howard (Ann Arbor, MI: OCSL Press, 1993), 157–62.

22. Sutton, "Contradicting Missions," 152.

23. "America's Best Colleges 2007," *U.S. News and World Report*, http://www.usnews.com/usnews/edu/college/directory/brief/drglance_16 71_brief.php (accessed December 2, 2006).

24. W. J. Wilson, *When Work Disappears: The World of the New Urban Poor* (New York: Knopf, 1996).

25. L. McKean and J. Raphael, *Drugs, Crime, and Consequences: Arrests and Incarceration in North Lawndale* (North Lawndale, IL: North Lawndale Employment Network and Center for Impact Research, 2002).

26. Duncan, "Beyond Love"; H. A. Giroux, *The Abandoned Generation: Democracy Beyond the Culture of Fear* (New York: Palgrave McMillan, 2003); Solorzano and Yosso, "Critical Race Methodology."

27. Ladson-Billings, "Silences as Weapons"; M. I. Philipsen, "Race, the College Classroom, and Service-Learning: A Practitioner's Tale," *Journal of Negro Education* 72, no. 2 (2003): 230–40.

28. Philipsen, "Race"; L. Valli, "The Dilemma of Race: Learning to Be Color-Blind and Color Conscious," *Journal of Teacher Education* 46, no. 2 (1995): 120–29.

29. Ladson-Billings, "Silences as Weapons," 81.

30. Sutton, "Contradictory Missions."

31. Delgado, *Critical Race Theory*; Duncan, "Beyond Love."

32. Duncan, "Beyond Love," 44.

33. L. Delpit, *Other People's Children: Cultural Conflict in the Classroom* (New York: Norton, 1995).

34. G. A. Duncan, "School Violence, Black Masculinities, and a Mother's Love: Reflections on (In)Formal Urban Pedagogies," in *Black Sons to Mothers: Compliments, Critiques, and Challenges for Cultural Workers in Education,* ed. M. C. Brown II and J. E. Davis (New York: Peter Lang, 2000), 71–92, 89.

8

❖ ❖ ❖

Racial Identity and the Ethics of Service-Learning as Pedagogy

ANNEMARIE VACCARO

Teaching undergraduates about complex social issues can be a challenging process, one not easily done through lecture and text alone. Engaging students in local environments provides opportunities for them to witness the social world and understand academic concepts in a richer way.

> As pedagogy, service-learning is education that is grounded in experience as a basis for learning and on the centrality and intentionality of reflection designed to enable learning to occur.[1]

A host of academic and developmental benefits of service-learning have been documented, including enhanced learning and skill building.[2] Using service-learning as a pedagogical tool can provide opportunities for students to understand course materials in the context of the "real world." Yet, the often invisible lens of racial identity development influences the way students see and interpret this world. Racial identity also influences how college students interact with community members at their service-learning site.

This chapter explores the intersections between service-learning, the racial identities of college students, and the identities of community members impacted through service-learning classes. This work was inspired by eight years of teaching service-learning courses at a private, predominantly White research university. This chapter is written from a markedly different perspective than many others in this volume. Instead of focusing solely on Black racial identity, this chapter is an attempt to interrogate the issue of White identity and White privilege as they relate to service-learning in communities of color. Far too much scholarship on service-learning focuses on the benefits of service-learning without acknowledging the complex ways Whiteness impacts communities of color. Traditional service-learning literature is steeped in hegemonic Whiteness and fails to acknowledge the potential harm done by White students in communities of color. In the following pages, White identity and service-learning are dissected to uncover the hidden effects of White privilege on communities of color. Actual student experiences reveal the vast discrepancies between the positive impact of students of color and the negative effects of White students in the local community. In short, the negative implications that White racial identity and privilege can have on Black communities is a central component of this work.

Since this chapter is informed by data collected from a host of communities, a variety of terms are used, including: *communities of color*, *people of color*, *African American*, *Black*, and *White*. Predominantly African American communities described in this chapter included people who identified as Black, mixed race, biracial, and others who did not self-identify as any race. Thus, throughout this chapter different descriptors are used to most accurately and respectfully describe the college student or community member in each example.

The overarching emphasis of this chapter is to explore the ethical issues related to racial identity and service-learning as pedagogy. However, it provides no solid answer as to whether service-learning is ethical. The intent of the chapter is to encourage the reader to grapple with the complexity of the intersections between learning, stereotypical attitudes, White privilege, microaggressions, ethical concepts, and racial identity development. It should be used as a starting point for reflection and dialogue among university and community members.

Ethical Concepts

Before proceeding with an analysis of service-learning, an overview of ethical concepts is necessary. In the realm of higher education, ethical codes of conduct and moral guidelines abound. Each discipline has one or more codes of conduct that higher education professionals are expected to follow. Information from the American Association of University Professors and College Student Educators International was combined with literature from higher education to shape three ethical concepts for use in this chapter:[3]

1. Ethical Concept #1: *Do no harm.* This principle can be found in most ethical codes of conduct and serves as an overarching concept for this chapter.
2. Ethical Concept #2: *Ethical relationships.* In addition to treating others with dignity and respect, this concept requires relationships be free from

deceit. Ethical relationships should be reciprocal and nonexploitative. Such relationships are necessary for the type of collaborative learning and collective investment that Evans describes in the preface to this book.

3. Ethical Concept #3: *Ethical guides.* The American Association of University Professors argues that professors should "adhere to their proper role as intellectual guides and counselors."[4]

Racial Identity Development

What happens when students at predominantly White institutions are asked to perform service-learning in communities of color? In this chapter, the racial identity development of both African American and White undergraduates is juxtaposed to the racial identity of people of color touched through service-learning courses. Although a host of racial identity development models are available,[5] Hardiman and Jackson's model of racial identity development was selected for this chapter.[6] This model is sometimes used to compare people from all races, yet the original research for this theory was completed with African American and White participants.[7] Table 8.1 presents a brief interpretation of the stages of this model.

TABLE 8.1. Interpretation of Selected Stages of Racial Identity Development for Both People of Color and Whites

Stage of Racial Identity	Hallmarks of the Stage of Racial Identity Development
Naïve	Little or no awareness of race
Acceptance	Active or passive acceptance of dominant White culture; Whiteness is valued and normalized while Blackness is the devalued other
Resistance	Increasing awareness and understanding of oppression, including both individual and institutional factors involved in racism
Redefinition	Creation of an identity not rooted in an oppressive system; Connection to like-minded and like-experienced others
Internalization	Incorporation of new identity and work toward social justice

Source: Adapted from R. Hardiman and B. Jackson, "Racial Identity Development: Understanding Racial Dynamics in College Classrooms and on Campus," in *New Directions for Teaching and Learning,* ed. M. Adams (San Francisco, CA: Jossey-Bass, 1992), 24.

According to Hardiman and Jackson, White students generally enter college in either active or passive acceptance.[8] Because of this, when White college students are referenced in this chapter, they are assumed to be in the racial identity stage of acceptance. In this identity stage, White individuals accept the views of the dominant culture and generally believe stereotypes and myths about people of color. Active acceptance can be seen in overt use of stereotypes and racist behavior. White people in passive acceptance usually do not see themselves as racist and are generally unaware of the covert ways they perpetuate racism. Unconscious stereotypes shape their attitudes about and behavior with people of color. Through college experiences, White students can move into the stage of resistance. However, this shift happens only when Whites learn that oppression is a reality, and that as White people, they receive privileges based on the color of their skin.

In contrast, African American college students generally arrive at predominantly White institutions in the racial identity stages of resistance or redefinition. In resistance, people of color refuse to accept the dominant White worldview and begin to question why things are "the way they are." The pain and frustration of constantly challenging dominant paradigms eventually force people of color to move into a place where they redefine who they are. A new identity is made independently of White supremacy and is often done within safe, racially homogeneous spaces. African American students are sometimes labeled "separatists" by Whites who do not understand the need for in-group support at this stage of racial identity.[9]

Youth of color in the local community will have a variety of racial identity levels, with young children presenting in the naïve or acceptance stages of racial identity. In the naïve stage, little or no consciousness of racial differences exists, but even very young children of color are socialized into an American culture where White is valued and Black is devalued. Through the socialization process, children of color move into the racial identity stage of acceptance where Whiteness is normalized as right, smart, and beautiful. By the time they enter middle or early high school, youth of color may have moved through acceptance into resistance.

What are the implications for interactions across racial identity stages at service-learning sites? Forthcoming sections provide insight into potential interactions between youth of color in local communities and college students doing service in those communities.

Service-Learning: The Benefits

There are a host of benefits associated with service-learning. First, universities that offer service-learning courses provide immeasurable sources of human capital to local communities. Many community agencies depend on volunteers for survival. Programs such as after-school tutoring and mentoring programs might not survive without the help of college students.

In addition to the benefits to local agencies, there are a plethora of rewards for college students. The benefits of service-learning for undergraduate students include enhanced learning, construction of an integrated identity, interpersonal skill building, and an increased sense of civic responsibility.[10] Other research shows that when students perform service in diverse settings, they become more open-minded and aware of social problems.[11] Using service-learning can be a powerful way to introduce college students to diverse populations and complex social issues. Giving students the opportunity to witness examples of social in-equalities in the local community can make learning relevant, intellectually stimulating, and emotionally impactful. Service-learning students say things like: "the course taught me a lot about the real world," or service "really opened my eyes to a lot of things." Sometimes, service-learning courses force students to question their biases.[12] At a service site, students may interact with someone of a different race for the first time. One woman, reflecting on her service experience said, "I became more aware of how my mentee thinks about her world, in the context of her culture and how she was raised. Our differences make sense and aren't so hard to get around."

Another student admitted that the service-learning class "got me out of my comfort zone . . . both physically and intellectually." A third student described her service experience as "stereotype shattering." Community managers also described students (usually White) as "being challenged about [their] assumptions about [social] issues." Some students even reported that their lives have changed as a result of engaging in service-learning. They have said things like "I learned so much and really grew as a person while taking this course."

College courses are often the first time that White students have considered racism a reality. Rarely have they grappled with the concepts of oppression or White privilege. Such learning experiences can be earth-shattering for White students, as is evidenced in the following quotes:

- The hardest thing for me to learn is that I am racist. I always thought that I was very good about treating people equally, but now I've learned this is not enough, because I willingly enjoy the privilege of being White.
- I learned a lot about myself and was truthfully ashamed of what I found out.
- I have learned . . . that I am an aversive racist. At times, I make prejudgments before being aware of all the facts. I would never have admitted this on the first day of class . . . partly because I really didn't think that I had racist tendencies. Even if I were to recognize [my] behavior, I would never have had the guts to share it with people!

These types of epiphanies are necessary for White students to cognitively and affectively move from the racial identity stage of acceptance into resistance, and toward a nonracist identity.

If we were to consider only the community agency needs and the growth of college students, we might consider service-learning ethical. A professor who strives to be an intellectual "ethical guide" might argue that service-learning is the best way to transmit meaningful knowledge. Unfortunately, service-learning involves more than just learning about course concepts and White privilege. Comprehension is shaded by students' racial identity development. Student interactions with people at service-learning sites are also influenced by racial identity.

Service-Learning: The Potential Harm

Just as there are benefits, potential risks are also associated with service-learning. This chapter does not address overt acts of racism, disrespect, or abuse of community members, as such actions are clearly unethical. Instead, psychological research is combined with actual service-learning experiences to explore three potentially hidden dangers of engaging White college students with communities of color. The analysis focuses on (1) the intersections of racial identity, racist attitudes, and worldviews; (2) the effects of aversive racism, microaggressions, and White privilege on youth of color; and (3) the reciprocity of relationships formed between college students completing service-learning and community members of color. As described in the introduction, the intent of the next sections is to interrogate Whiteness and its effects on Black communities. Quotes and observations of both White and Black service-learning students are contrasted throughout this section to highlight the vast racial differences regarding each of these three topics.

Student Worldviews: Shaped by Racial Identity

In reviewing three academic terms of service-learning evaluations at one Western institution, one-third of students strongly agreed that they became more aware of their own biases as a result of their service experience. What about the other two-thirds? Were their biases reinforced or did they remain the same? One community manager talked about White students being consistently introduced to diverse people who face daily inequalities. Yet, she laments that rarely can she "verify that it necessarily sinks in." The following paragraphs provide insight into the ways racist attitudes and stereotypes, harbored by Whites in acceptance, negatively affect African American communities.

Although stereotypes held by White students can be shattered through service, negative attitudes can also be learned and harmful stereotypes reinforced. Because their racial identity lens is different, perspectives and attitudes of White service-learning students and students of color can be markedly different. African American and White college students engaging in service-learning in the same public school viewed the community and its members in distinct ways. For White students in the stage of acceptance, racist stereotypes were reinforced. In one underperforming public school, Whites saw laziness, apathy, and bad behavior among youth of color. In a course paper, one White woman wrote, "I hate to say it, but it looked as though these people were lazy."

Students of color in resistance or redefinition did not view the community through the same lens. An African American woman wrote in her service-learning journal, "It was frustrating, because no matter how much I talked to the students, or helped them with their work, I knew that I could not fix many of the problems that were really causing the high volumes of apathy." College students of color in resistance or redefinition understand that the world is complex and ridden with inequalities. In the previous situation, the Black college student saw cultural and institutional racism as the root of student apathy, whereas her White counterpart saw only stereotypes. In another instance, a girl named Maria told her tutor that she was "too stupid and too slow" to complete her assignment. As a person of color himself, the tutor knew that her lack of self-esteem was partly the result of living in a racist society and attending a school system where youth of color were consistently given negative labels. He said, "I was ready to burst with frustration at her self-deprecation." The level of understanding, and consequently the reactions by service-learning students to youth of color, is shaped by racial identity. In Maria's case, White students in acceptance may have seen mere poor self-esteem, whereas a student of color recognized the racial context of the child's comment. Consider the level of understanding of another service-learning student of color who wrote in her journal about the double-edged sword her middle school students faced.

> On one hand, the students learned to be resilient and outspoken about issues that involve them, while on the other hand, they have internalized the fact that when labeled as a person of color, one has to fight for any chance to be successful because of that label.

Because they do not recognize that oppression exists, White students in acceptance may be unable to comprehend the racial inequalities inherent in the experiences of youth of color. Thus, White college students may have little awareness of the "fight" that youth of color engage in on a daily basis. Their privileged worldview overshadows every interaction White service-learning students have with community members. In sum, racial identity shapes the way individuals experience and interpret the world. Convergent realities for students in different stages of racial identity affect the ways service-learning students view and interact with youth of color.

Aversive Racism and Microaggressions

Even when White students enter communities of color with big hearts and good intentions, they still behave in ways shaped by their racial identity. Well-meaning White people bring to the community stereotypes they have learned their entire lives. Kozol laments a historic example of this phenomenon.[13] In the late 1960s and early 1970s he saw scores of "young [White] people who had the benefits of . . . successful education" enter Black schools to teach. Their good intentions resulted in immeasurable amounts of harm to African American youth in those schools. Similarly, through unintentional actions, contemporary college students may be doing harm to people in communities of color.

Even small, seemingly benign interactions between White college students in acceptance and people of color can be damaging. Discrimination in the twenty-first century is covert and at times unintentional. Instead of facing overt racist events, people of color face a consistent pattern of small, yet painful, racist happenings called "microaggressions."[14] Microaggressions are:

> [s]ubtle, stunning, often automatic, and nonverbal exchanges which are "put downs" of Blacks by offenders. The offensive mechanisms used against Blacks are innocuous. The cumulative weight of their never-ending burden is the major ingredient in Black–White interactions.[15]

Research has shown numerous negative effects of microaggressions on people of color. They include feelings of invisibility, self-doubt, frustration, exhaustion, helplessness, and racial tension.[16] In the previous section, Maria's lack of confidence and low self-image may be traced to the cumulative effect of microaggressions.

Microaggressions are related to aversive racism, which includes unconscious racist feelings and behaviors, usually by White people, who believe themselves to be nonracist or egalitarian.[17] Constantine found that even White counseling professionals with extensive antiracist training engaged in microaggressions with African American clients. If trained professionals perpetuated microaggressions, White service-learning students will likely do the same. College students may join the scores of individuals who add constant burdens or microaggressions to the shoulders of youth of color. By engaging in unintentional or unconscious racial slights, White students may perpetuate harm in communities of color. One community supervisor described a White service-learning student as very committed. Yet "she may not . . . be sensitive to cultural situations with the students." Another site supervisor talked about a White student's inability to seem "natural" around the children. In these cases, racial discomfort was obvious to both supervisors and community members. For youth of color, insensitivity and racial discomfort by Whites can reinforce the normalization of Whiteness.

White students in acceptance rarely understand or admit that they receive race privilege or benefits, assets, and opportunities based merely on the color of their skin. They can wield their privilege in ways that are offensive and painful to people of color. One community supervisor described a situation in which a privileged White tutor drove his Hummer to a middle school in a low-income neighborhood. A child of color walked up to the vehicle and spat on it. The supervisor explained that whether the White college student realized it or not, he was "flaunting his privilege." The college student was grossly offended by the middle school student's behavior, which only reinforced his stereotypes, racist beliefs, and his racial identity development stage of acceptance. The youth of color was likely in the racial identity stage of resistance, and was showing his disgust with White privilege by his actions. Franklin and Boyd-Franklin found that constant microaggressions can cause people of color to manifest internalized rage or immobilized frustration.[28] These feelings are also associated with the racial identity stage of resistance.

White privilege and its effects can be seen in another instance with a White college student. While serving as a mentor at a community center, a student reported that when people of color:

> started to complain that there is no work, I brought them a book of jobs and helped them find one they would enjoy. I heard every excuse why they shouldn't take the job. I couldn't believe that these people were turning down jobs. These jobs were paying more than most of my friends and I make!

Although she was trying to be helpful, her racial identity stage of acceptance led her to inflict a host of microaggressions. Community members of color in the racial identity stage of resistance experienced her as a privileged White woman with no understanding of their lives. To them, she represented all White people who believe stereotypes of laziness and lack of motivation. Her stated intentions may appear good on the surface, but going the extra mile to find job listings and suggest appropriate (but low-wage) jobs that people of color "would enjoy" was demeaning. Her actions spoke volumes about her belief in their inferiority. People of color in acceptance can also be hurt by behaviors that reinforce the idea that they are undeserving of services, jobs, or equality. Community members in resistance or redefinition would probably not return to the job center. Why should they return to a place where racist White people tell them what they are worthy of doing? In their research, Solórzano, Ceja, and Yosso found a pattern of African Americans not using services because of their frustration or discomfort with White service providers.[19] In this instance, community members of color who avoided the job center were consequently disenfranchised by a loss of access to material resources and opportunities.

Reciprocal Relationships

Sometimes community agencies seek out university volunteers so that community youth can "get the opportunity to see kids going to college." Many community supervisors hoped that college students would serve as leaders and role models. One described college students as "helpful and empowering." She believed the interactions between youth and college students helped "expand the reality of what is possible for these kids to achieve." But are all relationships between service-learning students and community members ethical? In order for a relationship to be ethical it must be reciprocal and free from exploitation. College students experience several benefits from service-learning, including skill enhancement, résumé-building experiences, and course credit. But what are the benefits for youth of color? If the benefits are not equal, are these relationships reciprocal and, thus, ethical?

Research has shown that as a result of aversive racism and microaggressions, people of color may fear or avoid relationships with White people.[20] Similar behavior is also a hallmark of the racial identity stage of resistance. In situations where it cannot be avoided, people of color may choose to engage in shallow relationships with Whites. Constantine found that African American people were less likely to trust White counselors.[21] African Americans expressed frustration at the lack of genuine relationships with White counselors who either unconsciously manifested racism or were unable to help them process racial events. Similar issues are apparent in examples where youth of color are able to express their true selves to mentors of color, but not to White service-learning students.

One community worker talked about the common occurrence of White college students entering communities of color hoping to be mentors. Often, they have "not been particularly well received." To be a role model, one must have respect. Additionally, teenagers will "be real" only with people they trust. For teens of color in resistance, White service-learning students represent an oppressive system. Thus, youth of color may not form substantial relationships with Whites. Conversely, teens of color in resistance or reintegration may be drawn to college students of color as mentors. In three years serving as a mentor in local schools, one college student of color has come to believe that mentors of color are more effective than White ones. Another service-learning student agreed that "it becomes more realistic to see a nontraditional (non-White) role model . . . someone who has been where you have been." Youth of color are more likely to share experiences with college students who have lived the realities of discrimination. Youth may talk openly with college students of color who may have had similar experiences of being profiled by police, followed by storeowners, or tokenized by teachers. One community supervisor described the phenomenon as "instant credibility." In an extreme case, one African American woman had childern reach out to her not only because she was a woman of color, but also because she had grown up in a local neighborhood. She knew that teens would never have confided in her about a neighborhood shooting if she had been a White person.

Community supervisors confirmed that White service-learning students are sometimes "unable to truly connect" with youth of color. When this happens, White students can have their racial identity of acceptance reinforced. When a White person's hopes of being a great mentor are dashed, said one site supervisor, negative opinions about people of color can be reinforced as White's "spiral into hurt, anger, and frustration." Such reinforcement is never the intent of service-learning, but unfortunately it is often an unintended outcome.

Conclusion

Tough Ethical Questions

This chapter offers an interrogation of Whiteness and exposes the potential harm of engaging White students with communities of color. However, it does not provide an answer as to whether service as pedagogy is ethical. Instead, it concludes with more unanswered and tough ethical questions. In the previous pages, student reflections, community voices, and research studies provided an image of service-learning that is layered with complexity. The benefits of service-learning are notable, but to focus solely on the benefits is to see only part of the picture.

By encouraging service-learning, universities are showing dedication to the public good. In many college towns, community agencies might cease to operate without students engaged in service-learning. Professors who use service as pedagogy provide powerful opportunities for growth and development of college students. Further, by witnessing oppression in the community, White students can experience the dissonance necessary to move into the racial identity stage of resistance. If White people are not challenged to move from acceptance to higher stages of racial identity development, they will continue to engage in active or passive racism in their everyday lives. For a society to exist free from racial stereotypes and microaggressions, the dominant group (Whites) must move through acceptance to higher stages of racial identity. Faculty members who teach service-learning courses can potentially guide White students on a journey toward acknowledging White privilege. But is it ethical for such learning experiences to be gained at a potential cost to communities of color?

Although service-learning may be a powerful learning tool, it can also be harmful. Whether the harm is intentional or unintentional, the impact on communities of color can be great. White students in acceptance may have significant negative effects on the youth they are serving. By engaging in microaggressions, White people can add to the sense of invisibility, frustration, and exhaustion of youth of color. In sharp contrast, college students of color engaging in the community may provide an invaluable service, more in line with the philosophical ideals of social change and community engagement. But, is it ethical to only send students of color to engage in service-learning? Is it ethical for college students of color to bear the burden of being role models and mentors to youth of color, especially when they must also maintain the emotional strength to fight micro-aggressions in their own lives?

In this chapter, it was argued that when White students engage in service-learning in communities of color, the relationships that develop may be nonreciprocal or devoid of true respect. In short, White students may benefit more from service-learning relationships than people of color. Such relationships can be exploitative and unethical. Once again, the thesis of this chapter emerges and the question remains. Could White college students potentially do more harm than good when engaging in service-learning with communities of color?

As I stated at the beginning of this chapter, no clear-cut determination of service-learning as ethical or unethical would be offered. Instead, my intention was to raise tough ethical questions about sending White college students into communities of color. The chapter covered topics rarely addressed in the service-learning literature with the hope of inspiring further conversations about these complex ethical issues. In sum, to determine whether service-learning is ethical, issues of White identity, privilege, aversive racism, microaggressions, and reciprocity in relationships must be acknowledged, understood, and analyzed.

Reconciling Ethics and Service-Learning: Thoughts for the Future

Because higher education institutions have the resources to meet community needs, ending service-learning could have vast negative repercussions in the community. Many community programs might not survive without the person-power provided by service-learning students. Yet, colleges and universities that wish to require or encourage service-learning have an ethical obligation to safeguard communities of color from harm. To make service truly ethical, aversive racism, microaggressions, and structural oppression must be extinguished. However, such lofty aims will require much time and a revisioning of society as a whole. In the meantime, there are six ways faculty and staff can reduce the harm done to communities of color.

1. *Teach from a critical perspective.* White students in acceptance only move to resistance when they learn that societal oppression and their privileges are a reality. Faculty who teach their disciplinary topic through the lens of social justice or critical race theory aid in this educational process. The more places White students learn about oppression, the more likely it is to sink in.
2. *Teach racial identity development models.* By learning racial identity development theory in service-learning classes, college students can better understand how their view of, and experiences in, the com-

munity are shaped by their racial identity. When students of color learn about racial identity development, they are learning the science of their lived experiences. Although the content may be no surprise, it can provide the theoretical framework and language to describe their experiences and an unspoken sense of validation.[22] Conversely, White students in the racial identity development stage of acceptance who learn about racial identity are faced with the reality of oppression and their race privilege. It is impossible for White students in acceptance to comprehend racial identity theory without acknowledging how oppression and privilege are a part of their daily lives. When teaching White students about privilege, faculty can help students become more self-aware and potentially reduce the amount of harm done in local communities.

3. *Support college students of color.* Students of color can provide invaluable resources to youth in local communities. We must take measures to ensure these students are not overburdened or unsupported in their efforts. It is important to remember that college students of color also experience the weight of microaggressions in their daily lives.

4. *Offer service options.* If it is obvious that a privileged White student may cause harm, educators have an obligation not to place them in an environment where they can negatively impact the lives of community members of color. Other service-learning sites, where they do not interact with people of color, should be offered as options.

5. *Require preservice social justice training.* Universities should offer preservice diversity training that stresses issues of privilege, respect, and care for others. One site director appreciated the implementation of diversity awareness training for her volunteers. She said, "We appreciate how well you encourage students to . . . broaden their experiences. The topic of White privilege . . . is very important."

6. *Dialogue with the community.* Only through strong relationships with community agencies can we build relationships of trust and honest communication. Through such relationships we are more likely to identify potential harm. We may not be able to eliminate every microaggression, but we have an obligation to stop harm when we recognize it.

Notes

1. B. Jacoby, *Service-Learning in Higher Education: Concepts and Practices* (San Francisco, CA: Jossey-Bass, 1996), 9; A. W. Astin and L. J. Sax, "How Undergraduates Are Affected by Service Participation," *Journal of College Student Development* 39, no. 3 (1998): 250–63.

2. S. R. Jones and E. S. Abes, "Enduring Influences of Service-Learning on College Students' Identity Development," *Journal of College Student Development*

45, no. 2 (2004): 149–66; G. B. Markus, J. P. Howard, and D. C. King, "Integrating Community Service and Classroom Instruction Enhances Learning: Results from an Experiment," *Educational Evaluation and Policy Analysis* 15, no. 4 (1993): 410–19; R. A. Rhoads, "In the Service of Citizenship: A Study of Student Involvement in Community Service," *Journal of Higher Education* 69, no. 3 (1998): 277–97.

3. T. L. Beauchamp, *Philosophical Ethics: An Introduction to Moral Philosophy*, 3rd ed. (Boston, MA: McGraw Hill, 2001); K. A. Strike and P. A. Moss, *Ethics and College Student Life* (Boston, MA: Allyn and Bacon, 1997); American Association of University Professors, "Statement on Professional Ethics," 1987, http://www.aaup.org/AAUP/pubsres/policydocs/statementonprofessionalethics.htm (accessed February 25, 2007); College Student Educators International, "Statement of Ethical Principles and Standards," 2006, http://www.myacpa.org/ethics/statement.cfm (accessed February 25, 2007).

4. American Association of University Professors, "Statement on Professional Ethics."

5. W. E. Cross Jr., "The Negro-to-Black Conversion Experience: Toward a Psychology of Black Liberation," *Black World* 20, no. 9 (1971): 13–27; J. E. Helms, *Black and White Racial Identity: Theory, Research, and Practice* (Westport, CT: Praeger, 1993); J. S. Phinney, "Ethnic Identity in Adolescents and Adults: Review of Research," *Psychological Bulletin* 108 (1990): 499–511.

6. R. Hardiman and B. Jackson, "Racial Identity Development: Understanding Racial Dynamics in College Classrooms and on Campus," in *New Directions for Teaching and Learning*, ed. M. Adams (San Francisco, CA: Jossey-Bass, 1992), 21–37.

7. For African American research, see B. W. Jackson, "Black Identity Development," in *Urban Social and Educational Issues*, ed. L. Golubschick and B. Persky (Dubuque, IA: Kendall/Hunt, 1976). For White research, see R. Hardiman, "White Identity Development Theory" (PhD diss., University of Massachusetts, 1979).

8. Hardiman and Jackson, "Racial identity Development."

9. B. D. Tatum, *Why Are All the Black Kids Sitting Together in the Cafeteria? And Other Conversations about Race* (New York: Basic Books, 1997).

10. Astin and Sax, "How Undergraduates Are Affected"; Jones and Abes, "Enduring Influences of Service-Learning."

11. Markus, Howard, and King, "Inegrating Community Service"; Rhoads, "In the Service of Citizenship."

12. Rhoads, "In the Service of Citizenship."

13. J. Kozol, *The Shame of the Nation: The Restoration of Apartheid in Schooling in America* (New York: Three Rivers Press, 2005).

14. C. Pierce, J. Carew, D. Pierce-Gonzales, and D. Willis, "An Experiment in Racism: TV Commercials," in *Television and Education*, ed. C. Pierce (Beverly Hills, CA: Sage, 1978), 62–88; D. G. Solórzano, M. Ceja, and

T. J. Yosso, "Critical Race Theory, Microaggressions, and Campus Racial Climate: The Experiences of African American College Students," *Journal of Negro Education* 69, no. 1/2 (2000): 60–73.

15. Pierce, Carew, Pierce-Gonzales, and Willis, "An Experiment in Racism."

16. M. G. Constantine, "Racial Microaggressions against African American Clients in Cross Racial Counseling Relationships," *Journal of Counseling Psychology* 54, no. 1 (2007): 1–16; A. J. Franklin and N. Boyd-Franklin, "Invisibility Syndrome: A Clinical Model of the Effects of Racism on African American Males," *American Journal of Orthopsychiatry* 70, no. 1 (2000): 33–41; Solórzano, Ceja, and Yosso, "Critical Race Theory."

17. Constantine, "Racial Microaggressions," 2.

18. Franklin and Boyd-Franklin, "Invisibility Syndrome."

19. Solórzano, Ceja, and Yosso, "Critical Race Theory."

20. Constantine, "Racial Microaggressions"; Solórzano, Ceja, and Yosso, "Critical Race Theory."

21. Constantine, Racial Microaggressions."

22. L. Rendón, "Validating Culturally Diverse Students: Toward a New Model of Learning and Student Development," *Innovative Higher Education* 19 (1994): 33–52.

9

◆◆◆

"We'll Understand It Better By and By"

A Three-Dimensional Approach to Teaching Race through Community Engagement

META MENDEL-REYES AND DWAYNE A. MACK

As has been argued frequently, the devastation caused by Hurricanes Katrina and Rita unmasked the vulnerability of African Americans that has been caused by embedded racial and class inequalities in American society. Although the inept and indifferent government response has often been attributed to systematic racism, there has been little consideration of the ways in which racialized perceptions of need have characterized and limited the responses of those volunteers motivated solely to "serve." Despite obvious differences in scale, the hurricanes revealed the centrality of race in community engagement, a subject that has been largely neglected in the literature of service-learning and other pedagogies of engagement in higher education. Unless the assumption that all are equally able to participate in democracy is questioned, the field will continue to neglect both the obstacles faced by African Americans (as illustrated by the many ways in which their votes have been suppressed) and their struggles to overcome these obstacles. Moreover, teaching through an African American lens can contribute to the redefinition of community engagement by applying the lessons of service-learning in that community to the best principles and practices for all.

Based on the service-learning experiences of an African American historian and a White political scientist and service-learning director at Berea College in Berea, Kentucky, this chapter offers a three-dimensional approach to teaching race through community engagement. We argue that the student's experience of interracial relations takes place on three levels: between the students and the community, among the students, and between the students and the professors. Narratives of two service-learning courses—one taking place in hurricane-ravaged Louisiana and the other involving a small African American church in Kentucky—demonstrate that teaching community engagement requires faculty to critically examine their own racial and cultural identities and facilitate identity development on the part of their students. Moreover, such self-examination is an ongoing process guided by the African American spiritual "We'll Understand It Better By and By."

Community Engagement, African Americans, and Berea College

Nearly all of the growing body of literature about community or civic engagement neglects or marginalizes issues of race, even those written from a critical perspective. There will be an occasional passing reference to multiculturalism or diversity but no attention is given to the small but significant body of scholarship focusing specifically on service-learning and African Americans. As indicated by Evans in the preface to this book, scholars have ignored the history of African American traditions of service, and the unrecognized contributions of African American educators to the theoretical foundations of service-learning and community engagement.[1]

There is also a growing body of literature about teaching courses on race and inequality through community engagement.[2] However, these scholars emphasize just one dimension of the student experience: interaction with a racially different community. Little or no attention is paid to interactions among students or between students and faculty. Moreover, these educators focus almost entirely on the challenges faced by White, middle- and upper-middle-class students serving in low-income communities of color. Economic differences map onto racial differences, making it difficult to explore the particular impact of race. A related limitation characterizes studies of community engagement at traditional African American colleges and universities (historically black colleges and universities), where students and the community generally share a common racial identity.[3] Due to Berea College's distinct mission, however, the authors have had the opportunity to work with students and communities of different races but a common low-income economic status. The impact of race stands out in these interactions, which are also more typical of those likely to occur in the broader community. Following graduation, most students will resume their roles in communities and workplaces that are segregated according to race and income. Interracial interaction will occur, albeit infrequently, toward the lower end of the economic spectrum, but usually in the form of competition for scarce jobs and resources.

Founded in 1855 by abolitionist John G. Fee, Berea College was the first fully integrated institution of higher education in the South. Racial coeducation in a slaveholding state was a monumental experiment; in fact, the founders were run out of town and only returned after the end of the Civil War. During the second half of the nineteenth century, Berea College educated low-income students from the Appalachian region, approximately half African American and half White. However, in 1904, the Day Law, aimed specifically at Berea College, outlawed integrated education in Kentucky, forcing the college to limit itself to educating poor, White Appalachians only. Although the college established Lincoln Institute, near Louisville, as a school for African Americans, Berea College itself was not reintegrated until the repeal of the Day Law in 1950. Today, Berea College retains its commitment to the education of low-income Appalachians and African Americans (approximately 20 percent of the student body). All students, whose income must not exceed a maximum level, receive a full-tuition scholarship and work between ten and fifteen hours on campus or in the community.[4]

Therefore, unlike most college students, Berea College students come from a socioeconomic background similar to the people in the communities they serve. As a result, racial dynamics between students and the community—the first dimension of interracial interaction—can be more easily distinguished and analyzed. Similarly, despite their shared class status, it is the first time that many of the White students, especially those from the isolated mountains, take classes with African American students or have an African American teacher. This brings out the second and third dimensions: the impact of race among the students and between the students and the professors.

Berea College's approach to service-learning reflects its commitment to the integration of "learning, labor, and service":

> Service-learning is an educational experience based upon a collaborative partnership between college and community. Learning through service enables students to apply academic knowledge and critical thinking skills to meet genuine community needs. Through reflection and assessment, students gain deeper knowledge of course content and the importance of civic engagement.[5]

The Courses: Toward a Three-Dimensional Pedagogy

Course One: General Studies 102: Rebuilding Community: Lessons from Katrina Taught by Dr. Meta Mendel-Reyes and Ms. Betty Hibler during the 2006 January Short Term

Course narrative. In this service-learning course, race and community engagement were placed front and center. The students themselves were diverse: eight were White and five were African American. During the first week, the class studied the racialized nature of the disaster: the disproportionate impact on poor African Americans, the slow government response, and the sensationalized media coverage. They critically examined the outpouring of people wanting to help, asking whether and how the good intentions were translated into actions that truly benefited the community. During this week, the students worked in teams to research specific topics, including the impact of race.

The next two weeks of the class were spent in the rural area surrounding New Iberia, Louisiana, working with the Southern Mutual Help Association (SMHA), a local grassroots organization that linked disaster relief to long-term community development.[6] The students tore out sheetrock and bleached floors alongside diverse families, from an elderly African American couple to a four-generation family of Cajun fishermen. After their return, the students presented their findings to a senator and a member of the House of Representatives,[7] thereby transforming community engagement at the local level into civic engagement at the national level. In addition, students organized an interactive campus presentation of their experiences. The student research teams designed posters and displays around their topics and invited the audience to sample Cajun food and enjoy souvenirs illustrating the varied cultures of Louisiana. As their journals demonstrated, the course was largely successful in helping students recognize the strengths of the so-called victims and the need for service with rather than to the community. As one student reflected afterward:

> Of all the courses that I have taken at Berea College, the course Rebuilding Through Service: Lessons from Katrina has had the greatest impact on me. It has been a week since the class ended, and already I miss the people, the stories, [and] the experience. I found it strange that human beings bond over trauma and destruction. By trudging through the pain, loss, and sorrow, relationships are solidified. . . . "Community" is being redefined in the Gulf. Neighbors are helping neighbors, families have come together, and an already tight sense of culture and belonging is being strengthened further.[8]

Preparation for service-learning. In designing the course, I paid the most attention to preparing students for interactions with the community. The SMHA was chosen as our community partner because of its commitment to racial and economic justice, its interracial staff, and the diverse area in which it works. The SMHA was founded in 1969 in response to the oppressive conditions facing African Americans in the Louisiana sugar cane fields. The SMHA continues to "work primarily with agricultural and pervasively poor communities, women and people of color. We help build rural communities through people's growth in their own empowerment and the just management of resources." In line with the focus of our course, the SMHA distinguishes between direct service and social justice. Throughout its history, the organization "confronted policies that did not change people's lives, because they were based on service not on systematic change."[9] This approach made an impact on the class, as expressed in a student journal:

> Working with SMHA helped me to realize that it takes more than a band-aid to heal wounds placed upon citizens such as those affected by both Hurricane Katrina and Hurricane Rita. . . . You have to start at the root of the problem and help people to help themselves.

The first week's readings, classroom activities, and discussions were intended to orient the class to the racial dynamics exposed by the hurricanes and by the response to them. Because the course took place less than six months after the hurricanes, there were almost no scholarly materials to assign. The main course reading was a just-published book by *Time* magazine,[10] supplemented by print and electronic media. These included articles and essays written shortly before the hurricanes (August 2005) to the time of the course (January 2006). I realized that many in the class, particularly the White students, would share the initial hesitation, as described by one White student:

> As [a] chemistry major I rarely take courses, with the exception of general requirements, that force me to examine and discuss such issues as poverty, racism, and the media. I was tentative about placing myself outside my comfort zone.

To facilitate this transition beyond the comfort zone, our journey to rural Louisiana included a stop in New Orleans, where the class both observed the devastation of the storm and met with residents determined to rebuild.

In terms of the students themselves, I anticipated that the subject of race could cause tensions among a diverse group of students, especially in the intense atmosphere of living and working together. However, beyond a few introductory exercises, I expected that regular reflective writing and discussions would resolve these tensions at the time they surfaced. The course design did not consider potential tension between the students and me. In retrospect, I must have assumed that my commitment to teaching on race would be sufficient; despite years of experience in teaching this type of course, I failed to recognize and prepare adequately for the fact that student interracial interactions would occur on three levels.

Students and the community. Of the three levels, the interaction between the students and the community appears to have caused the fewest tensions, due in large part to the extensive preparation. Nevertheless, the reality of desperate poverty, in addition to the devastation from the hurricane, made many students visibly uncomfortable. This took on a racial edge because the most distressed community we visited was the African American town of Abbeville. However, the experience of working with Black families to rebuild their homes helped the students see them as empowered survivors. As a community member explained, "These people here are the kind of people who don't sit around and wait for a miracle . . . we roll up our sleeves and get back on our feet!" Students also had the chance to experience the strength of the Abbeville community by participating in the annual Martin Luther King Day parade.

Another bridge across racial differences was the strong religious faith shared by both the African American and White Appalachian students with the Black community in Louisiana. Many students wrote in their journals about one elderly African American in particular:

> I especially appreciated the many times that she sat down with my team and I to talk about the goodness of God and the hope she had for the future. In fact, she was probably more of a blessing to me than I was to her!

Students and students. Although the Martin Luther King Day parade was a highlight for all of us, it also led to tensions between some of the Black and White students. In a journal entry, one African American student suggested that the Whites saw only poverty instead of community:

> Some of [them] pointed out that the [B]lacks, in the neighborhoods we walked, were obviously poor . . . [but] their situations are nothing new to me. Instead I saw "uncle," "mama," "sister," "gramps," and "granny" all relaxing, indulging, and having a genuinely good time. . . . I saw a real [B]lack community. One that prided itself in not necessarily being pressed or overwhelmed by circumstances, but, rather, looking forward in the mind[-]set of "how can I progress?"

Similarly, while religion created a common bond, it also took on racial overtones. On one Sunday, some of the African American students walked out of an interracial church service recommended by an SMHA staff member and went across the street to a wholly Black church. As one student stated, "Whoa! The beat of the drums could be heard outside of the church and I immediately felt a sense of right and comfort." Instead of an opportunity to appreciate different styles of worship, there seemed to be an unspoken competition over which worship experience was "better." The combination of religion and race also exacerbated what started out as a simple misunderstanding about food. One of the African American Muslim students was on a restricted diet and on two occasions the students who did the grocery shopping and cooking bought and prepared the wrong food. These students felt that the Muslim was overreacting to honest mistakes, while one of her friends wondered why it was so easy for everyone to keep track of her own allergy to soy. Perhaps the combination of African American race and a so-called terrorist religion desensitized the other students.

As an instructor, I interpreted these tensions as typical for a group of relative strangers spending twenty-four hours together in an unfamiliar location. In our daily group reflections, we addressed these and other incidents through the perspective of team building. Lacking a fully-developed African American lens, I failed to grasp or deal with the underlying racial themes. The importance of our service project kept everyone working together, but a full airing of our differences would have enhanced student learning about the depth of racial and cultural divisions in this country.

Students and faculty. The least anticipated tension turned out to be the most painful for me and two of the Black students with whom I worked most closely. During a visit to a home that was in poor condition even though it had not sustained hurricane damage, I called attention to the fact that the family needed to use gas burners on the stove to heat the house despite the apparent danger. While I thought of this as an attempt to explain one consequence of poverty, at least one of the Black students saw the following:

> Someone so susceptible to racism, even though they are honestly against it, to the point that they would act ignorantly towards others. I realized, in that moment, that the person was unaware of her actions. Nevertheless, I was personally offended because it was so blatant. . . . I just saw the similarities between myself and the [family]. Sometimes it was necessary for us to heat up the house by using the stove. A single mother supporting seven kids did not always allow for the best living situation. Nevertheless, that was my life.

I was surprised and hurt when these reactions were shared during our team reflection that evening, but I stifled my first response to defend myself. Instead, I made myself listen, which led to a real "learning" experience for all of us. The same Black student wrote later in her journal:

> The person was sincerely affected and apologetic. I can in no way hold anything against the individual. We all fall victim to racism in some way. This was just a stark reminder that it still exists. I feel that we all needed this experience.

The discussion led to a deeper understanding of racism and poverty. In this student's words:

> I have observed that we often look at what impoverished people don't have or need instead of focusing on what they do have. . . . It is ok to help people if they want and accept it. However, never assume that you

are needed or the savior of the day. Black people have a long history of making the most out of the least. No assumptions, please, simply offer your help; help me to help you and I'll help you to help me. That way there will be no room for inferiority.

Although this challenge led to new insights about service-learning in the African American community, it also demonstrated the potential costs of neglecting one of the three dimensions of interracial interaction.

Course Two: History 386: The Civil Rights Movement in America taught by Dr. Dwayne Mack, during the Fall 2006 semester

Course narrative. As an African American professor and emerging scholar, I have approached service-learning as a way to strengthen relations between the campus and the Black community and as a way to increase student learning. I designed this course to teach advanced history majors how to conduct oral histories to document the history of a local Black church during the Civil Rights era. For the community partner, I chose my own place of worship, Farristown Church, which has been serving the rural African American community of Berea since 1883. The centerpiece of the service-learning experience was a series of video interviews with ten elders who discussed their personal experiences of civil rights and the role that the church played socially, politically, economically, educationally, and spiritually in uplifting the community. As apprentice historians, my students became active learners and listeners. Instead of only reading history, they documented and wrote history.

Because I wanted the community to help define our service-learning project, I worked closely with Ray Reed, a church deacon and community activist. Deacon Reed suggested producing a short documentary adapted from the video interviews, which would offer the congregation, especially the children, a glimpse into the history of African Americans in Berea. Throughout the project, Deacon Reed served as a guide and mentor to the students.

After completing the interviews and conducting research, the students produced a thirty-minute film entitled *Documenting the Role of the Black Church in the Civil Rights Movement in Madison County through Oral History*, using Pinnacle software. In addition, they collected documents, such as church programs and photographs, and created bulletin board displays. Together, these final products complemented other historical projects conducted by the church and helped preserve communal memory.

Preparation for service-learning. The experience of teaching courses such as this has deepened my awareness of the racial dynamics involved in community engagement. I recognized that most of the students in this particular class, four Caucasians and one African American, had minimal experience with the Black community and limited knowledge about the Civil Rights Movement and service-learning itself. However, they did share a common entry point to the course content: their Appalachian roots, including deep religiosity. To acculturate my students to the Black church, I required them to attend five worship services or Bible studies. I hoped that their attendance would help them bond with the congregation and ease their anxieties about interviewing people they perceived as different from themselves.

To orient them to the region, I assigned literature on race and ethnicity in Appalachia.[11] The readings also addressed the cultural dynamics of Berea's Black community and other black communities during the Civil Rights Movement. To prepare my students for the process of field interviewing, I frequently referred to Cynthia Stokes Brown's *Like It Was: A Complete Guide to Writing Oral History*.[12] I also assigned one of my own Civil Rights Movement articles to illustrate the way in which some Berea students, faculty, staff, and local residents forged a strong alliance to combat racial discrimination.[13]

Nevertheless, despite these preparations and my experience, I discovered that I had not anticipated the full impact of racial dynamics on interactions between this interracial group of students and the community and between the students and myself.[14]

Students and community. Even before we entered the field, it became clear that some of the Caucasian students had trouble understanding the effect of racism on the lives of African Americans. During one classroom discussion on violence against Blacks during the Civil Rights era, a White student stated that she identified with this form of racial oppression. As evidence, she claimed that a group of Black youths had committed a criminal act against her family. I explained that her isolated incident could not be compared to the systemic terror during the Civil Rights era or to the continuation of White privilege today.

As an African American and member of one of Berea's Black churches, I assumed that the students could interact comfortably with the Black community with minimal orientation. However, I was incorrect. Although the lone African American student wrote that she readily "connected" with the members of the congregation, who reminded her of relatives back home, a White student described experiencing "awkwardness and discomfort." Sometimes, these feelings were expressed obliquely, as in the comment that the church services and prayer sessions were "too long." Students also described feeling like outsiders. They had mistaken an exclusively African American church congregation for African American segregation. Ironically, the community also had initial doubts about the project, which they saw as a threat to their privacy.

In response, I encouraged the students to express their concerns in their journal reflections and in open classroom discussions. However, the most effective strategy was to invite the students to attend church social events with me. While sharing meals in this less formal environment, they built relationships with their community partners. According to Mendel-Reyes, this form of socializing "demonstrates subtly that community does not just happen but must be built through ritual and effort."[15] Social events also built on key features of the students' shared Appalachian heritage, such as the emphasis on church, communal meals, and respect for elders. For example, one Caucasian student came to understand that the prayer circle reflected the "close-knit" structure of the Black church and that of the White church.

The relationship between the students and community deepened when the students volunteered to work at Farristown's annual Family Fun Day. The team reflected in their journals about the fun they had interacting with church members and the public who attended the event. One described how, while setting up a game, a classmate became drenched with water after a water balloon blew up in her face. This light moment further eased tensions between the students and the congregation. The students' act of volunteerism allowed them to become unofficial members of the church. During that moment, the color lines were blurred, bridging the cultural and racial gap.

The strategy of involving Deacon Reed in designing and guiding the project also helped promote trust between the community and the students. One student commented that it was "exciting to see members of the community interested in and become involved in our project." Deacon Reed was also able to reassure the elders about their privacy so that they became more comfortable about sharing their stories with the students.

Students and faculty. Race also affected a tension that arose between the students and me over the intensive demands of the project. In addition to the anticipated workload, the college alumni magazine decided to feature my class in an upcoming issue, creating a much tighter time line than I had anticipated. Because the amount of work is a typical source of stress in courses, I was not surprised to read in a journal that a student "felt overwhelmed." However, I was disappointed to learn that some students had taken their concerns to a White member of the service-learning staff and not to me. As an African American professor, I am familiar with my authority being questioned. In fact, one of the reasons for assigning my own scholarship is to establish my professional credibility with the students. Still, it is especially painful when even African American students complain to a Caucasian colleague.

Because I understand this as a relic of slavery, I think it is important to help all my students learn to recognize and appreciate African American authority. In this case, the service-learning staff came directly to me with the students' concerns. This allowed me to devise a strategy that addressed the issue in a positive way. Without making accusations, I invited all the students to come directly to me with any concerns that they might have. I also tried to be more intentional about recognizing and affirming their work. In the future, if the course schedule has to be changed for external reasons, I will make a point to discuss the situation with the students and invite them to help design a feasible work plan.

As with the interaction between the students and the community, the church visits served as the best strategy for building trust between the students and me. They had the opportunity to observe my interactions with the local community and with my wife and children. As they came to realize that my life had much in common with theirs, we were able to develop a strong working relationship. I think that it is particularly important to bond with a diverse group of students outside the intimidating "ivory tower."

At the conclusion of the course, we received positive feedback from the Black community. In reference to the documentary, Dr. Gerald Smith, the pastor of Farristown Church, said that it offered a "personal and insightful understanding of the role of the black church in historically rural communities. It broaden[ed] the perception and appreciation for local history."[16]

It was just as gratifying to observe the growth in my students. One White student wrote:

> The symbols in the stained glass were almost identical to the ones in my church back home. I recall that it seemed pathetic and sad that we, as people, are so comfortable with the segregation of church. I'm guilty of it, too. I know, but it is so commonplace that we do not generally seem to mind. It really bothers me that I did not feel immediately at home simply because of racial differences. It does not bother me at all in school . . . so why, then, at church?

Conclusions and Recommendations

The three-dimensional approach to teaching community engagement through an African American lens leads to specific recommendations for each type of interracial interaction experienced by students. With respect to *students and the community*, we recommend the following three things: using a project model to involve students from the beginning in developing and sustaining a reciprocal relationship with the community partners; taking advantage of opportunities for relationship building beyond the project, such as church services and social gatherings, in which students can experience cultural similarities and differences; and inviting honest reflection on student–community interaction throughout the semester, rather than relying exclusively on the initial orientation and readings.

Recommendations for addressing conflicts related to interracial actions *among the students* include the following three things: using the project model, in which the need for cooperation to complete the task encourages working out differences; recognizing that the likelihood of conflict increases as students spend more time together, especially twenty-four hours a day during a service trip setting; and giving students tools and skills to work out their own conflicts, rather than solving their problems for them.

In terms of *student–faculty* interactions, we suggest the following three things: anticipating that there will be misunderstandings and tensions, whether the instructor is Black or White; understanding that, while all professors should examine their own identities throughout the course, White professors have a particular responsibility to recognize their privilege inside and outside the classroom; and being willing to acknowledge mistakes and act to correct them through new teaching strategies and, when needed, an apology.

In conclusion, we would like to comment on our own interactions and collaborations over the years, including coauthoring this chapter. As a young African American, Christian male working closely with an older Caucasian, Jewish female, our interactions have paralleled those discussed in this chapter. Our professional relationship has been a wonderful, often challenging, journey that has helped both of us become better teachers of race and community engagement. We hope that the strategies offered in this chapter will help other instructors "understand it better by and by."

Notes

Meta Mendel-Reyes: I co-taught the course with Betty Hibler, the associate director of the Center for Excellence in Learning Through Service, who is Caucasian. Although we consulted on every aspect of the course, I had primary responsibility for it as a member of the teaching faculty. For that reason, this section of the chapter is written in my voice alone.

1. See the preface to this volume, pages xi–xx.
2. R. L. Coles, "Race-Focused Service-Learning Courses: Issues and Recommendations," *Michigan Journal of Community Service Learning* 6 (Fall 1999): 97–105; M. R. Dunlap, "Voices of Students in Multicultural Service-Learning Settings," *Michigan Journal of Community Service Learning* 5 (Fall 1998): 58–67; S. Evans, "The Right to Grow: African American Women's Intellectual Legacy," *International Journal of the Humanities* 3, no. 7 (2006): 163–74; J. A. Galura, P. Pasque, D. Schoem, and J. Howard, *Engaging the Whole of Service-Learning, Diversity, and Learning Communities* (Ann Arbor: OCSL Press at the University of Michigan, 2004); S. Marullo, "Bringing Home Diversity: A Service Learning Approach to Teaching Race and Ethnic Relations," *Teaching Sociology* 26, no. 4 (October 1998): 259–75.
3. B. W. Jones, "Reclaiming the Historical Tradition of Service in the African American Community," in *Connecting Past and Present: Concepts and Models for Service Learning in History*, ed. I. Harkavy and B. Donovan (Washington, DC: American Association for Higher Education, 2000), 139–47; C. S. Stevens, "Unrecognized Roots of Service-Learning in African American Social Thought and Action, 1890–1930," *Michigan Journal of Community Service Learning* 9, no. 2 (Winter 2003): 25–34; P. Brotherton, "Connecting the

Classroom and the Community; Service learning Programs Allow Students to Apply Real-World Experience with Classroom Study," *Black Issues in Higher Education* 19, no. 5 (April 2002): 22–24; G. D. R. Scott, "A Historically Black College Perspective," in *Civic Responsibility and Higher Education*, ed. T. Ehrlich (Phoenix, AZ: Oryx Press, 2000), 263–78.

4. Berea College, "Berea College," http://www.berea.edu (accessed January 30, 2007).

5. Center for Excellence in Learning Through Service, "Service-Learning," http://www.berea.edu/celts/servicelearning (accessed January 30, 2007).

6. Southern Mutual Help Association, "Southern Mutual Help Association," http://www.southernmutual.help.org (accessed January 30, 2007).

7. Senator Mitch McConnell, nationally recognized as a senior leader of the Republican Party, and Congressman Ben Chandler, District 6, in his first full term.

8. Except where indicated, all quotations from students come from student journals written during the course. To protect their identities, their names have been removed.

9. Southern Mutual Help Association, "Southern Mutual Help Association."

10. Editors of *Time* magazine, *Hurricane Katrina: The Storm That Changed America* (New York: Time, 2005).

11. W. Hayden, "Appalachian Diversity: African American, Hispanic/Latino, and Other Populations," *Journal of Appalachian Studies* 10, no. 3 (2004): 293–306.

12. C. S. Brown, *Like It Was: A Complete Guide to Writing Oral History* (New York: Teachers and Writers Collaborative, 1988).

13. D. Mack, "Ain't Gonna Let Nobody Turn Me Around: Berea College's Participation in the Selma to Montgomery March," *Ohio Valley History* 5, no. 3 (Fall 2005): 43–62.

14. In this class, there was no obvious tension among the students, perhaps because there was only one African American student. In my experience, conflict is more likely when the racial numbers are closer to even, as in the course discussed earlier by my coauthor.

15. M. Mendel-Reyes, "A Pedagogy for Citizenship: Service Learning and Democratic Education," *New Directions for Teaching and Learning* 73, no. 10 (Spring 1998): 37.

16. G. Smith, personal communication, January 12, 2007.

PART 3

◈ ◈ ◈

Community-Based Research

DeMond S. Miller

I was going to study the facts, any and all facts, concerning the American Negro and his plight, and by measurement and comparison and research, work up to any valid generalizations which I could. I entered this primarily with the utilitarian object of reform and uplift; but nevertheless, I wanted to do the work with scientific accuracy. Thus, in my own sociology, because of firm belief in a changing racial group, I easily grasped the idea of a changing developing society rather than a fixed social structure.

—W. E. B. Du Bois, *The Autobiography of W. E. B. Du Bois*

The final group of chapters in this volume presents research, reflections, and strategies designed to combat decades of racial discrimination, a lack of community empowerment, and equitable access to resources through the building of effective community partnerships that are evaluated and modified, when needed, for their effectiveness. Community-based research (CBR), in its most basic form, is a collaborative partnership that forges connections with universities and the communities that lie beyond their campuses. At first, I thought it was an idea to get students out of the classroom; however, when I became a professional educator, I realized the promise of partnerships among students, faculty, and community stakeholders in solving problems and effecting meaningful social change. "These partnerships have resulted in a plethora of outreach initiatives in which a number of students and faculty are participating in tutoring and sports programs; internships in areas such as education, social work, and psychology; research projects; and the provision of other services to

149

their local communities."[1] CBR is a model of community–higher education collaboration that combines various forms of action-oriented research with service-learning to support social action for social justice.

So, with external funding and the fully committed institutional support of Rowan University (Glassboro, New Jersey) in terms of administrative backing financial and institutional mission institulization, my students, colleagues, and I embarked on a four-year partnership with community groups (in the Parkside and Cramer Hill sections of the city of Camden, New Jersey, just across the river from Philadelphia, Pennsylvania—where Du Bois had conducted his pioneering community research a century earlier. Camden groups welcomed the assistance offered by our HUD-funded Community Outreach Partnership Center). As a result of the Community Outreach Partnership Center initiative and ongoing partnerships, I have watched over the past eight years as numerous community groups—namely, Parkside Business and Community in Partnership, Camden's Promise Middle School, and Camden Academy Charter High School—heightened the quality of the citizens' lives and enhanced the surrounding environment.

While the tradition of community-based research dates back nearly two centuries, those of us engaged in the practice embrace the newness of each experience. The multidisciplinary origins of community-based research stem from the late 1800s when the staff of Hull House, co-founded in 1889 by Jane Addams and Ellen Starr, undertook a large land-use mapping research project in Chicago. As the project developed, Hull House involved community residents as a way of educating the staff, students, and residents. Soon, the community research became a part of Hull House's social service and social action agenda and influenced empowerment planning in Chicago.[2] However, the first systematic attempt to study African Americans was undertaken by W. E. B. Du Bois, who noted in his article, "The Study of Negro Problems": "It is not *one* problem, but rather a plexus of social problems, some new, some old, some simple, some complex; and these problems have their one bond of unity in the act that they group themselves about those Africans whom two centuries of slave-trading brought into the land."[3]

African American social thought has become responsive to the community by merging social theory and action. Charles Stevens maintains in the *Unrecognized Roots of Service-Learning in African American Social Thought and Action, 1890–1930* that many of the service-learning activities employed in the African American community today are part of initiatives stemming back to the late 1890s designed to promote race pride and influence social change. Stevens's work places into historical perspective the importance of such work, which incorporates service-learning ideals, although not specifically identified as such, is organized social action for community building used by African American social activists, women's groups, and educators interested in social justice and community empowerment. I am most inspired by the work of Du Bois because he clearly articulated that the complex social problems facing African Americans during his lifetime were valid for the nation to consider when African American issues were not on the research agendas of any leading scholars of the day. With Du Bois' application of sociological theory and methods, a variety of quantitative, qualitative, historical, statistical, and demographic approaches were applied to under-standing the conditions of African Americans as a result of the African Diaspora in America, with a particular interest in Philadelphia.[4] Du Bois' empirical orientation led to a methodology based on direct and prolonged observation. In Philadelphia, for example, he used participant observation by living in the seventh ward for a year, "in the midst of . . . dirt, drunkenness, poverty, and crime."[5] He used the term *car-window sociologist* in reference to sociologists who, while attempting to understand the South or Black Americans, spent a few leisurely hours on holiday riding in a Pullman car through the South, generally not venturing into communities.[6] Du Bois recognized early on that CBR involved more than a study from afar; his actions led to other researchers adopting and using methods to scientifically study and understand marginalized groups to this very day. In the next section, I will focus on the contributions of W. E. B. Du Bois as the pioneer in the movement to address the social concerns of the African American community through the rigorous principles of social scientific CBR.

William Edward Burghardt Du Bois (1868–1963)

Du Bois's major sociological work, *The Philadelphia Negro: A Social Study*,[7] is highly regarded among his many publications. It is the earliest large-scale empirical study in the history of American sociology. Gunnar Myrdal referred to *The Philadelphia Negro* as the best model of "what a study of a Negro community should be."[8] In the book, Du Bois surmises that complex problems are "a group of symptoms, not a cause, . . . as a long historical development and not a transient occurrence."[9] To demonstrate his commitment to using a scientific approach to study communities while spreading cultural understanding and social equality, he expanded his research to include communities in Georgia and Virginia. Du Bois was firm in his commitment to the use of sociological measurement to describe and delimit social phenomena. He felt that proper measurement of social conditions would provide a rational basis for sound social judgments. Implicit in this belief was a more general belief in the worth of a quantitative, empirically-based sociology that, if properly practiced, would form the foundation of social policy.[10] So influential was his research that between 1898 and 1904, the U.S. Department of Labor financed and published other studies written by Du Bois that were modeled after *The Philadelphia Negro*.[11] Although his research involved community data collection, he was viewed as an outsider during his time. This view was attributed to the fact that he not only represented the elite academic establishment, but he was also funded by a variety of private and federal sources, which the community did not recognize as an "end product" that would meet their needs.

Contemporary models of CBR draw on the work conducted in Chicago by Hull House and in Philadelphia by Du Bois. Today's CBR uses three foundation tenants that serve as guiding principles used by communities, universities, and colleges to address social problems. According to Strand et al.,

- [CBR] is a collaborative enterprise between academic researchers (professors, staff, and students) and community members.
- [CBR] promotes the use of multiple methods of discovery and dissemination of the knowledge produced.
- [CBR's] goal is to implement social change for the purpose of achieving social justice.[12]

The first feature, collaboration, is important because it brings the academy into an accessible forum, positioning scholars in a place where they can be engaged. Also, collaborations within the university are enhanced as the "university," via the outreach team members, works to address problems. Finally, such collaboration can work to empower community residents in the process of demystifying the research process. By way of collaboration, the research process helps the organization become self-sufficient to the point where it may no longer need outside experts but could draw on them when necessary.[13] In essence, the information obtained from the primary relationship becomes a way to build a community's capacity.

Moreover, CBR uses multiple sources of data to validate the data gathered. To understand the fullness of the problems confronting the community, multiple measures that go beyond statistical-demographic measures are used to give "life" to the community's story while also using multiple venues to present the story of a community. This goal of CBR reflects the teams' integrity in telling the comprehensive story while eliminating the tendency to not view it through a set of prescribed theories or preexisting demographic data. Although these sources of information are insightful, they do not tell the story of the community.

For the research collaboration, tangible results are important. The work is not a scholarly exercise, but rather a way of explaining and bringing about change using the knowledge produced from this endeavor. The results of both examples of earlier research, Hull House and *The Philadelphia Negro*, led to a greater understanding of the problems of their time. In the case of Du Bois, "[He] not only suggested a course of research[,] he demanded that this research lead to social action. His cultural orientation may have been prudish and conservative, but his insurgent intellectual activities still challenge us to make our social science relevant to social transformation."[14]

Hence, the goal of community-based research is to produce information that might be substantial in bringing forth needed change of a long and lasting nature. Change that improves the lives of individuals in the community, organization, or association, or that affects a larger social agenda for comprehensive social action brings about social change (e.g., the Environmental Justice Movement). Moreover, with reference to health and minority community health care issues, CBR research is preferred when conducting research with vulnerable populations as a way to reduce racial and ethnic disparities in health. This part of the book explores CBR in various settings—charity-related service-learning, social justice service-learning, action research, and participatory research. The following chapters illustrate and reflect on how CBR, based in different settings, theories of society, and approaches to community work, may combine or conflict.

This part draws on the long tradition of civic engagement in the form of CBR using mixed methods while working with a wide range of community-based organizations to address a host of social problems in the African American community. In chapter 10, "Black Like Me: Navigating Race, Gender, Research, and Community," Fleda Mask Jackson maintains that negotiating the space between community concerns and the mandated rigors of research demands sensitivity, reciprocity, and, most importantly, respect for the lives and realities community partners face. In doing so, this chapter contributes to the field by viewing the challenging role of an African American female researcher; examining the implicit ways in which race and gender research are essential in questions of social justice, equity, and CBR as a component of the community empowerment aspect so implicit in CBR; and analyzing the promises and perils of capturing the authentic experiences of race and racism for translation into measures and interventions to improve health outcomes. These themes are expounded in the next chapter.

In chapter 11, "A Partnership with the African American Church: IMPPACT and S.P.I.C.E.S. For Life," Micah McCreary, Monica Jones, Raymond Tademy, and John Fife are engaged in two community faith-based partnerships with Spring Creak Baptist Church. One is a grant-funded initiative called IMPPACT (I Must Pause Pray Analyze Chill and Take Action), for which the goal is to provide a culturally congruent family-based program for increasing positive family relationships, spirituality, and problem-solving skills. The second project is the group's research with the Baptist General Convention of Virginia in which they share an ongoing relationship to decrease health care disparities via the S.P.I.C.E.S (Spiritual, Physical, Intellectual, Cognitive, Emotional, and Social) For Life Program.

This collaborative approach to community engagement and CBR is grounded in a theoretical perspective that incorporates counseling psychology, multicultural theory, liberation teaching philosophy, and African American psychology. The partnership incorporates the values and behaviors of unity, strong kinship bonds, inherent feelings of cooperation, and sharing, within an overarching religious orientation that focuses on wellness.

In chapter 12, "'I Have Three Strikes Against Me': Narratives of Plight and Efficacy among Older African American Homeless Women and Their Implications for Engaged Inquiry," Olivia Washington and David Moxley document the nature of the helping network in Detroit, Michigan, that is emerging to support older African American homeless women and to identify the principal dimension of this intervention strategy, which operates though a university–community partnership by way of the Leaving Homelessness Intervention Research Project. The chapter's title refers to an interview in which one participant identified herself as having three strikes by stating: "I have three strikes against me: I'm a woman, poor, and black." The multilevel and mixed-methods research highlights the work of an African American faculty member who, as part of an multidisciplinary team, incorporates narrative strategies through which project personnel support women in their efforts to tell their stories. In doing so, the members of the team highlight the issues African American women face that increase their vulnerability to homelessness, the forces that push them into homelessness, and their personal strengths and needs.

In chapter 13, "A Culturally Competent Community-Based Research Approach with African American Neighborhoods: Critical Components and Examples," Richard Briscoe, Harold Keller, Gwen McClain, Evangeline Best, and Jessica Mazza implement an approach that addresses a culturally competent neighborhood-based research endeavor to promote healthy, productive, and successful children within a neighborhood setting by employing overlapping individual, group, and organizational strategies to improve behavior. The overall approach addresses the challenges and barriers of neighborhood-based research in African American neighborhoods, families, and children. Its primary goal is to employ a culturally competent framework so that mutual impact informs both the research process and the neighborhood residents to successfully implement a culturally competent neighborhood-based strategy in a real-world setting. This chapter culminates by sharing valuable lessons that are conducive to building and maintaining a culturally competent framework.

In chapter 14, "Community Engagement and Collaborations in Community-Based Research: The Road to Project Butterfly," GiShawn Mance, Bernadette Sánchez, and Niambi Jaha-Echols assess the intervention of Project Butterfly. Project Butterfly is an Afro-centered program designed to meet the needs of adolescent African American girls. It is rooted in African-centered philosophy and values and is dedicated to supporting young women and girls of African descent through the transitions of life. The intervention was devised to help them gain a greater understanding of who they are and to help them gain personal power and strength. Most importantly, these authors argue that with African Americans' researcher–community collaborations, it is central to keep in mind that cultural considerations of the population are most valuable in the engagement process. Additionally, connectedness and relationships are essential to maintaining an effective collaboration. The authors conclude by asserting that research must focus on engaging the African American community in practicing the cultural values of reciprocity, connectedness, and mutual respect.

In all, these works address the following questions often asked of CBR: What is meant by successful community–institutional partnerships for CBR? What are the factors that contribute to successful CBR in the African American community? What are the barriers that interfere with successful CBR in the African American community? By using tangible examples, the five research partnerships included in this part offer a wealth of understanding about the mechanics of how to develop structures and maintain processes that effect positive social change for both sides of the partnership; how to build community capacity; how to plan for sustainability; and how to seek ways to change public policy. They all suggest that the effect of their research on the community be considered. Just as Du Bois was treated as an outsider by some and welcomed by others, these researchers have overcome obstacles that they have reflected on and documented to illustrate the research–researcher dynamic. Moreover, they also reflected on the impact that CBR has had on the academic institutions they represent. Most importantly, CBR efforts build on the strengths and assets of both partners, in turn facilitating an environment that engenders trust and mutual respect.[15] By providing culturally relevant, sound perspectives that not only inform the current discussion on CBR in African American communities, but also adds greater depth, richness, and clarity to the future directions of the field, these research collaborations and researcher reflections where race is placed in the center of town-gown engagement.

Notes

1. D. J. Maurrasse, *Beyond the Campus: How Colleges and Universities Form Partnerships with Their Communities* (New York: Routledge, 2001); K. Strand et al., *Community-Based Research and Higher Education: Principles and Practices* (San Francisco, CA: Jossey-Bass, 2003), 3.

2. Maurrasse, *Beyond the Campus*; Strand et al., *Community-Based Research.*

3. T. Zuberi, "W. E. B. Du Bois's Sociology: The Philadelphia Negro and Social Science," *Annals of the American Academy of Political and Social Science* 595 (2004): 146–56.

4. Zuberi, "W. E. B. Du Bois's Sociology."

5. W. E. B. Du Bois, *The Autobiography of W.E.B. Du Bois: A Soliloquy on Viewing My Life from the Last Decades of Its First Century* (New York: International Publishers, 1968), 195.

6. D. S. Green and E. D. Driver, eds., *W. E. B. Du Bois: On Sociology and the Black Community* (Chicago: University of Chicago Press, 1978).

7. W. E. B. Du Bois, *The Philadelphia Negro: A Social Study* (Philadelphia: University of Pennsylvania Press, 1899).

8. Green and Driver, *W. E. B. Du Bois*, 113.

9. Zuberi, "W. E. B. Du Bois's Sociology," 148.

10. Green and Driver, *W. E. B. Du Bois*.

11. Zuberi "W. E. B. Du Bois's Sociology."

12. Strand et al., *Community-Based Research*, 8.

13. R. Stoecker, "Making Connections: Community Organizing, Empowerment Planning, and Participatory Research in Participatory Evaluation," *Sociological Practice* 1 (1999): 209–32; Strand et al., *Community-Based Research*.

14. Zuberi, "W. E. B. Du Bois's Sociology," 156.

15. D. Brugge and H. P. Hynes, eds., *Community Research in Environmental Health: Lessons in Science, Advocacy and Ethics* (Aldershot, UK: Ashgate, 2005); E. Freeman et al., "Challenges of Conducting Community-Based Participatory Research in Boston's Neighborhoods to Reduce Disparities in Asthma," *Journal of Urban Health* 83 (2006): 1013–21; B. A. Israel et al., eds., *Methods in Community-Based Participatory Research for Health* (San Francisco, CA: Jossey-Bass, 2005); M. Minkler and N. Wallerstein, eds., *Community-Based Participatory Research for Health* (San Francisco, CA: Jossey-Bass, 2003); J. Shoultz et al., "Finding Solutions to Challenges Faced in Community-Based Participatory Research between Academic and Community Organizations," *Journal of Interprofessional Care* 20 (2006): 133–44.

10

◆◆◆

Black Like Me

Navigating Race, Gender, Research, and Community

Fleda Mask Jackson

As I awaited the doctor's return to the examination room, I glimpsed a poster affixed to the wall. In columns and rows were warnings about potential hazards to the growth of a developing fetus. No surprise, the absence of vital nutrients and environmental toxins were included among the risk posed to the unborn. What I did not anticipate as a risk for baby and mother was also printed on the poster in bold letters: **African American.**

This account describes my own experience during a prenatal visit and, in fact, forecasted my emersion into research aimed at solving the mystery of reproductive disparities among African American women. My expression of disbelief to the idea that race alone can affect reproductive outcomes was met by the doctor's unconvincing and dispassionate reply, "That's what the science says." His unsuccessful efforts to defuse my anger and suspicion of what I perceived as a racial assault on the reproductive capacities of African American women capitulates the spoken and unspoken tensions and opportunities in health disparity research.

For decades, scientists have pursued explanations for the disproportionate rates of preterm delivery and low birth weight babies born to African American women as compared to women from other racial and ethnic groups. The data indicate that African American women are nearly twice as likely to give birth to babies born prematurely or with low birth weights, placing those babies at greater risk for fetal death or permanent disability. Because biological factors and class indicators fail to fully account for the reproductive disparities seen among African

American women, the search for answers turned to psychosocial risks, particularly stress, as a significant contributor to reproductive disparities.[1] With clear indications that "racism matters" as a psychosocial risk for reproductive outcomes, scientists are explicitly directing their efforts toward the discovery of the link between psychosocial stress connected to race and the physiological responses that trigger poor reproductive outcomes.[2]

Documentation of the authentic experiences of race and gender as they potentially imperil health outcomes demands close scrutiny of the research process. Community-based participatory research, as an ideal approach for capturing the lived experiences of African American women, is a paradigm shift designed to reposition the community and investigator so as to produce a more equitable exchange for scientific inquiry.[3] Negotiating a space between community concerns and the mandated rigors of research demands sensitivity, reciprocity, and, most importantly, respect for the lives and realities of community partners.[4] This chapter will offer the insights and actual processes for conducting community-based participatory research on racialized and gendered stress and coping as risks and mediators for adverse reproductive outcomes and health disparities among African American women. Its intent is to delve into the sometimes difficult yet stimulating task of collecting the voices of African American women sharing their lived experiences of gendered racism and its connection to health outcomes. Most importantly, this chapter probes the issues and responses in research where race was explicitly significant for the objectives and process for a body of research on reproductive disparities.

Atlanta: Intersecting Contexts of Race, Gender, and Class

The research discussed in this chapter describes a series of investigations conducted in Atlanta, Georgia, from 1996 to 2004. Internationally recognized as the Black Mecca, metropolitan Atlanta has seen unprecedented growth as part of the reverse migration of African Americans to the South over the past two decades. The lure of the city and surrounding suburbs includes (1) a long-standing reputation as a hub for civil rights activities, (2) the prosperity of African American residents evidenced by a burgeoning middle- and upper-class population, and (3) the political clout won and sustained by African American politicians over the past thirty years. The city is also notable as the location of the largest consortium of Black colleges and universities in the world, educating African American luminaries, including Dr. Martin Luther King Jr., for nearly two centuries. The schools within the Atlanta University Center complex have a long history of educating African American women. Atlanta University (now Clark–Atlanta University), the oldest university in Atlanta, opened its dormitories to women students in 1870.[5] Spelman College, one of two remaining colleges for African American women, was founded in 1881.

Populated by generations of college-educated African American women, the signs of prosperity and progress in Atlanta coexist with poverty and hopelessness. At least 25 percent of Atlanta's African American population lives below the poverty level, and women and their families comprise a significant segment of the poor in the city.[6] According to a report on the 2004 U.S. Census data by the Urban League, in 2004 Atlanta led the nation in child poverty.[7] The highly visible prosperity among Atlanta's elite also masks the signs of instability for middle- and working-class individuals and families. Recent reports designate Atlanta as having the second highest foreclosure rate in the country, a phenomenon that is attributable to corporate layoffs, change in pension plans, and variable mortgages.[8]

Atlanta is a tale of two cities, divided by the haves and the have nots, separated by race. Known during the Civil Rights era as a "city too busy to hate," coalitions across racial lines subverted the explosive campaigns and violence seen in other major southern cities.[9] While these coalitions persist, Atlanta remains a residentially segregated city, populated by neighborhoods representing the spectrum of socioeconomic backgrounds. In the 1980s and 1990s disparate distribution of commercial and residential development resources were apparent across racial lines even in affluent African American neighborhoods, where redlining lending practices shamefully denied needed services.[10]

Pressing issues surrounding education, employment, and housing are indicative of class and race. Equally profound is the state of health outcomes for Atlanta's African American population. Comparable to national data, the city's Black population experiences disproportionately higher rates of chronic diseases and death.[11] African American women in Atlanta are nearly twice as likely to give birth to babies born prematurely and with low birth weights. Most astoundingly, there is evidence that education and income fail to ameliorate African American women's adverse reproductive outcomes. Over a decade ago research was conducted in Atlanta comparing the birth outcomes of African American and White female college graduates.[12] The results revealed that, as compared to their White counterparts, African American women with college degrees are nearly twice as likely to experience adverse birth outcomes. Furthermore, the data shows that the rates of preterm delivery and low birth weight for African American women are comparable to White women who are only high school graduates. The gap between the adverse birth outcomes of African American women and women from other racial, ethnic, and educational backgrounds persist in Atlanta as throughout the country. Yet, explanations for reproductive disparities remain elusive.[13]

Finding Answers: Grounded in the Voices of African American Women

A series of community-based studies was conducted to (1) collaborate with communities of African American women documenting the experiences of race and gender and their connection to health outcomes and (2) to translate those experiences for the development of a racialized and gender stress measure. Since biological and genetic explanations are inconclusive, the impetus for the research was to explore psychosocial risk for adverse birth outcomes. Specifically, findings indicate that babies born to native Africans and women from the Caribbean have birth outcomes that are comparable to Whites, and there are also indications of much better birth outcomes for poor Mexican women.[14] But the challenge for exploring psychosocial risk, stress in particular, is determining the best way to assess the unique stressors confronted by African American women and to establish a direct or intermediary link between the lived experiences of stress and strain and poor birth outcomes.

The process for this research is grounded in the belief that African American women possess the authoritative knowledge to make the connection between their lived realities and heath outcomes. Therefore, the voices of African American women, from all walks of life, informed every phase of a community-based approach designed to uncover the explanations for poor reproductive outcomes. In the absence of measures to explicitly assess the stressors of race and gender, this research sought to develop a tool that captured the authentic lived experiences of race and gender for African American women. This objective was achieved through a robust research process that combined qualitative and quantitative methods shaped by the insights and participation of nearly six hundred African American women between the ages of seventeen and seventy-seven. Focus groups and interviews informed the creation of statements representing the stressors of race and gender that were transformed into items for a stress measure. Research collaborators critiqued the statements for the measure, and based on their responses, along with contents and psychometric analysis, the Jackson, Hogue, Phillips Contextualized Stress Measure was developed.[15] This seventy-one-item tool is arranged in subscales with items that measure racism (e.g., I have to deal with racism directed at my children), burden connected to gendered roles and responsibilities (Everyone expects me to be strong for them), physical and emotional abuse (I have experienced physical abuse in my relationship with a man), and workplace oppression—race and gender (Because I am a woman, my employer is not usually open to suggestions from me). The measure also includes assessments of stress mediators in the form of social support, religiosity and spirituality, and individual coping. The Jackson, Hogue, Phillips measure is validated with measures of anger, anxiety, and depression.[16] Race continues to matter in a city that is emblematic of economic progress alongside disparities in health, housing, and education. The items from the scale are representative of what women shared about their racialized lives throughout the life course. As indicated by the responses of one woman, race mattered as she awaited the birth of her child:

It [the pregnancy] scares the life out of me because I am pregnant with a Black boy and [I] know how Black boys are treated in this society. And because I've seen them, it worries me because I wonder if I can give this baby boy what he needs in order to function in this racist society.

Race shaped the experiences in the workplace where women encountered discrimination and disregard for their abilities. One collaborator talked about the beginning of her career as an engineer:

> I came to Atlanta because of the offer for a particular job. . . . So ambitious, young, all that. I could do whatever I chose. Each job was progressively worse . . . very low pay, I was the lowest paid . . . we were treated as if were clerks . . . we were technically tokens.

As participants articulated their stressors, they also shared their capacity to mediate racial and gendered encounters:

> Oh yes, we do have so many [stressors], I think that it is our ability to survive in the midst of everything that's going around and I look at some of the Black women on the jobs. Some of the positions that they are in, and they have to deal with a lot.

Race and gender were issues as women negotiated the lack of services for themselves and their families within their neighborhoods. Women talked about the lack of grocery stores, which caused them to have to go outside of the neighborhood for the food and supplies they needed.

The quantitative findings from the scale items confirm the strain that racism imposes on the lives of African American women, educated and noneducated. Each activity conducted with the women peeled away the layers of racial experiences underscoring the complexities of race and racism in Atlanta. Only 25 percent of the responses agreed, "Racism is a problem in my life." Yet nearly half (48 percent) of the responses agreed, "I have to deal with racism directed at the African American children I interact with." Other responses showed that women felt that "I have to work harder than White women to get the same recognition" (63 percent).

Most importantly, the research uncovered gendered racism as the intersectionality of racial and gendered stress as the women talked about how race exacerbates their roles and responsibilities as nurturers and caregivers. Statistical analysis confirmed the strong associations for racial encounters and anticipations and the burdens of role overload, financial instability, and uncertainty.[17] Furthermore, gendered racism as the intersection of racial and gender stressors is correlated with anger ($r = .39, < .01$) and anxiety ($r = .31, < .01$), indicating a noteworthy relationship between gendered racism, anger, and anxiety as a potential risk for the development of chronic diseases.[18]

These findings from the scale items coupled with what the women said offer a comprehensive portrait of race in the lives of African American women. This collection of the voices and responses is the result of an iterative process in which each phase informed a sequential process for discovery that was sensitized to the knowledge and perceptions of African American women as they confronted challenges and demonstrated resistance and resilience to the struggles of race and gender.

Health Disparity Data: A Matter of Race

At the outset, groups of African American women from college alumnae groups, churches, public housing communities, work sites, and other settings were shown data on health disparities and prompted to provide their own explanations for the disproportionate rates of diabetes mellitus, heart disease, and other chronic conditions. They were asked, "What do you think accounts for the higher rates of sickness and death for African American women?" Responses to the data plotted on the graphs illustrating the significant gaps in the health consequences for Black and White women ranged from shock to disbelief. While the women offered lifestyle and genetics as contributors to poor health outcomes, they unanimously named stress as a major risk for health disparities.

For most of the audiences of potential research participants, the research was their first exposure to population data on the health of African American women. Health disparities data comparing the outcomes of Blacks and Whites are commonplace among health professionals. In contrast, discussions of health, sickness, and death within communities of African American women are understood and experienced in terms of the immediate and long-range impact of illness in a woman's life and in her role as a caregiver for ill family members— with little comparison of health experiences across racial lines.

The presentation of health disparity findings ignited some protest over the issue of race, resulting in several women challenging the validity of the data. Reproductive disparities data indicating the comparable rates of low birth weight and preterm delivery for college-educated African American women and noncollege-educated White women brings to the forefront the assumptions and fallacies of race in health research.[19] Since Blackness is historically and by design associated with poverty and Whiteness is seldom perceived as indication of lower socioeconomic status, these data suggesting the preeminence of race, and the psychosocial risks attached to race, also can infer racial deficits. Predictably, during the introductory sessions where women were shown the data on health disparities, including reproductive outcomes, there were individuals who asked, "Where does this data come from?" and "Who conducted the analysis?" At one of the gatherings, a woman asserted, "You know people lie with statistics." Implicit in their questioning are challenges to the comparisons of Black and White with the health of Whites represented as the standard for optimal health outcomes. Skepticism similar to my response in the doctor's office remained for some of the women despite my attempts to argue for the legitimacy of the data.[20] Women were only convinced of the need for an examination of the reproductive health of African American by the brief yet powerful stories of the birth of premature and underweight babies shared by individuals in the audience. But conceding the need for the exploration of the causes of reproductive disparities did not completely erase the challenges to racialized health disparity data with suspicions about how the data was collected and its ultimate application for policy and practice.

A biracial team of investigators and research staff conducted the studies, but it was the African American investigators, as the lead and collaborating investigators (principal and coprincipal investigators) and research staff who had the main responsibility for data gathering and the interpretation of the findings. Members of that team represented diverse ages and childhood socioeconomic and regional backgrounds. Interviews, focus groups, and the administration of psychosocial tools were conducted at colleges, churches, community centers, shopping malls, school grounds, in automobiles, at work sites, and in the homes of research participants.

The presence of a minority investigator does not eliminate the distrust of research within African American communities. The paucity of African American investigators exacerbates challenges to the authority and decision making of African American investigators. Comparable to the absence of African American physicians, the numbers of African Americans who are researchers is also abysmal.[21] The challenges and responsibilities for this African American researcher are shaped by assumptions about the identity of an investigator that are informed by community expectations and perceived obligations alongside skepticism about scientific studies within African American communities.[22] I was confronted with spoken and unexpressed questioning about my presence and authority as an African American investigator. After completing a focus group session, one of the participants asked me, "Who is in charge of this research; who is *really* in charge?" While I assured her that I was a principal investigator, doubts lingered about my role and authority for the project. In contrast, another participant queried, "How did you get your position? I can't recall having seen an African American researcher." Her curiosity about my work was neither a challenge to the research nor my role as an investigator. Rather, it was in some respects her way of acknowledging my role as investigator as an indicator of racial progress.

Defining Community: Place and Membership

The aim of community-based research is to reconfigure the hierarchical arrangement that typically characterizes a research endeavor. In other words, community-based research is an attempt to employ the knowledge and expertise of participants in a reciprocal relationship with investigators. This is accommodated by the perceptions of what community is and, most importantly, the acknowledgement of the assets within a community.[23]

Unfortunately, there remain lingering perceptions of "the community" as a place inundated by deficits with few possibilities for sustained positive interventions. Even with the discourse surrounding community-based research, community and what it brings to the research process is viewed, in many instances, as "separate and unequal" in comparison to the sphere of the investigator.

Early in the research, we attempted to define community as we made plans for recruiting participants. Recruitment was opportunistic, an organic process occurring in collaboration with the women as we identified enclaves of African American women from diverse socioeconomic and educational backgrounds. The majority of the participants were college-educated (60 percent), and they resided throughout the city, whereas the women who were noncollege educated and with lower incomes were recruited from two public housing communities. Some women from the public housing communities earned less than $10,000 annually, and other individuals residing in luxurious homes scattered throughout the city and in subdivisions had combined annual household incomes of well over $100,000 annually. Collaborators included young adults entering the work world alongside retirees.

We discovered the fluidity of the networks of African American women transcending class, witnessing the web of multiple and overlapping community affiliations for individual women. It was across these networks where women shared information and resources, thus enhancing community assets. I, too, navigate among multiple communities in both my professional and my personal lives. My life operates in the spaces of my predominantly African American neighborhood, the school my son attends, the church where my family worships, and a range of social and civic associations. The cornucopia of shared experiences we observed among the women and experienced ourselves captures what the significance of community as both place and affiliation meant to the research.

Culture and Competency

An ability to illuminate the particular pathways from racial oppression to chronic disease begins with a process driven by an emphasis on deep structure cultural competence, rather than a simplistic approach that is limited to rituals, symbols, and language. This is particularly important for understanding the complexities of race, especially as it interacts with the gender roles of women simultaneously assumed and embraced.

Deep-structure sensitivity encompasses the idea of "peoplehood," capturing group identification social factors, historic and geographic dimensions.[24] An orientation toward deep-structure sensitivity is demonstrated through intimate knowledge of the context for the perspectives, behaviors, and experiences of community collaborators shaped by race, gender, and class. These dimensions are significant for defining the boundaries and borders of "community," and for examinations of the interactive dimensions for investigator and community, particularly as shaped by race and gender.

The questioning of my authoritative role in the design, implementation, and ultimately the interpretation of the data points to the centrality of my identity in a process shaped by deep-structure sensitivity. Implicit in the questioning of my identity was not only an inquiry about me individually, but it also was a challenge to what I potentially represented as a faculty member at a predominantly White institution that had experienced highly publicized contentious racial incidents. It was, therefore, my identity as a graduate of Spelman College and other associations within Atlanta that facilitated our entry into the communities of African American women throughout the Atlanta metropolitan area.

Intimate knowledge of the inner workings and culture of African American communities set the framework for interrogating the lives of African American women from across the life span as they navigate the present circumstances shaping their lives. In particular, understanding the nuances embedded in the culture of African American women living in the South was critical for entering diverse communities throughout the city. This knowledge translated into my meeting with representatives from the various communities rather than a staff member making the initial face-to-face contact. I understood that for some of the communities and their representatives, my presence signaled recognition of their position and status in the community as equivalent to my status as an investigator and university professor. To some extent, this type of engagement helped address perceptions about the intent of the research, challenges to the validity of health disparity data, and questions about my identity as an African American woman investigator.

Our research team understood the cultural expectations about the appropriate times to call, how individuals should be addressed, and, most importantly, who were the key contacts for making entry into communities. There were instances in which I had to demonstrate reciprocity by agreeing, when asked by collaborators, to give informal talks to community groups or share information about resources that were not necessarily related to the research.

An Equitable Exchange:
Reciprocity and Accountability

The goals of reciprocity and accountability can best be achieved when every attempt is made to ensure that the process is of mutual benefit for the community and the investigator. I recognized that, for the investigator, the residuals of a research project extend well beyond the period of data collection. Analysis, papers, and presentations can be a never-ending process. At the same time, community partners expressed their desire for an immediate application of the findings to address their needs. To demonstrate that we valued their time and contribution to the project, participants were compensated, but in no way was the exchange of money for information the only form of reciprocity. However, I discovered that if an authentic partnership is forged between community and investigators, the exchanges of money for participation could have a residual impact.

A graduate chapter of Delta Sigma Theta sorority was invited to be a collaborator in the research. I explained to one of the chapter officers the goals and process, including the compensation for participating in the study. Her enthusiastic response exceeded my expectation until she revealed how the goals of the research were aligned with the agenda for their organization. Their commitment to various community service projects throughout the city meant that funds had to be raised for those activities. Mental health was on the national agenda for the organization, and the goal of acquiring funds for local projects was foremost. Members of the chapter elected to combine their individual compensation from the research to support their community service; hence, their involvement in the research became a fund-raiser for projects that were, in effect, interventions for the stressors that women described in the research.

Payment for the women required considering who they were and where they lived and worked. One of the sessions was conducted in a community center adjacent to a public housing project. As with all participants, these women were to be paid, but how they were compensated had to be carefully planned. Women from other locations were given checks after they completed an activity. Recognizing that the women from a public housing community are unlikely to have bank accounts and would be assessed fees to cash checks or money orders, we decided that cash was the most equitable way to compensate them. Because cash was distributed during a late evening session, our staff and staff from the center collaborated to ensure the safety of the women and especially my safety because I carried a large amount of cash.

Compensation was a motivation for some of the women, but equally important for many was the opportunity to give voice to their experiences of racial and gendered oppression. Some interviews were emotional and extended beyond the planned time, as women cried while talking about racial assaults, confrontations in the workplace, and fears for their children. In response, our staff offered information for counseling and other resources.

As women acknowledged the therapeutic benefits of the focus group sessions, they lamented the absence of opportunities for ongoing stress interventions elsewhere. In the absence of psychological support—freestanding or as part of routine health care—and because of the stigma attached to mental health and illnesses, prior to their participation, the women experienced a few gatherings to address the stressors in their lives. A number of them requested additional sessions beyond the scope of the research. However, what I observed as the attraction of the focus groups is that the sessions allowed the women to be vulnerable while remaining mindful of their resilience and resistance to hopelessness from the exposure to multiple forms of oppression. In this respect, the sessions were empowering because the participants saw that their lives, with all the challenges and successes, mattered. This allowed them to affirm themselves, assist others in their struggles, and create sustainable interventions.

From Research to Intervention and Beyond

Because of the notorious abuses of the Tuskegee syphilis study and other research atrocities, stringent guidelines are in place to protect research participants from research abuses.[25] In comparison to the attention on entry and procedures for ensuring informed consent, there is relatively little focus on how a research project should end in a fashion that is accountable and not exploitative.

I constantly struggled over the mismatch between the required procedures for the research and the collaborators' expectation for the immediate application of the research to arrest stress in their lives. To a certain extent, what the women sought from the research was provided through the therapeutic exchanges that took place during the focus groups. Nonetheless, I wondered how to employ a more intentional process for further demonstration of the authoritative knowledge of the collaborators. The women's evaluations of the focus groups led to the development of an activity designed to disseminate the preliminary findings while offering an opportunity to share and display the research participants' stress interventions. Over the course of the study, two day-long events assembled the women to hear the progress of the research and participate in "talking circles," where the focus was on ways to ameliorate the particular racial and gendered stressors uncovered during the research. Sessions led by collaborators offered a forum for continued exchange especially around individual and community responses to racialized stress. In these groups, the women discussed workplace stressors, financial issues, self-care, and the development of friendships. The women were also invited to display on the stage items representing their individual approaches for stress reduction. Garden tools, books, candles, and other items lined the stage as illustration of self-care during stressful periods. Most importantly, the events were arranged to give the women ample opportunities to demonstrate their authoritative knowledge of health and to initiate a community conversation about how to organize as they confronted the health risk of gendered racism. As an explicit refocusing from health disparities to health assets and equity, the events presented a framework for the contemplation of individual and collective pathways to health and wellness fostered by community action.

The interactions among the women had residual effects, such as initiating relationships and continuing discussions well after the event and the women's participation in the research concluded. These interactions also resulted in lingering connections between the research collaborators and me. Countless times, I encounter women from the first phases of the research who remind me of their participation and, in some instances, update me on the events in their lives. There are also times when I am in the same space with women who shared, during the interviews I conducted, the intimate details of their lives. We simply nod at each other with the assurances of confidentiality and knowledge of my remaining a resource for information, particularly for mental health referrals, as needed.

Conclusion

The research that began as an exploration of psychosocial risks for reproductive disparities evolved to include an articulation of health assets and equity. This transformation was a response to the lingering tensions between the deficits of health disparities and the empowerment objective of community-based research that was made apparent by the reactions of the participants. Race mattered not only as the women shared their lived experiences of confronting racism in the workplace, in their neighborhoods, and within their families, it was also implicit in their critique of the research process. Their questioning of the data and my role in the research was resonating with the racialzied concerns of the women about stereotypes, discrimination, and exploitation.

Community-based participatory research is designed to bring keen focus to the insights and expertise of community participants; it also has implications for the investigator. As a researcher, I had the formidable task of negotiating and balancing the needs of the community with the demands of scientific rigor. While I understood the expectations of me as a scientist, I was also mindful of my identity as an African American woman who had reacted to the information on reproductive disparities in a way that was similar to the responses of some of the women. For me, this intersection of race and science translated into a particular focus on ensuring that the research, aimed at creating a measure of race and gender, was both accountable and reciprocal. It was these commitments that led to the creation of a dissemination activity that was not part of the original research design.

The emphasis on reciprocity placed high demands on me as a researcher. There were instances when I was asked by the collaborators to respond to needs that went outside the scope of the research. But requests for information about colleges, jobs, and other resources never detracted from the aims of the research; rather, they provided further context for interpreting the experiences of race and gender. Race mattered as I not only understood the expectations and mechanisms for exchange between myself and research collaborators but also that my acquiescence to those requests were viewed as affirmation of my authenticity as a member of an African American community, thus establishing respect and trust. It was this trust, and admittedly perceptions of my racialized life, that gave me and members of the team access to the racial struggles articulated by the women. It is from the vantage of our shared racialized and gendered lives that we have advanced scholarship for understanding and measuring challenges and opportunities that impact the health and well-being of American women.

The process for conducting this research underscores the critical importance of sensitivity as a component of the insights needed for uncovering the authentic experiences of race and racism. The insights for conducting research on race and health require introspection on the role and identity of the investigator and the researcher's own experience and responses to race and racism. As health disparities research increasingly explores interventions, it is vital that these activities acknowledge the centrality of race and racism in the production of disparate outcomes and, most importantly, employ processes and perspectives that ultimately result in equitable health outcomes.

Notes

1. N. Anachebe, "Racial and Ethnic Disparities in Infant and Maternal Mortality," *Ethnicity and Disease* 16, no. 3 (suppl. 3) (2006): 53–71; S. Hoffman and M. C. Hatch, "Stress, Social Support and Pregnancy Outcomes: A Reassessment Based on Recent Research," *Paediatric Perinatal Epidemiology* 10, no. 4 (1996): 380–405; F. Jackson, *Race, Stress, and Social Support: Addressing the Crisis in Black Infant Mortality* (Washington, D.C.: Joint Center for Political and Economic Studies, August 2007); V. K. Hogan and C. Ferre, "The Social Context of Pregnancy for African American Women: Implication for the Study and Prevention of Adverse Perinatal Outcomes," *Maternal and Child Health Journal* 5, no. 2 (2001): 67–69; T. Stancil et al, "Stress and Pregnancy among African American Women" *Paediatric and Perinatal Epidemiology* 14, no. 2 (2000): 127–35.

2. J. F. Culhane et al., "Maternal Stress Is Associated with Bacterial Vaginosis in Human Pregnancy," *Maternal and Child Health Journal* 5, no. 2 (2001): 127–34.

3. D. Blumenthal, "A Community Coalition Board Creates a Set of Values for Community-Based Research," *Preventable Chronic Diseases* 3, no. 1 (2006): A16; G. Corbie-Smith, A. S. Ammerman, and M. L. Katz, "Trust, Benefit, and Burdens: A Randomized Controlled Trial to Reduce Cancer Risk through African American Churches," *Journal of General Internal Medicine* 18, no. 7 (2003): 531–41; I. C. Williams and G. Corbie-Smith, "Investigator Beliefs and Reported Success in Recruiting Minority Participants," *Contemporary Clinical Trails* 27, no. 6 (2006): 580–86.

4. F. Jackson, "Considerations for Community-Based Research with African American Women,." *American Journal of Public Health* 92, no. 4 (2002): 561–64.

5. C. A. Bacote, *The Story of Atlanta University: A Century of Service, 1863–1963* (Princeton, NJ: Princeton University Press, 1969).

6. D. Sjoquist, *The Atlanta Paradox* (New York: Russell Sage Foundation, 2000).

7. M. McArdle, "Poverty, Concentrated Poverty and Urban Areas, National Urban League, Policy Institute, 2004, http://www.nul.org/publications/policy institute/factsheet/PovertyFactSheet.doc (accessed November 1, 2007).

8. "Metro Atlanta Foreclosure Up to 36 Percent," *Atlanta Business Chronicle*, September 25, 2006, http://www.bizjournal.com/atlanta/stories/2006/09/25/dialy2.html (accessed March 1, 2007).

9. V. Hein, "The Image of 'A City Too Busy to Hate': Atlanta in the 1960's," *Phylon* 33, no. 3 (1972): 205–21.

10. E. Wyly, "The Color of Money Revisited: Racial Lending Patterns in Atlanta's Neighborhoods," *Housing Policy Debate* 10, no. 3 (1999): 555–600.

11. Centers for Disease Control and Prevention, *Chronic Diseases: The Leading Causes of Death in Georgia* (Atlanta, GA: National Center for Chronic Disease, 2006).

12. G. A. McGrady et al., "Preterm Delivery and Low Birth Weight among First-Born Infants of Black and White College Graduates," *American Journal of Epidemiology* 136, no. 3 (1992): 226–32.

13. Fleda Mask Jackson et al., "Examining the Burdens of Gendered Racism: Implications for the Pregnancy Outcomes of College-Educated African American Women," *Maternal and Child Health Journal* 5, no. 2 (June 2001): 95–107.

14. R. David and J. Collins, "Differing Birth Weights among Infants of U.S. Born Blacks, African American Blacks and U.S.-Born Whites," *New England Journal of Medicine* 337, no. 17 (1992): 1209–14.

15. F. Jackson et al. "The Development of a Race and Gender Specific Stress Measure for African American Women: The Jackson, Hogue, Phillips Contextualized Stress Measure," *Ethnicity and Disease* 15, no. 4 (October 2005): 594–600.

16. Jackson, "The Development of a Race and Gender Specific Stress Measure," 594–600.

17. Jackson, "The Development of a Race and Gender Specific Stress Measure," 594–600.

18. Jackson, "Examining the Burdens of Gendered Racism," 95–107.

19. G. Corbie-Smith, "Distrust, Race, and Research," *Archives of Internal Medicine* 162, no. 22 (2002): 2458–63.

20. J. Wasserman et al., "Raising the Ivory Tower: The Production of Knowledge and Distrust of Medicine among African Americans" *Journal of Medical Ethics* 33, no. 3 (2007): 177–80; S. Thorburn and L. Bogart, "Conspiracy Beliefs about Birth Control; Barriers to Pregnancy Prevention among African Americans of Reproductive Age," *Health Education Behavior* 32, no. 4 (2005): 474–87.

21. M. Nunnez-Smith et al., "Impact of Race on the Professional Lives of Physicians of African Descent," *Annals of Internal Medicine* 146 (2007): 45–51; M. Christian and E. L. Trimble, "Increasing Participation of Physicians and Patents from Underrepresented Racial and Ethnic Groups in National Cancer Institute—Sponsored Clinical Trials," *Cancer Epidemiology, Biomarkers and Prevention* 12 (March 2006): 277s–83s.

22. L. Serrant-Green, "Black on Black: Methodological Issues for Black Researchers Working in Minority Ethnic Communities," *Nurse Researcher* 9, no. 4 (2002): 30–44.

23. Jackson, "Considerations for Community-Based Research, 561–64; F. Jackson, "Evaluating Service Learning," in *Rethinking Tradition: Integrating Service and Academic Study on College Campuses*, ed. T. Kupiec (Denver, CO: Education Commission of the States, 1993), 129–36.

24. K. Resnicow and R. Braithwaite, "Cultural Sensitivity in Public Health," in *Health Issues in the Black Community*, ed. R. Braithwaite and S. Taylor (San Francisco, CA: Jossey-Bass, 2001), 516–33.

25. V. Fremith et al., "African Americans' View on Research and the Tuskegee Syphilis Study," *Social Science and Medicine* 52 (2001):797–803; J. Jones, Bad Blood: The Tuskegee Syphilis Experiment (New York: Simon and Schuster, 1993); T. Murphy, *Case Studies in Biomedical Research Ethics*. Cambridge, MA: MIT Press, 2004.

11

◈◈◈

A Partnership with the African American Church

IMPPACT and S.P.I.C.E.S. For Life

MICAH MCCREARY, MONICA JONES,
RAYMOND TADEMY, AND JOHN FIFE

Our approach to community engagement and community-based research with African American churches and communities is grounded in a theoretical perspective that incorporates counseling psychology, multicultural theory, liberation teaching philosophy, and African American psychology.[1] Our model of engagement and research is grounded in the values and behaviors of unity, strong kinship bonds, inherent feelings of cooperation and sharing, an overarching religious orientation that provides structure and direction, and a focus on wellness.[2] Our work is further informed by a core belief that there are multiple origins to the challenges, weaknesses, and problems of our constituency. Thus, our approach involves multiple components.

First, we have cultivated a philosophy and an approach to community engagement and community-based research that emphasizes the importance of the individual, family, and community from an interpersonal-family systems-ecological-cultural perspective. We approach our work from a perspective of the whole. We attempt to remain keenly interested in investigating the quality of the relationships within the community with a focus on how relationships enhance and hinder self-expression, self-respect, and self-actualization.

Our team is concerned about the patterns of family and community conflicts over the lifespan. We pay close attention to family and community alliances, coalitions, triangles, and boundaries. Our engagement and research approach consist of assessing and intervening with the various ecosystems that the family and community contacts. Our goals for engagement and research are simple. We want families and communities to grow relationally, socially, psychologically, and behaviorally. We want them to take action toward their well-being—to change their awareness about their relationships and their positions regarding external structures. We want families to realize that they are not victims, but victorious. This philosophy of engagement and research has grown from our personal experiences with children, adolescents, couples, families, and communities.

Second, as partners with the community, we must offer a product and a process that facilitates African American academic and social success. We must empower one another as we engage one another. We are, therefore, compelled to eradicate the mismatch between the needs of the university and the needs of society, particularly African Americans and other people of color. We feel obligated to develop programs with the African American community and church that are mutually beneficial, foster economic development, and produce social progress. Our primary method of accomplishing our research agenda is through relationships. No partnership will be effective without a trusting relationship. No trusting relationship will exist without dialogue and effective communication. Thus, our community-church-university partnership is maintained and reinforced by our liberation and teaching philosophy.[3]

We focus our intervention and engagement efforts on and around the practice of freedom, democracy, compassion, justice, equity, and respect. All of our engagement and research goals are based on the principles and values of integrity, virtue, and authenticity. Ultimately, we strive to assist African American communities in the development of critical thinkers (i.e., people who are critically aware and engaged in the struggle for freedom) and revolutionary healers (i.e., people involved in helping others obtain health, healing, and wholeness). This engagement and research philosophy includes awareness of race, sex, ethnicity, and class. As partners with the African American church and community, we operate with a fierce commitment to harmony and open, honest dialogue.

African American Psychological Philosophy

Volumes of scholarly works have been published affirming and criticizing African American psychology as a discipline.[4] Our purpose here is not to survey African American psychology, but to state that its underlying premises have influenced and informed our research and engagement efforts. We consider African American psychology to be an outgrowth of third world philosophy. It is a psychological perspective born from a need for applied solutions, strong empirical support of the African American psychological experience, and to develop a psychology that did not see African Americans as culturally deprived.[5] Kambon described four characteristics of an African American psychology relevant to our work: (1) it generates the construction of African social reality from the framework of the history, culture, and philosophy of African civilization; (2) it recognizes and articulates the basic continuity of the African worldview throughout the diverse African population around the globe; (3) it recognizes and articulates the basic distinctness and independence of the African worldview, relative to any other; and (4) it projects the African survival thrust as the center of African social reality.[6]

In the current chapter, we will use two programs, IMPPACT and S.P.I.C.E.S., to discuss our community engagement and community-based research efforts with African Americans. The acronym IMPPACT stands for "I Must Pause Pray Analyze Chill and Take action." The Spring Creek program was previously titled IMPACT: I Must Pause Analyze Chill and Take action.

IMPPACT is a culturally congruent family–church-based program designed to apply salient dimensions of African American religiosity and cultural values to the cultivation of resilience and self-efficacy outcomes among African American families. IMPPACT has been conducted in the community since 2001 and applies salient dimensions of African American religiosity and cultural values to the cultivation of resilience and self-efficacy outcomes among African American families.

Conceptually, IMPPACT aims to address multidimensional and multi-domain influences of social disorganization (e.g., deviant peer groups, crime, poverty, violence exposure, and unemployment) on youth attitudes and behaviors. The program generally applies a social development model that marshals the social capital resources of a faith-based institution to foster social bonding among youth while also enhancing youth self-efficacy and resilience. The effects of social bonding result in the acceptance and adherence of positive behavioral and attitudinal norms that reflect the values of one's affiliated institution. IMPPACT seeks to investigate the role of several known risk factors associated with adolescence, such as the chronic social demands of economic deprivation and disadvantage.[7] The program is also concerned with the effect of institutionalized racism, unemployment, and poor educational outcomes on the everyday lives of the youth and families participating in the program.[8]

IMPPACT is further interested in peer influence, quality of parental and peer relationships, and their relationship to antisocial and risky behaviors among adolescents.[9] The effects of peer influences seem most dramatic when parental or family relationships are weak or when there are few affiliations with affirming institutions or nurturing adults.[10] Peer relationships can become the strongest influence on behaviors of youths when not moderated by protective factors, including parental monitoring and caring adult relationships.[11] Again, we believe that our engagement and involvement with the church is paramount to gaining a more accurate understanding of peer influence and peer rejection.[12]

S.P.I.C.E.S. is a program conducted in collaboration with a Baptist church convention. The focal points of the program are demonstrated by what the acronym, stands for Spiritual, Physical, Intellectual, Cognitive, Emotional, and Social. This program was designed to decrease health disparities in the African American community through a holistic approach to educating African American church members about healthy lifestyles.

In addition to the health facts and knowledge provided by the S.P.I.C.E.S. program, the endorsement from the church, the spiritual component, and support group format contributed to the success of the project. The rapport that was established between the targeted population and the church was particularly important to the introduction of the health education program to the community. Research has suggested that collaborations between the church and community groups are essential for disseminating beneficial information to minority populations. This relationship allows for added rapport from the initiation of intervention programs. The endorsement of pastors, ministers, and other trusted church leadership of community projects increases the credibility of the organization, in addition to increasing the likelihood that the participants will take the program more seriously.

The spiritual component also enhances the program, especially for use with the African American population. Studies suggest that spirituality emerges as an important cultural variable for many ethnic minorities. This is an essential aspect of the identity of many African Americans, and the inclusion of spirituality is important to make intervention efforts culturally sensitive to the population.

Last, the support group format of the program has been found efficacious. Information that is taught and discussed in this environment seems to have more of an impact on participants. This group setting also appears most conducive for a predominantly female sample as there is consistently the finding that females are more relational in nature and are more open to group processes that foster this orientation.

Through IMPPACT and S.P.I.C.E.S. we pay close attention to the principles of community engagement as they relate to research and interventions in the African American church. We view community engagement as a powerful tool used to create partnerships, alliances, and coalitions that work together to obtain and maintain resources. Strategies for community engagement in the African American community have been found to differ from that of European Americans or other ethnic minority groups due to exclusion and rejection from the greater civic culture of mainstream society.[13] Prejudice and discrimination impact the desire and capacity for civic engagement in the African American.[14] Effective community engagement within the African American community tends to involve both the family and the church.[15]

The social development model provides a theoretical explanation for how a protective factor, such as religiosity among African American youth, can foster resilience through the operation of a dual-process model.[16] According to Catalano and associates, individuals who experience greater attachment and commitment to a formal socializing unit are more likely to exhibit prosocial behaviors and values than individuals who do not experience positive social units.[17] This positive social support, a primary goal of our programs, helps adolescents cope and create positive pathways, while preventing the occurrence of other behavioral and emotional problems.

Resilience

Despite exposure to multiple risk factors, many African American youth, including those in low-income, urban environments, develop into well-functioning and productive adults.[18] These positive outcomes, in the face of multiple risk factors, indicate the existence of protective factors that reduce exposure to these risks or promote effective coping responses on exposure to risk factors. Resilience has been defined as the attainment of normal developmental outcomes and the maintenance of uninterrupted psychological functioning in the face of adversity.[19]

Resilience is generally fostered through individual, family, or community-based protective factors.[20] Although individually based factors have been the primary focus of research, prevention and intervention programs and family factors such as a positive relationship with at least one parent have been associated with resilience in youth.[21]

Community-Based Research

Community-based protective factors, such as religious involvement, extended families, and fictive kin, are known to protect youth from negative outcomes.[22] Thus, transcending the walls of academia is important to create enduring change through culturally significant institutions, such as the church. The African American church represents a crucial entity within the Black community to increase community engagement and facilitate community-based research. Its impact can truly change lives through intervention and prevention strategies, but also through the presentation of African American mentors and role models outside the immediate family; thus, we moved our programs from the university to the church.

Community-based research efforts can still meet with reluctance in the African American community due to distrust in the medical profession and previous research debacles where African Americans were treated cruelly and unjustly (e.g., the Tuskegee syphilis experiment and the recent AIDS medication research with African American foster children).[23] Both projects failed to provide adequate information to those involved and their families and had the potential to cause significant harm to the participants. The word *research* has the potential to elicit various negative images and connotations for African Americans. Engaging in research through the church may help build trust.

African American Church

A discussion of community engagement in the African American community would be incomplete without including a closer examination of the African American church. Because religious concepts are interwoven into daily living among African Americans, the church represents a primary institution of socialization.[24] Available research indicates differences in religious involvement between African Americans and other ethnic groups.

The focal point of religious and spiritual traditions within the African American community extends to Africa. Traditional and contemporary African societies revere the presence of spiritual beings and often involve themselves in religious practices reflective of this reality.[25] African spiritual traditions have historically held a central place in African American communalism and were vital to survival during the time of slavery.[26]

Wills, Yaeger, and Sandy found that many highly religious youth feel that drug use is immoral and therefore are able to abstain even when exposed to peers, friends, or other drug use influences.[27] They also found that religious attitudes toward drug use mediated the buffering effects of religiosity on drug use. Religiosity also had buffering effects on stress and other factors associated with drug use.[28]

Haight hypothesized that resilience among African American children may be cultivated by nurturing and caring relationships with adults as part of their affiliation with religious institutions.[29] The purpose of the research with IMPPACT and S.P.I.C.E.S. is to look at whether religiosity (i.e., religious involvement) increases African American children's access to social support resources. Furthermore, our research endeavors seek to show that community-based research and engagement efforts with the African American church are viable.

The African American church has served as a setting for organization and mobilization of community resources and has provided consistent support to African American families.[30] The term *African American church* encompasses any predominantly African American congregation, even if it is part of a predominantly White American religious denomination. The African American church is often acknowledged as the pulse of the African American community. Moreover, scholars have noted that no other institution in the United States can claim the loyalty and attention that the African American church claims.[31] Despite an individual's religious group affiliation or nonaffiliation, the African American church has served political, social, emotional/relational, and financial functions in the African American community.[32]

One of the main goals of IMPPACT and S.P.I.C.E.S. is to show how African Americans use religious values to promote a sense of connectedness and to shape the parishioners' understandings of their moral obligation to the community and society. In this vein, the African American church has been used to empower the community and to address social and political issues. Thus,

IMPPACT and S.P.I.C.E.S. are two programs that continue to model the connection between the African American church and various social-political issues. The African American church was at the center of the Civil Rights Movement, with Martin Luther King Jr., a young minister, leading the charge for social and political justice. The movement was a true example of the intersection between race and religion. From his writings and speeches, King clearly showed that the impact of race and racial experiences on the religious experience of African Americans must be understood.

Giving special attention to the counseling psychology theory of multicultural counseling to engage the African American church has been beneficial in our community-based research efforts.[33] Using tradition, culture, and knowledge to obtain participation and collaboration among church members has been crucial to our research. Cultural sensitivity to African American culture, in addition to the culture of the church environment, is essential for engagement. Being adept in acquiring information about the church's current practices, such as faith practices, prayer, and music, are important components leading to successful community-based programming.[34] According to program participants, our knowledge of the African American church has made IMPPACT and S.P.I.C.E.S. very meaningful. For example, we work diligently to engage the pastor of the church and purposefully seek to include other congregants in important church roles and positions, such as deacons and elders.

University–Community Partnerships

Our university–community partnership is made possible based on the fact that we are faculty and graduate students at Virginia Commonwealth University (VCU), located on two downtown campuses in Richmond, Virginia. VCU ranks among the top one hundred universities in the country in sponsored research and enrolls thirty thousand students in more than 195 certificate, undergraduate, graduate, professional, and doctoral programs in fifteen schools and one liberal arts college. Medical College of Virginia hospitals, clinics, and health sciences schools of VCU constitute the VCU Medical Center, one of the leading academic medical centers in the country. As an urban university, VCU has made a strong commitment for collaboration and work within the urban community of Richmond. The Psychology Department at VCU has a long history of education and relevant work in community engagement and community-based research.

In 1998, Drs. Micah McCreary, Kevin Allison, and Faye Belgrave received a three-year grant from the Department of Health and Human Services, Center for Substance Abuse Prevention. Project IMPACT was funded to conduct a substance abuse prevention intervention research program with children ages six to eight whose parents were current or former substance abusers. This grant project was a partnership between Richmond Behavioral Health Authority, the primary agency responsible for assessment of residents with substance abuse problems, several Richmond public schools, and VCU's Department of Psychology. Richmond Behavioral Health Authority was contracted to provide case management to the recruited families. The Richmond Public Elementary Schools provided access to the children and their facilities. The VCU faculty and staff provided the program and evaluation services.[35]

After the conclusion of our grant project we moved our program to Spring Creek Baptist Church as a summer institute. The program was changed from a substance abuse prevention program to a resiliency, skill development, and problem-solving program. The program was also changed to include Christian and value education to facilitate and enhance our community engagement and community-based research. Participants are recruited from the church and the community. The name IMPACT was changed to IMPPACT to more clearly reflect the value education focus of the program.

Evaluation of IMPPACT

Several methods have been undertaken to evaluate the IMPPACT program implementation and delivery efforts. Process evaluation was used to provide on-going feedback to project staff regarding success at meeting objectives and implementation efforts. Evaluation activities were needs assessment, on-site observations, staff meetings, and feedback from parents.

Overall, the evaluation results indicate that the program was rewarding for both staff and participants. According to the evaluation, the strength of the IMPPACT program lies in its generation and maintenance of high levels of interest and engagement among participants and parents. The evaluators suggested that these factors combine to give the program a strong reputation that is significantly reinforced by word-of-mouth advertising by both children and parents. Parent satisfaction surveys and interviews with participants and staff further reinforce these points.

It was discovered that the children's satisfaction was largely driven by the variety of activities within an environment that provides multiple levels of academic, social, and physical stimulation. Parental satisfaction seems largely derived from energized children who regularly share what they learned and what they did at IMPPACT. These factors coalesce in session-ending programs that generally feature dramatic skits, dances, or musical performances by the children in front of an audience of their parents. The session-ending program provides the children with public recognition, and high levels of individual validation.

Some of the program's biggest challenges are embedded with its general strengths. First, the variety of program activities and events require advance planning and allocation of resources (i.e., transportation) for effective and timely execution. Program staff seemed particularly concerned by the frequency of changes in schedules and events due to staffing changes. They perceived these changes as negatively impacting the program. Program staff also mentioned the variety of events and activities demanded that staff have a strong background in child management and time management.

To emphasize the importance and power of evaluating our community–university partnership, we have included the eleven excellent recommendations from the summer evaluation, which suggested how we might enhance and develop the efficacy of IMPPACT.

1. Staff should begin to plan for the summer sessions well in advance of the camp.
2. Incorporate the entire existing curriculum into daily sessions or modify if necessary.
3. All social interactions and activities should emphasize the IMPPACT model.
4. Maximize the high adult–children ratios by providing more one-on-one attention.
5. Facilitators and staff should refer to and apply the IMPPACT model during their interactions with the children.
6. Separate the children into age-appropriate groups.
7. Use the older children to mentor the younger children.
8. Incorporate physical fitness (e.g., martial arts, yoga, and nutrition) into a specific component that addresses "the body as a temple" ideal.
9. Language acquisition, cultural knowledge, and other formal learning opportunities should be used as opportunities to build individual academic achievement efficacy while also identifying intellectual or academic challenges.
10. Christian education should be integrated into all activities.
11. Staff must be able to work with parents to help make significant attitudinal or behavioral changes.

The S.P.I.C.E.S. For Life Program

Our collaboration with the Baptist General Convention of Virginia, which began in 2002, is another example of a research-based university–church relationship. The Baptist General Convention of Virginia is a predominantly African American, faith-based organization serving approximately eleven hundred churches and thirty associations throughout Virginia. The S.P.I.C.E.S. For Life Program was designed to decrease health disparities within the African American community through a holistic approach to teaching healthy lifestyles. The convention's purpose for implementing the S.P.I.C.E.S. For Life Program was to (1) identify chronic diseases/health concerns for African Americans; (2) explore intervention and preventive health care methods; and (3) develop community contacts to facilitate their efforts.

Each of the S.P.I.C.E.S. concepts contributes to a framework used by the Baptist General Convention of Virginia to facilitate the exploration of the mind-body-spirit connection and promote optimal health. The program is comprised of health education, skill building, and an increased ability to attain necessary health resources.

We have evaluated 245 participant surveys collected during the 2004-2005 grant year for the S.P.I.C.E.S. For Life Program. The sample is predominantly female (84.6 percent), with 55.3 percent between the ages of fifty and seventy-nine. The churches were all located within urban and rural segments of Virginia. Thirty-seven percent of the respondents were single, 34 percent were married, 6 percent were separated, 6 percent were divorced, and the remaining 17 percent were widowed. Thirty-nine percent of the individuals within the random sample had completed high school and 36 percent had acquired some postsecondary education. Twenty-six percent of the participants in the random sample declined to answer the education question.

Ninety-one percent denied any current illnesses, and 9 percent currently described themselves as "ill." Some of the miscellaneous illnesses reported by the sample were nosebleeds, diabetes, back pain, acid reflux, heart problems, hypertension, overweight, arthritis, and cancer.

Overall, the sample reported moderately healthy behaviors and attitudes at pretests and posttests as evidenced by most answers being "4" or "5" on a five-point Likert-type scale of increasing health knowledge. Despite the initial level of knowledge and behavior exhibited by the group, there were changes indicated in each of the six domains targeted by the program: spiritual, physical, intellectual, cognitive, physical, and social health.

The sample displayed high levels of spiritual health, although there were increases in spiritual health knowledge as a result of the program. Ninety-two percent of participants found that their personal beliefs were meaningful to their lives after completing the program, compared with 86.1 percent who felt that way before going through the program. Ninety percent of participants felt that their lives were meaningful after the program versus 84 percent who felt that way before the program. Ninety-two percent of the group felt that their personal beliefs provided them with strength to face difficulties after the program, while 84 percent reported such beliefs before the program. Eighty-seven percent of program participants stated that they felt their personal beliefs helped them understand life, while 82 percent felt this way before.

The participants were also more pleased with their overall physical health following the program implementation, with 64.1 percent rating their health as "satisfied" or "very satisfied" before the session, and 73.7 percent giving the highest rankings after the program. Eighty-two percent of program participants felt they would have a greater capacity of energy for daily functioning as a result of the program, versus 71.8 percent who felt this way before the program. There was also an increase in knowledge about the importance of sleep to health and perceived ability to perform daily activities after the program. Participants also felt better able to perform a variety of work tasks after the workshop in comparison to their initial reports prior to the project.

The intellectual and cognitive components of the curriculum focused on goal setting and thinking ability. Seventy-six percent of participants felt that they were better able to concentrate after the program versus 63 percent prior to the program. The participants also felt greater confidence in their ability to access appropriate health services following the workshop.

Regarding emotional health, 81.1 percent of participants reported feeling very happy with themselves at the initiation of the group, compared with 78.3 percent before the program. Eighty-five percent of program participants conveyed acceptance of their body image following the execution of the S.P.I.C.E.S. For Life Program versus 81.5 percent before the program. More participants reported that they were also more satisfied with themselves after the program (94.8 percent), compared with 89.2 percent prior to the program.

Social health was the last element of the S.P.I.C.E.S. For Life Program. It focused on relationships and physical environment. Participants had a greater value for the importance of their friends for support following the project. They felt better able to improve the safety of their home and community after the program (92.1 percent) versus before the program (89.1 percent). Ninety-two percent of the group reported greater satisfaction about their living space after the program versus 89 percent before the program. This likely reflects a better ability to judge appropriate living conditions.

The results of the S.P.I.C.E.S. For Life Program identified change in knowledge of health issues within all six domains of interest: spiritual, physical, intellectual, cognitive, emotion/mental, and social health. This has the potential to create a lasting change in the manner in which the participants are able to make decisions about their health. An increase in knowledge may also lend itself to an increase in the participants' self-efficacy in regard to their health behaviors. When individuals perceive their own ability to engage in certain behaviors, participation in said behaviors increases.[36] The impact to the African American community through this type of outreach project can be an effective approach to the subject of health among a community that suffers from health disparities.

Summary

Developing a successful community-church-university partnership is a challenging endeavor. Successful community and church engagement is facilitated by a relationship based on building social and political capital and enriching the educational experience of all involved. Our approach to community engagement and community-based research with African American churches and communities is grounded in a theoretical perspective that incorporates counseling psychology, multicultural theory, liberation teaching philosophy, and

African American psychology. Our model of engagement and research is grounded in the values and behaviors of unity, strong kinship bonds, inherent feelings of cooperation and sharing, and an overarching religious orientation that provides structure, direction, and a focus on wellness.

Communities, churches, and universities are experiencing new and unique challenges to their effectiveness and well-being, particularly as we enter a new era of increased regulation and reduced funding. From our experience, we offer two suggestions to enhance community engagement with African American churches: (1) cultivate a philosophy and an approach to community engagement and community-based research that emphasizes the importance of the individual, family, and community from an interpersonal-family systems-ecological-cultural perspective; and (2) pay close attention to the nature and quality of the community and church relationships, maintaining a focus on how your relationships enhance or hinder self-expression, self-respect, and self-actualization.

This chapter discussed two community-church-university research programs: IMPPACT and S.P.I.C.E.S. For Life. The creation of a church, community, and university program offers more accurate evaluations and improved programming. We have found that church programming without appropriate evaluation hinders program effectiveness and the ability to replicate the programs in other communities. Also, the church offers an optimal environment for dissemination of essential information to African Americans. Culturally appropriate tools and strategies for evaluation can be determined through an assessment of the population and goals of the project. Relationship building is fundamental in working with this population. It is the relationship that facilitates rapport and trust and eliminates the stigma of the community toward research.

Notes

1. P. Freire, *Pedagogy of the Oppressed* (New York: Continuum, 1993); b. Hooks, *Teaching to Transgress: Education as the Practice of Freedom* (New York: Routledge, 1994); D. A. Y. Azibo, *African Psychology in Historical Perspective and Related Commentary* (Trenton, NJ: Africa World Press, 1996); K. A. Burlew, C. W. Banks, and H. P. McAdoo, *African American Psychology: Theory, Research and Practice* (Thousand Oaks, CA: Sage, 1992); R. L. Jones, ed., *Black Psychology*, 3rd ed. (Berkeley, CA: Cobb and Henry, 1991).

2. A. M. Jackson, "A Theoretical Model for the Practice of Psychotherapy with Black Populations," in *African American Psychology: Theory, Research, and Practice*, ed. A. K. H. Burlew, W. C. Banks, H. P. McAdoo, and D. A. Azibo (Newbury Park, CA: Sage, 1992), 321–29; J. G. Ponterotto, J. M. Casas, L. A. Suzuki, and C. M. Alexander, eds., *Handbook of Multicultural Counseling*, 2nd ed. (Thousand Oaks, CA: Sage, 2001).

3. Freire, *Pedagogy of the Oppressed*; Hooks, *Teaching to Transgress*.

4. Azibo, *African Psychology*; F. Z. Belgrave and K. W. Allison, *African American Psychology: From African to America* (Thousand Oaks, CA: Sage, 2006); T. A. Parham, J. L. White, and A. Ajamu, *The Psychology of Blacks* (Upper Saddle River, NJ: Prentice Hall, 2000).

5. Azibo, *African Psychology*; Belgrave and Allison, *African American Psychology*; Parham, White, and Ajamu, *The Psychology of Blacks*.

6. K. K. K. Kambon, "The Africentric Paradigm and African American Psychology and Liberation," in *African Psychology in Historical Perspective and Related Commentary*, ed. D. A. Y. Azibo (Trenton, NJ: Africa World Press, 1996).

7. A. Franklin, "Therapeutic Interventions with Urban Adolescents—Ethnic Minority Research: Research Trends and Directions," in *Minority Mental Health*, ed. E. Jones and S. Kornich (New York: Praeger, 1982), 267–95; J. T. Gibbs, "Black American Adolescents," in *Children of Color: Psychological Interventions with Minority Youth*, ed. J. T. Gibbs, L. N. Huang, and Associates (San Francisco, CA: Jossey-Bass 1989), 179–223; M. A. Zimmerman et al., "A Longitudinal Study of Stress-Buffering Effects for Urban African American Male Adolescent Problem Behaviors and Mental Health," *Journal of Community Psychology* 28, no. 1 (2000): 17–33.

8. R. Reed, "Education and Achievement of Young Black Males," in *Handbook of Mental Health and Mental Disorders among Black Americans*, ed. J. T. Gibbs (Westport, CT: Greenwood Press, 1988); J. Spurlock, "Development of Self-Concept on African American Children," *Hospital and Community Psychology* 37 (1986): 66–70.

9. R. F. Catalano et al., "The Importance of Bonding to School for Healthy Development: Findings from the Social Development Research Group," *Journal of School Health* 74, no. 7 (2004): 252–61.

10. Catalano et al., "The Importance of Bonding to School"; R. F. Catalano et al., "Positive Youth Development in the United States: Research Findings on Evaluations of Positive Youth Development Programs," *ANNALS of the American Academy of Political and Social Science* 591, no. 1 (2004): 98–124; J. Garbarino and K. Kostelny, "Child Maltreatment as a Community Problem," *Child Abuse and Neglect* 16, no. 4 (1992): 455–64.

11. M. Allen et al., "Comparing the Influence of Parents and Peers on the Choice to Use Drugs: A Meta-Analytic Summary of the Literature," *Criminal Justice and Behavior* 30, no. 2 (2003): 163–86.

12. M. J. Prinstein and A. M. La Greca, "Childhood Peer Rejection and Aggression as Predictors of Adolescent Girls' Externalizing and Health Risk Behaviors: A 6-Year Longitudinal Study," *Journal of Consulting and Clinical Psychology* 72, no. 1 (2004): 103–12; M. J. Prinstein et al., "Peer Functioning, Family Dysfunction, and Psychological Symptoms in a Risk Factor Model for Adolescent Inpatients' Suicidal Ideation Severity," *Journal of Clinical Child Psychology* 29 (2000): 392–405.

13. J. Phinney et al., "Ethnic Identity and American Identification among Ethnic Minority Youths," in *Journeys Into Cross-Cultural Psychology*, ed. A. Bouvy, F. van de Vijver, P. Boski, and P. Schmitz (Amsterdam: Swets and Zeitlinger, 1994), 167–83; M. Sanchez-Jankowski, "Minority Youth and Civic Engagement: The Impact of Group Relations," *Applied Developmental Science* 6 (2002): 237–45.

14. Sanchez-Jankowski, "Minroty Youth and Civic Engagement."

15. J. G. Smetana and A. Metzger, "Family and Religious Antecedents of Civic Involvement in Middle Class African American Late Adolescents," *Journal of Research on Adolescence* 15, no. 3 (2005): 325–52.

16. Catalano et al., "Positive Youth Development."

17. Catalano et al., "Positive Youth Development"; Catalano et al., "The Importance of Bonding to School."

18. D. Cicchetti and N. Garmezy, "Prospects and Promises in the Study of Resilience," *Development and Psychopathology* 5 (1993): 497–502.

19. A. S. Masten and J. D. Coatsworth, "The Development of Competence in Favorable and Unfavorable Environments: Lessons from Research on Successful Children," *American Psychologist* 53, no. 2 (1998): 205–20.

20. K. E. Grant et al., "Protective Factors Affecting Low-Income Urban African American Youth Exposed to Stress," *Journal of Early Adolescence* 20 (2000): 388–417.

21. Masten and Coatsworth, "The Development of Competence"; N. Finkelstein et al., "Building Resilience in Children of Mothers Who Have Co-Occurring Disorders and Histories of Violence: Intervention Model and Implementation Issues," *Journal of Behavioral Health Services* 32, no. 2 (2005): 141–54; N. Garmezy, "Children in Poverty: Resilience Despite Risk," *Psychiatry* 56, no. 1 (1993): 127–36; Finkelstein et al., "Building Resilience in Children"; J. M. Merdinger et al., "Pathways to College for Former Foster Youth: Understanding Factors That Contribute to Educational Success," *Child Welfare* 84, no. 6 (2005): 897–96.

22. D. L. DuBois et al., "Effectiveness of Mentoring Programs for Youth: A Meta-Analytic Review," *American Journal of Community Psychology* 30, no. 2 (2002): 157–97; D. L. DuBois and N. Silverthorn, "Characteristics of Natural Mentoring Relationships and Adolescent Adjustment: Evidence from a National Study," *Journal of Primary Prevention* 26, no. 2 (2005): 69–92; J. B. Grossman and J. E. Rhodes, "The Test of Time: Predictors and Effects of Duration in Youth Mentoring Relationships," *American Journal of Community Psychology* 30, no. 2 (2002): 199–219; Masten and Coatsworth, "The Development of Competence."

23. R. L. Jones, *Black Psychology*; J. H. Jones, *Bad Blood: The Tuskegee Syphilis Experiment* (New York: Free Press, 1993); D. Montero, "AIDS Tots Used as Guinea Pigs: Probe of City Foster Center's HIV RX Tests," *New York Post*, February 29, 2004, A5–A6.

24. P. W. Wielhouwer, "The Impact of Church Activities and Socialization of African American Religious Commitment," *Social Science Quarterly* 85, no. 3 (2004): 767–92.

25. Belgrave and Allison, *African American Psychology*.

26. J. S. Mbiti, *African Religions and Philosophy*, 2nd ed. (Oxford, UK: Heinemann, 1990).

27. T. A. Wills, A. M. Yaeger, and J. M. Sandy, "Buffering Effect of Religiosity for Adolescent Substance Use," *Psychology of Addictive Behaviors* 17, no. 1 (2003): 24–31.

28. Wills, Yaeger, and Sandy, "Buffering Effect of Religiosity."

29. W. L. Haight, "'Gathering of the Spirit' at First Baptist Church: Spirituality as a Protective Factor in the Lives of African American Children," *Social Work* 43, no. 3 (1998): 213–22.

30. C. Adkison-Bradley et al., "Forging a Collaborative Relationship between the Black Church and the Counseling Profession," *Counseling and Values* 49 (2005): 147–54.

31. N. Boyd-Franklin, *Black Families in Therapy: A Multisystems Approach* (New York: Guilford, 1989); B. L. Richardson and L. N. June, "Utilizing and Maximizing the Resources of the African American Church: Strategies and Tools for Counseling Professionals," in *Multicultural Issues in Counseling: New Approaches to Diversity*, 2nd ed., ed. L. C. Courtland (Alexandria, VA: American Counseling Association, 1997), 155–70.

32. Wielhouwer, "The Impact of Church Activities."

33. J. G. Ponterotto, J. M. Casas, L. A. Suzuki, and C. M. Alexander, eds., *Handbook of Multicultural Counseling*, 2nd ed. (Thousand Oaks, CA: Sage, 2001).

34. Adkison-Bradley et al., "Forging a Collaborative Relationship."

35. For more information on this grant project, see M. L. McCreary, F. Z. Belgrave, and K. W. Allison, *Final Project Report for Project Impact: A Family Based Psychoeducational Prevention Project for Substance Abusing Families* (Richmond: Virginia Commonwealth University, 2001); M. L. McCreary, J. N. Cunningham, K. M. Ingram, and F. E. Fife, "Stress, Culture, and Racial Socialization: Making an IMPACT," in *Handbook of Multicultural Perspectives on Stress and Coping (International and Cultural Psychology)*, ed. P. Wong and L. Wong (New York: Springer, 2006), 487–513.

36. A. Bandura, "Self Efficacy: Toward a Unifying Theory of Behavioral Change," *Psychological Review* 84 (1977): 191–215.

12

◇◇◇

"I Have Three Strikes Against Me"

Narratives of Plight and Efficacy among Older African American Homeless Women and Their Implications for Engaged Inquiry

OLIVIA G. M. WASHINGTON AND DAVID P. MOXLEY

Perhaps one of the greatest challenges facing urban universities resides in the linkage of civic engagement to research that focuses on urban issues, particularly those emanating from poverty.[1] Over the past seven years, the authors have struggled with such a challenge as they sought to address the problem of homelessness among older African American women. Addressing this challenge through multiple strategies, the investigators have linked civic engagement, social research and development, and the humanities in a manner that amplifies the problem of homelessness among older African American women in the city of Detroit, Michigan. In this chapter, we document the nature of the service network emerging in Detroit to support older African American homeless women and identify the principal dimensions of this form of service, which operates through action research in a matrix of university–community partnerships.

Knowledge emanates directly from older African American women's perspectives on their lived experience with homelessness, and the resolution of the substantive issues they must overcome to move their lives forward infuse the project with practical aims. Insight into this lived experience, inherent in each woman's biography of homelessness, can guide academic researchers, particularly those in the helping professions, in the design of relevant action in partnership with homeless women.[2] Such collaboration can reduce the chasm of relevance that often divides academic researchers and community members, and it can strengthen the link between research and application in health and human services through responsiveness to those issues community members define as important.[3] The multilevel and mixed-methods research incorporates narrative strategies in which project personnel support women in their efforts to tell their stories and highlight the issues they face in the life course that increase their vulnerability to homelessness, the forces pushing them into homelessness, and their strengths and needs.

Homelessness as a Social Issue for Older African American Women

In the United States, as members of the baby-boomer generation move closer to retirement, the lack of safe, affordable, and adequate housing, the inadequacy of retirement benefits, and the high costs of living, people fifty years of age and older are increasingly joining the ranks of the homeless. A heightened potential for becoming homeless is true of older African American women, who now number some 360,000 of the homeless and whose ranks are growing rapidly.[4] African Americans—representing approximately 49 percent to 50 percent of the homeless—experience this serious social issue at higher and disproportionate rates than other ethnic or racial groups.[5] Serious personal consequences can result when race, gender, and poverty intersect.[6] Continuous stress associated with living in poverty, transient living environments, and harsh living conditions, aggravated by poor nutrition, can create serious negative consequences for older African American women, often resulting in adverse physical and mental health outcomes.[7] While these women face numerous health problems, the present state of public support may force them back into the job market where they may qualify for only marginal jobs.

The literature on homelessness among older women and, in particular, among African American women is limited, although ethnographic research indicates that older women move into the ranks of the homeless for a variety of reasons. The problem is mainly social and structural: older women simply do not have many resources to successfully negotiate the economic and social barriers they confront (i.e., limited involvement in the workforce, changes in marital status due to divorce or the death of spouses, and the high costs of daily life). Homelessness is hard living, according to Liebow, the toll of which is serious and debilitating.[8]

We began to see signs of this emerging problem in the late 1990s when we found increasingly larger numbers of older African American women residing in shelter care, receiving mental health services designed to reach homeless people, and living in makeshift accommodations on city streets. The completion of a community assessment revealed the inadequacies of human services to address the needs of these women and the absence of advocacy and support sensitive to their gender and age-related issues.[9]

The Founding of the Leaving Homelessness Intervention Research Project

What began as a traditional applied social science research project in 1999 transitioned into an action research effort by 2004, and then by 2005 the desire of participants to become increasingly involved in project activities imbued the project with participatory qualities inherent in action. Such a change in the purpose of the project (from illumination to action) heightened the civic engagement of academic personnel and fostered a culture in which collaboration became an essential ingredient.[10] The subsequent evolution in the role of participants required the women's involvement in leadership development and governance and in the formulation of research strategy since they sought more significant levels of engagement. Participants have reframed what homelessness means among African American women in later life from a personal and private tragedy to a public issue.

As the women sought to tell their stories, they discovered a commonality among themselves rooted in social structure, the intersection of racial and gender experience, personal and cultural histories, and direct experience with oppression. Their own engagement in the generation of alternative ways of knowing, deeply grounded in self-expression, achieved through the use of poetry, scrapbooks, photography, and quilting, strengthened the bonds among the women and served as catalysts for a transformation in personal agency.[11] The storied nature of the research, achieved through its incorporation of multiple forms of narrative, reveals how help and services can be shared among academics, social and health service personnel, and homeless and formerly homeless women.[12] Through engagement in partnerships in which social action is central to the challenge of healing from the negative consequences of homelessness, or in which the focus is on prevention of homelessness from occurring is a possibility, the mission of the project is to create a model of service informed by the participant's direct experience with homelessness.

Engagement of academic social and health services faculty with vulnerable populations is an important feature of the project and amplifies the participant witnessing that the lived experience of homelessness requires academics who can easily isolate themselves from direct involvement with human vulnerability. Engaged inquiry is a form of getting close to a particular social issue through partnerships with those who directly experience the negative consequences of the issue.[13] As one participant has emphasized during the project, "I have three strikes against me: I'm a woman, poor, and black." Certainly, it is this type of statement that challenges both the relevance and responsiveness of university-based research in a domain like homelessness, one that necessitates the interplay of action, knowledge, and service.[14]

The Leaving Homelessness Intervention Research Project (LHIRP) is an effort to respond to the unmet needs of homeless and formerly homeless older African American women. It has sought to build over time a network of advocacy and support that is responsive to the women's needs and situations, mindful that a more systemic prevention strategy is in order, but must materialize as an outcome of concerted effort within a community.[15]

Distinguishing Features and Aims

The project has several distinguishing features: action research in health promotion,[16] collaboration,[17] and social action. The community-based participatory action research project operates within the context of university–community partnerships,[18] including collaborative work with homeless and formerly homeless women, faith-based organizations, and university faculty and students. The aim of these partnerships is to form and sustain a continuum of support, rooted deeply in civic engagement, and is designed to help older African American women get out of and stay out of homelessness. The project itself reflects a growing movement in higher education to link with communities, particularly those facing health disparities as a result of poverty.[19]

The principal aim of the project is to serve and support women while the investigators and participants build knowledge and practices useful in creating a continuum of transition effective in helping women get leave homelessness successfully and remain domiciled. The continuum itself is formative—it takes shape through the participatory research of LHIRP and elements of it have emerged as the investigators have accumulated increasingly higher levels of information and knowledge about this issue through the testing of practice strategies that make the most sense to the participants. It is this strategy, "knowledge through action," that imbues the project with a dynamic character.

The homeless experiences of the participants shape and inform the research, which enables the investigators to identify promising directions, formulate specific practices, and test practices in action, that is, within the context of helping and service. Interweaving basic research on the problem of homelessness among older African American women with the design and testing of actual helping components and engagement in service has become a hallmark of LHIRP.

Narrative

The Centrality of Narrative within LHIRP

To ensure relevance, the investigators rely heavily on the first-person accounts of homelessness among participants. Narratives offer a flexible strategy for gaining insight into a person's life.[20] They can reveal the dynamics of the lived experience[21] and produce a rich portrayal of a personal life story.[22] Narrative method helps the project capture the experience of homelessness: it amplifies how each woman enters, struggles with, and resists debilitating situations. The narratives are rich in context, personal history, details about homelessness, and ideas about what each woman found (or did not find) helpful. A woman's story holds centrality within the project, a view consistent with narratology.[23]

Forms of Narrative

Contextualized narratives place considerable burden on participants since interviews and dialogues between participants and investigators often reveal serious personal issues and consequences emanating from poverty, trauma, negative life events, and nonproductive decisions, themselves products of each woman's efforts to surmount or survive poverty.[24] To respect such revelation and buffer the negative psychological effects of reliving trauma, the investigators have modified traditional research methods as they engaged the women in such demanding conversations. Consistent with narrative method,[25] interviews become shared dialogues out of respect for the deeply held personal experiences the participants may be reluctant to share initially. Conversations require a give and take, but it has been important for the investigators to realize (and respect) that a story is the sole possession of the participant, something that belongs to her. The story, as a woman frames it and develops the plot, must remain under her control. Thus, participants are not research subjects nor are they objects of curiosity. They are colleagues, and together investigators and participants seek a mutual understanding of a lived experience that neither party truly understands in its complexity and multiplicity of layers at the beginning.

Each story possesses a revelatory quality;[26] as dialogue proceeds, both parties are awakened to the forces that prepare a woman for homelessness (marginalization by economic forces), ready her to tip into homelessness, sustain her homelessness, and help her emerge from such a difficult and life-altering situation. Engagement is inherent in such situations; the investigator and participant engage one another—demanding sincerity, openness, trust, and vulnerability. They also need to engage the social forces that create and sustain homelessness. By speaking "truth to power," such storytelling gives the participants freedom to characterize their own lived experience by responding to the forces that are so powerful in their ability to dramatically alter the trajectory of a life.[27] By listening closely and actually witnessing this lived experience, investigators can literally embrace a new perspective on homelessness as it is expressed in a particular woman's biography.

By engaging participants—as agents who actively cope with their homelessness and who make strategic decisions about how to handle or manage their situations—investigators gain more insight into the lived experience than if they view participants from the perspectives of passivity and victimization. Understanding participants as active agents illuminates possibilities for gaining insight into resilience, strengths, and strategies that are easily obscured when participants identify only personal weaknesses. The narratives themselves inform action within the project and facilitate strategic direction. For example, the narratives of participants illuminated the many issues they faced and established the need for advocacy to help participants resolve the challenges that keep them from moving out of homelessness.[28]

Stories yield narratives because it is the latter that are the written and formalized products of the dialogues the investigators have undertaken with participants. The investigators have relied on three sources of narrative content to gain insight into the lived experience of homelessness among older African American women: (1) in-depth narrative interviews of eight older African American homeless women who exemplify the eight pathways into homelessness in late life (the women were selected from a large sample of homeless women since their stories captured the various ways of becoming homeless); (2) rich clinical narratives that illuminate the experience of homelessness among thirty African American women; and (3) the content of an innovative social action installation and educational forum constructed through civic engagement, university–community partnerships, and collaboration with formerly homeless African American women. The exhibit includes performative features in which the women demonstrate their cultural and racial knowledge, forms of knowing that bolstered their coping, and their self-efficacy in the face of adversity.

The Importance of Witnessing

The multiple forms of narrative become a way of witnessing the women's experience of deprivation during the life course through the illumination of the numerous issues they found overwhelming before, during, and after homelessness. The investigators' experience with the LHIRP suggests a particular type of method project personnel refer to as "participant witnessing," an approach that blends engaged inquiry, the provision of direct assistance, and collaborative engagement in social action. Witnessing alters the role of the investigator: from dispassionate observer to that of documentarian connected to the narrator within a crucible of pain, injustice, and vulnerability.[29] The investigator is likely changed by such engagement and comes to understand through the narrative the context, culture, and history within which homelessness becomes real for an older African American woman. Participants likely find some solace in telling their stories to those who are attentive; by unburdening themselves of nonproductive emotions they can gain more clarity and energy. A staff member amplifies such an outcome: "The participant smiled saying 'what better way to spend an hour and a half than talking to somebody who is really listening to you, OK, let me slow down, I'm just happy to be part of anything that might help me.'" Witnessing can join the investigator and participant more closely and prepare each for further collaborative inquiry, the hallmark of participatory action research.

This witnessing, made salient to participants through the investigators' attentive listening and empathic responding, is rooted in the ability of investigators to recognize the resilience and strengths of the women, something the women themselves may easily overlook given the heightened level of distress they experience. Witnessing requires the investigator to move beyond the role of bystander.[30] The investigator becomes more engaged by the lived experience and the suffering it entails. Listening, seeing, hearing, and empathic responding are all required of the secondary witness,[31] the person who sees suffering through the eyes of the primary witness who, in this case, is the homeless woman. Fully appreciating a woman's story is vital within the context of the project because they can easily overlook their strengths as many engage in self-blame. Framing the narrative as an opportunity to reflect on the full experience of homelessness, including early life experiences and challenges, opens the vistas of participants to a consideration of how social forces are influential in the creation of homelessness.

From the perspective of narrative, and as an act of witnessing, engaged inquiry requires an investigator to be tuned into the expression of efficacy and resilience as well as plight and predicament. Plight, predicament, and frustration are most salient in narratives because the women literally exist in a pressure cooker, an apt metaphor that communicates the immediate demands and life-threatening qualities of the situations that place the women under constant pressure. Located in marginal situations, such as living within shelters or in makeshift circumstances on city streets, the participants will likely approach investigators in a paradoxical manner. Their approach can be described only as a "wary eagerness" in which the countenance of a woman is one of caution while she demonstrates an eagerness to form a relationship with investigators, if they are successful in expressing an authentic interest in the woman's situation. In traditional clinical interviewing, the stage is set for the investigator to discern the weaknesses and vulnerabilities of the woman. Alternatively, in engaged inquiry, the investigator is attuned to qualities of efficacy, strength, and character. Narrative inquiry can reveal resilience in the face of adversity.

Resilience in the Face of Adversity

What are these strengths that the investigator comes to witness in the lived experience of the older homeless African American woman? There are multiple ones that echo the Black experience in the face of adversity, ones that serve as virtues:

An Inherent Belief in the Strength of Black Women

It is likely that a narrative reveals early life experiences in which the women have been exposed to stories of strong Black women by those who reared them.

The narratives of participants reveal stories of their mothers, aunts, grandmothers, older sisters, and neighbors or surrogate parental figures who nurtured them, taught them to believe in themselves, and offered them insight into navigating adversities. Themes of managing in the face of discrimination, deprivation, and poverty likely emerge within a woman's narrative as she relates how a nurturing figure showed her how to handle adversity early in life. Some women commented on how for some time they had not thought about these nurturing figures and their legacies until investigators inquired into whether and how women served as powerful role models early in their lives.

One participant elaborated on her strategy to cope with the psychological consequences of homelessness by recreating the biography of her grandmother and, in writing, amplified this loved one's own strengths and character. The project rekindled the participant's relationship with her deceased grandmother and in frequent conversations with this beloved figure she recalled the manner in which her grandmother nurtured her, what her grandmother stood for, and the deep love they shared. Grandmother, for this participant, stood as an icon of inspiration and figured into the participant's own process of recovery. The biography, which actually went unwritten but persisted as an idea, was nonetheless a powerful project useful to the participant as a way of sustaining herself in the face of adversity. It is common for powerful Black women to emerge in the narratives of participants as important role models for navigating and overcoming adversity. Reflecting on such role models can facilitate the participants' control over their situations and remind them of their own resilience and capacity to face adversity.

Faith and Spirituality

A number of diverse forms of spiritual expression emerges within the narratives of the participants, illuminating the importance spirituality plays as a positive resource for coping with the homeless experience. These forms include prayer, membership in a congregation, reading spiritual material, participation and involvement in worship, seeking the advice of spiritual practitioners, and engaging in contemplation.[32] Prayer offers a good example of a resource for the women as they communicate what is important to them in a higher power.[33] Prayer often is an ongoing conversation with a higher power about getting out of homelessness, mustering one's strength, and unburdening oneself of anxiety and self-incrimination. The object of prayer may be the well-being of children, relief from addiction, overcoming depression, or gaining employment.[34] The request often involves bolstering or strengthening the self in the face of adversity. Prayer as narrative captures the lived experience of homelessness: women may seek guidance in overcoming their situations and contemplating new opportunities. It also reflects the importance of spirituality in the African American tradition, and the role of religion in sustaining African American people in the face of racism.[35]

Dignity in the Face of Adversity

Assessment and appraisal of written narratives based on the women's stories reveal their retention of dignity even in the face of adversity. Certainly homelessness makes a direct impact on resources women have available to manage their appearance, suitable and appropriate clothing, and good grooming. Dialogues with participants about their self-care inevitably raise issues of self-care and public presentation in the face of limited resources. Nonetheless, clinical narratives, those in which research staff prepare written statements that capture the theme of a woman's homeless experience and organize the trajectory of homelessness as a lived experience, contain statements about how, in preparation for dialogues with research staff, participants went to great lengths to find appropriate clothing, to groom themselves, and to care for their hair. The women present themselves in interviews in dignified ways, which was apparent from their dress. Such presentation is more than what social scientists refer to as "impression management." Dignity in the face of adversity, its expression through dress and grooming, is a form of hope that for the participants expresses deep faith. One African American woman emphasized in her narrative, "I'm getting out of this, and I ain't coming back." When the interviewer inquired into how she would manage this, the genesis of her strengths emerged: "Because I am praying to get out. God won't let me down." Still, when the interviewer probed further, the woman indicated that she saw how her mother and grandmother handled adversity. "I will handle this," the woman said emphatically. "I saw my granny handle a lot more."

Certainly biographies of powerful Black women reflect such processes of self-development and hardiness, which is handed down generationally through vicarious learning supported through great love of the maternal figure for the daughter. Chana Kai Lee, Fannie Lou Hamer's biographer, characterized the principal source of the great Civil Rights activist's hardiness:

> Fannie Lou was deeply inspired not only by Lou Ella's sad past, but also by the efforts her mother made to ensure that the Townsend family could survive physically and spiritually. Lou Ella Townsend was indeed, the quintessential "outraged mother," moved by anger and determined to "make a way out of no way," if only for her children's sake. Through her life, Hamer was deeply impressed with her mother, whom she often referred to as a "strong woman."[36]

A correspondence of strong faith in the face of adversity and salient vicarious learning facilitate coping in adult life. Strong spirituality strengthens resilience in the face of racism. Bridges states in the preface of her study on African American spirituality that resilience means being "less malleable to racial, social, and economic exploitation and more able to live with some sense of dignity and cultural cohesion as a community."[37] Witnessing such dignity offers academics a portal through which they can see how older African American women "keep going on," as one participant referred to her efforts. Such persistence reflects a cultural resilience passed from a member of one generation to another.

Reaching Out to Other Black Women

Still another strength visible in project narratives is the idea that women should not have to experience homelessness alone. There is a movement toward other women who share the same experiences or who potentially become friends or even surrogate family members. In the Telling My Story Project, a subproject of LHIRP in which eight participants helped the investigators understand their trajectories into and through homelessness, the participants spoke of the other women as sisters or in one case a participant referred to another woman as her mother, metaphorically communicating the nurturing role this particular participant assumed for the group as a whole. A focus group conducted with these eight women identified the power inherent in the support the women offered one another.

The participants used the concept of camaraderie to express their mutuality and further developed this idea with the following words and phrases: *closeness, sisterlike/sisterhood, allegiance, support, partners,* and *collaborators.* Encompassing the idea of comradeship is the women's attitude that "we will get through it together." But it is actually more than an attitude, it is a practice involving celebrating important occasions together, sharing resources, staying in touch, keeping an eye on one another, and helping in times of crisis. The homeless experience solidified relationships among these eight women, but their traditions of care and support, handed down from one generation to the next, further strengthened group identity.

Telling My Story: Narrative as a Form of Representation

In 2005, the action research team expanded both its membership and its concept of engagement to include an artist/curator with considerable experience in linking the arts and social action. Gathering together narrative content, photographs of their homeless experiences, poetry, scrapbooks, and physical artifacts (taken from the streets and apartments) that served as remnants of the homeless experience, eight women worked closely with the artist to create eight large conceptual portraits. Each portrait captured a woman's interpretation of her homelessness. For Godfrey, conceptual portraits possess a reflexive character in which the configuration of materials within a particular portrait refers to the object of representation, which in the case of this project is the lived experience of homelessness.[38]

In June 2006, the women's exhibit Telling My Story: At the Edge of Recovery—Eight African American Women's Journey from Homelessness in Detroit (www.tellingmystorydetroit.org) premiered in the rotunda of a large corporation located in the central part of the city.[39] Ninety-seven visitors attended the opening, out of 125 who were invited. The women served as docents of their portraits, which were hung from specially designed wood trusses. The women engaged visitors in telling their stories and elaborated on their own experiences with homelessness. Visitors then participated in an educational forum on homelessness in which each woman offered brief vignettes of her experiences, and the visitors obtained information on LHIRP and the social problem of homelessness. The women performed selections from their poetry, dramatic readings, and inspirational songs, which served as vehicles for dispelling myths and negative stereotypes about homeless people, and highlighting the strengths of the women. The inclusion of these performative features demonstrated the personal qualities of the women that enabled them to transcend homelessness. Performance is yet another form of narrative.[40]

Conclusion

We have sought to outline an expanded view of engaged inquiry in which civic engagement serves as a vehicle for bringing academic researchers closer to a particular phenomenon in partnership with those who experience it firsthand. Broadening engagement in the context of this particular social issue requires academics to engage the African American experience as well as homelessness. Narrative in its diverse forms can expand the awareness of investigators about the strengths women bring to an overwhelming situation. While women succumb to homelessness, investigators can appreciate how they overcame this situation by drawing from core traditions within the African American experience, and the linkage of art and humanities offers ways of knowing and understanding that other modalities may simply not achieve, further expanding the possibility of engagement.[41]

Expanding the concept of engaged inquiry through the linkage of social science, helping services, and the arts and humanities within a framework of informed action is a central theme of this chapter. Engagement of the public through the translation of narrative and other sources of knowledge concerning the lived experience of homelessness among African American women in later life offers a way of engaging the public in awareness building and education. It is here that the work of the LHIRP transcends collaborative research. The project seeks to engage homeless women and the African American experience as solutions to the challenging problem of homelessness. Thus, the project demonstrates how civic engagement can serve as a central foci of academic research.[42]

"Knowledge is best constructed in collaborative action research projects where people work together to experiment, test, elaborate, and articulate goals, values, and ideas."[43] Such knowledge and the action it informs is a product of engaged inquiry; when investigators appreciate the strengths of a particular group, they gain insight into the creation of partnerships necessary for bringing about change. Ultimately, in the case of the LHIRP, helping components informed by the lived experience likely will be more responsive and relevant than if those components were designed by academic researchers working independently of those who possess the critical knowledge the project requires—older homeless African American women.

Notes

This chapter was supported by grants from Wayne State University's Humanities Center and the Institute of Gerontology.

1. Office of University Partnerships, *Scholarship in Action: Applied Research and Community Change* (Washington, DC: Office of University Partnerships, U.S. Department of Housing, 2006).

2. R. Josselson, and A. Lieblich, "Narrative Research and Humanism," in *The Handbook of Humanistic Psychology,* ed. K. J. Schneider, J. Bugental, and J. Pierson (Thousand Oaks, CA: Sage, 2001), 275–88.

3. D. Moxley, "Engaged Research in Higher Education and Civic Responsibility Reconsidered," in *University-Community Partnerships: Universities in Civic Engagement,* ed. T. M. Soska and A. K. Johnson (Binghamton, NY: Haworth, 2004), 235–42; S. D. Seifer, and S. Sisco, "Mining the Challenges of CBPR for Improvements in Urban Health," *Journal of Urban Health* 83, no. 6 (November 2006): 981–84.

4. R. Rosenheck, E., Bassuk, and A. Salomon, "Special Populations of Homeless Americans," in *Practical Lessons from the 1998 National Symposium on Homeless Research,* ed. L. B. Fosburg and D. L. Dennis (Washington, DC: U.S. Dept. of Housing and Urban Development, 1999), http://aspe.hhs.gov/progsys/homeless/symposium/toc.htm (accessed November 8, 2000).

5. Interagency Council on the Homeless, "Homelessness: Programs and the People They Serve," *Findings of the National Survey of Homeless Assistance Providers and Clients, December 1999,* http://www.huduser.org/publications/homeless/homeless_tech.html (accessed February 3, 2004).

6. M. de Chesnay, "Vulnerable Populations: Vulnerable People," in *Caring for the Vulnerable: Perspectives in Nursing Theory, Practice, and Research,* ed. M. de Chesnay (Boston, MA: Jones and Bartlett, 2005), 12.

7. Rosenheck, Bassuk, and Salomon, "Special Populations of Homeless Americans."

8. E. Liebow, *Tell Them Who I Am: The Lives of Homeless Women* (New York: Penguin, 1993).

9. O. G. M. Washington, "Identification and Characteristics of Older Homeless African American Women," *Issues in Mental Health Nursing* 26, no. 2 (September 2005): 117–36.

10. S. L. Percy, N. L. Zimpher, and M. J., Brukardt, eds., *Creating a New Kind of University: Institutionalizing Community–University Engagement* (Bolton, MA: Anker, 2006), 3–22.

11. O. G. M. Washington, D. P. Moxley, and L. Garriott, "Use of the Quilt Workshop in Group Work with Older African American Women Recovering from Homelessness," *Journal of Psychosocial Nursing*, in press.

12. A. J. Schultz, B. A. Israel, E. A. Parker, M. Lockett, Y. Hill, and R. Wills, "Engaging Women in Community-Based Participatory Research for Health: The East Side Village Health Worker Partnership," in *Community-Based Participatory Research for Health*, ed. M. Minkler, N. Wallerstein, and B. Hall (San Francisco, CA: Jossey-Bass, 2002), 293–315.

13. M. Sullivan and M. Willis, "Collaboration: A Broad-Based Methodology," in *Collaborative Research: University and Community Partnership*, ed. M. Sullivan and J. Kelly (Washington, DC: American Public Health Association, 2001), xix–xvi.

14. P. Nyden, A. Figert, M. Shibley, and D. Burrows, *Building Community: Social Science in Action* (Thousand Oaks, CA: Pine Forge Press, 1997).

15. S. A. Amuwo and E. Jenkins, "True Partnerships Evolve Over Time," in *Collaborative Research: University and Community Partnership*, ed. M. Sullivan and J. Kelly (Washington, DC: American Public Health Association, 2001), 22–44.

16. M. Minkler, "Community-Based Research Partnerships: Challenges and Opportunities, *Journal of Urban Health* 82 (suppl. 2) (June 2005): ii3–ii12.

17. M. Minkler and N. Wallerstein, eds., *Community-Based Participatory Research for Health* (San Francisco, CA: Jossey-Bass, 2003), 293–315.

18. T. M. Soska and A. Johnson Butterfield, *University-Community Partnerships: Universities in Civic Engagement* (Binghamton, NY: Haworth, 2004).

19. A. Eisinger and K. Senturia, "Doing Community-Driven Research: A Description of Seattle Partners for Health Communities," *Journal of Urban Health* 78, no. 3 (September 2001): 519–34.

20. J. Elliott, *Using Narrative in Social Research: Qualitative and Quantitative Approaches* (Thousand Oaks, CA: Sage, 2005).

21. A. L. Cole and J. G. Knowles, *Lives in Context: The Art of Life History Research* (Walnut Creek, CA: AltaMira, 2001).

22. D. J. Clandinin and E. M. Connelly, *Narrative Inquiry: Experience and Story in Qualitative Research* (San Francisco, CA: Jossey-Bass, 2000); M. Van Manen, *Researching the Lived Experience: Human Science for an Action Sensitive Pedagogy* (Albany: State University of New York Press, 1990).

23. D. E. Polkinghorne, *Narrative Knowing and the Human Sciences* (Albany: State University of New York Press, 1988).

24. J. Harvey, *Embracing Their Memory: Loss and the Social Psychology of Story telling* (Needham Heights, MA: Allyn and Bacon, 1996).

25. S. Wortham, *Narratives in Action: A Strategy for Research and Analysis* (New York: Teachers College Press, 2001).

26. R.Coles, *The Call of Stories* (New York: Mariner, 1990).

27. A. Dorfman, *Manifesto for Another World: Voices from Beyond the Dark* (New York: Seven Stories Press, 2004).

28. O. G. M. Washington, D. P. Moxley, and J. P. Crystal, "Souls in Extremis: Using Narrative to Illuminate the Challenges Homeless Older African American Women Face in Their Process of Recovery," working paper, September 2007.

29. J. Groopman, *The Anatomy of Hope: How People Prevail in the Face of Illness* (New York: Random House, 2004).

30. S. Bloom, *Creating Sanctuary: Toward an Evolution of Sane Societies* (New York: Routledge, 1997).

31. D. Apel, *Memory Effects: The Holocaust and the Art of Secondary Witnessing* (New Brunswick, NJ: Rutgers University Press, 2002).

32. O. G. M. Washington, D. P. Moxley, L. Garriott, and J. P. Crystal, "Five Dimensions of Faith and Spirituality of Older African American Women Transitioning Out of Homelessness," *Journal of Religion and Health*, in press.

33. O. G. M. Washington and D. P. Moxley, "The Use of Prayer in Group Work with African American Women Recovering from Chemical Dependency," *Families in Society: The Journal of Contemporary Human Services* 82, no. 1 (2001): 49–59.

34. Washington and Moxley, "The Use of Prayer."

35. R. J. Taylor, L. M. Chatters, and J. S. Levin, *Religion in the Lives of African Americans: Social, Psychological, and Health Perspectives* (Thousand Oaks, CA: Sage, 2004).

36. C. K. Lee, *For Freedom's Sake: The Life of Fannie Lou Hamer* (Chicago: University of Illinois Press, 2000), 10.

37. F. Bridges, *Resurrection Song: African American Spirituality* (Maryknoll, NY: Orbis, 2001), ix.

38. T. Godfrey, *Conceptual Art* (New York City: Phaidon, 2006).

39. J. J. Fulmer, O. Washington, and D. Moxley, *Telling My Story: At the Edge of Recovery—8 African American Women's Journey from Homelessness in Detroit* (Grand Blanc, MI: Looking Glass Press, 2006).

40. W. Wadlington, "Performative Therapy: Postmodernizing Humanistic Psychology," in *The Handbook of Humanistic Psychology*, ed. K. J. Schneider, J. Bugental, and J. Pierson (Thousand Oaks, CA: Sage, 2001), 491–501.

41. P. B. Allen, *Art Is a Way of Knowing* (Boston, MA: Shambhala, 1995).

42. M. J. Brukardt, S. L. Percy, and N. L. Zimpher, "Moving Forward Along New Lines," 3–22, and J. Wergin, "Elements of Effective Community Engagement," 23–42, in *Creating a New Kind of University: Institutionalizing*

Community–University Engagement, ed. S. L. Percy, N. L. Zimpher, and M. J. Brukardt (Bolton, MA: Anker, 2006).

43. M. F. Belenky, L. Bond, and J. S. Weinstock, *A Tradition That Has No Name: Nurturing the Development of People, Families, and Communities* (New York: Basic Books, 1997).

13

◈◈◈

A Culturally Competent Community-Based Research Approach with African American Neighborhoods

Critical Components and Examples

RICHARD BRISCOE, HAROLD R. KELLER,
GWEN MCCLAIN, EVANGELINE R. BEST,
AND JESSICA MAZZA

A fundamental change in the traditional methods of community-based research is needed to meet the multiple and complex needs of African American children, families, and communities. This chapter introduces and describes a framework for the implementation of a culturally competent research approach. This approach is action oriented with the goal of neighborhood improvement and includes collaboration between researchers and local residents, knowledge of culturally competent values and principles, and the use of multifaceted research methods. The aim of this approach is to enhance the traditional methods of community-based research conducted within a neighborhood to improve the well-being of African American children and families. An overview of this approach is presented, and five culturally competent community-based research projects are used to outline the implementation of the components.

Issues, Challenges, and Barriers

Engaging in community-based research in African American communities is challenged by contextual barriers, including historical, interpersonal, and organizational.[1] Scholars have often conducted research in African American communities from a conceptual frame of "pathology," particularly within low-income African American communities.[2] African American communities are frequently the objects of study, and some African Americans feel that they are constantly being researched.[3] A more pervasive problem is that research often provides more benefits for the researchers (in the form of promotions, raises, and prestige) than for the people who are researched. They often feel that the questions addressed in traditional (investigator-driven) research are not important or relevant to their communities. Many African Americans perceive the researchers as employing interventions that are intrusive and unbeneficial.[4] Conducting community-based research in the context of service-learning and action research does not necessarily remove these perceptions.

Social class, racial, and cultural discrepancies (with accompanying disparities in values, attitudes, and behaviors) between researchers and neighborhood residents are also challenges to effective research.[5] This includes traditional research paradigms antithetical to community-based research, so efforts may not be well-received by community members until trust is established. Matching researchers and residents by racial or ethnic group does not always eliminate the challenge of trust building. Generally, universities and African American communities are culturally different; therefore, African American faculty members who have assimiulated to university culture in terms of language, dress, and mannerisms often must also use culturally competent strategies to establish trust with community members.

African American communities are typically underresourced, as are the community organizations in which residents participate. Due to the history of alienation from researchers and professionals, the lack of perceived relevance or benefits from research and the disparities between academic and African American communities, communities and organizations have little time or patience for research. Collaboration with community-based agencies in African American communities requires considerable efforts to build and maintain trust, to mobilize resources that increase the capacity of local agencies and communities, and to include other community organizations (such as local churches and civic organizations).

Critical Components of the Research Approach

The work to implement culturally competent community-based research is informed by a variety of principles and conceptual frameworks. This project adopted several theoretical frameworks: participatory action research methodology;[6]

TABLE 13.1. Elements for the Critical Components of the Research Approach

Critical Components	Activities
Community–university partnership	Mutually beneficial and equal partnership that guides the structure for all aspects of research activities.
Cultural competence	Preserves and enhances the historical, cultural, socioeconomic, and political circumstances and experiences of participants
Community-based	Identification of the target population as a group of people who form a functionally cohesive group within their perceived boundaries
Community driven	Active participation of community members in central decision-making at all levels.
Strengths-based	Emphasizes identifying and enhancing natural supports, networks and assets
Capacity-building	Resources are made available to the group that can be sustained after the completion of the research
Comprehensive services	Recognize that children, youth, and families have multi-system needs and require supports, resources and services to become self-sustaining.
Multifaceted research	Emphasizes mixed methods, data emerges and will promote relevant solutions

grounded theory approach;[7] strengths-based;[8] system of care;[9] and community development.[10] The approach evolved as the result of collaborative efforts of interdisciplinary research teams from the University of South Florida working with African American communities. This comprehensive effort blends cultural competence principles and service interventions with relevant and authentic research methodologies. These principles and methodologies have overlapping emphases and each perspective adds to the whole. The addition of each perspective maximizes the effectiveness of a culturally competent appoach. The three critical components of all of the projects highlighted in this chapter are community–university partnerships, values and guiding principles, and use of a multifaceted research methodology (see table 13.1).

   Participatory action research. Participatory research is an applied social process that involves a partnership between trained evaluation personnel and practice-based decision makers, organization members with program responsibility, or people with a vital interest in the program, the primary users of the program. Participatory action research may be characterized by direct involvement and influence in the real-world experience of participants. It frames community issues, determines possible solutions to address these concerns, places solutions into practice, and then studies the outcomes. Local practitioners play central roles in simultaneous action and enlightenment through the process of problem framing, planning, action, observation, and reflection.

Grounded theory involves the gathering and analysis of data that are grounded in the reality of the lived experiences of the target popluations (African American families). This grounded theory draws heavily on the oral tradition of African Americans, and this mode of communication facilitates the ability of the researchers to engage in discussions directly with the people living within their own communities and the extensive awareness they have about their own everyday living experiences.

Strengths-based research.[11] The focus on strengths in terms of African American family lifestyles began in the late 1960s with the work of Robert Hill. His research on the strengths of African American families revealed that their lifestyles consisted of strong kinship bonds, strong work orientation, adaptability of family roles, high achievement orientation, and strong religious orientation. In contrast to previous research models that have examined African American families and communities from a "deficit-perspective," this approach looks at African American families from a strengths-based perspective. Strengths-based approaches conceptually are closely linked to asset mapping. Asset mapping involves a concerted effort to identify resources within a community, including financial, structural, organizational, human, and interpersonal assets.

System of care.[12] The system of care is child/family centered and emphasizes multiagency involvement, community-based nonresidential services, a strong partnership between parents and professionals, accountability, and meeting the needs of ethnically and racially diverse populations. The system of care approach supports the advancement of community-based programs to meet the needs of this multiple and varied population of children while also placing emphasis on family and culturally sensitive approaches. A community-based system of care changes the focus from that of the individual child to the broader network of family, churches, friends, and other supports available in the community.

Community development.[13] The potential role of universities and university-based researchers in community development is tremendous. Community engagement as part of university–community partnerships is designed in part to specifically address economic and community development. There is a growing understanding of the importance of community engagement to the well-being of both society and major research universities. The Brookings Institution has articulated the role of higher education as a major asset in community revitalization and community development.

Community–University Partnerships

The initial step in creating a culturally competent community-based research program is a steadfast commitment to building a mutually beneficial community–university partnership, which guides the structure for all aspects of research activities. It is critical to the process that all members of the partnership understand and accept the framework of the research approach.[14] The Carnegie Foundation describes community engagement as "the collaboration between institutions of higher education and their larger communities . . . for the mutually beneficial exchange of knowledge and resources [e.g., research, capacity building, and economic development] in a context of partnership and reciprocity."[15] Community engagement consists of scholarly and curricular activities that are carried out via collaborative interactions between groups and organizations in the municipality or region that contains the university, with potential benefits for all involved.

The community–university relationship generates a context that enables university faculty to participate in culturally competent community-based research and simultaneously gives members of African American communities the opportunity to observe faculty who are committed to sustained partnerships with community stakeholders. Before initiating a partnership, the university team should have a history with and understanding and knowledge of research and program evaluation methods with cultural groups. University researchers should also have a thorough understanding of African American functioning at the individual, family, and community levels. The university team must quickly develop an understanding of the specific community targeted for research.[16] With this understanding, the partners will analyze community issues together, develop the purpose and goals, and design the research project. Community members will actively participate in developing research questions, identifying indicators of success, and gathering and evaluating data.

Values and Guiding Principles

Researchers, practitioners, policy makers, and community residents have actively advocated for guidelines, principles, and values that promote and sustain culturally competent research practices. For example, Cross, Bazron, Dennis, and Isaacs asserted that research conducted with "the consent, consultation, and participation of . . . the community—from planning to dissemination" needs to be developed and implemented.[17] Members of the Minority Initiative Resource Committee of the Child and Adolescent Service System Program (CASSP) reported that the "meeting participants were unanimous in their view that culturally competent research is needed if [they are] to adequately address the current and critical minority-oriented research issues in child mental health."[18] These values and principles were adopted from consumer empowerment case management models and by system of care best practices. The values and guiding principles, including the critical value of cultural competence of research practices in African American communities, will be discussed. This discussion is followed by a description of research, which is community based, community driven, and strength based, and includes capacity building and comprehensive services.

Cultural competence. A variety of efforts have been made to enhance the ability of practitioners and others working with individuals and families from diverse cultures to respond in ways that are effective, culturally congruent, and culturally sensitive to their collective diversities. The goal of this type of culturally competent intervention is to always preserve and enhance the interests, dignity, and integrity of children and families and the diverse cultural communities in which they live.

Our overall philosophy and values are committed to culturally competent research protocols that are grounded in their awareness of the historical, cultural, socioeconomic, and political circumstances and experiences that have significantly affected African American's physical, mental, and psychological well-being and survival. Each community–university team explored their own level of cultural awareness, cultural sensitivity, and self-inventory of beliefs, information and knowledge, personal identity, and cross-cultural skills developed over time in working with children and families living in these communities.

Community based. The community is the basic unit of social change. The term *neighborhood* is not used as a geographic concept but rather as a sociological construct, and it is not exchangeable with the word *community*. Neighborhood is used to indicate an emphasis on the locality and history of a group of people who form a community. Formal boundaries such as a district, a city, or a county may differ from the borders of a functionally cohesive neighborhood informally perceived by local residents. The identification of target populations and geographical areas has value for organizing services and neighborhood efforts to address the issues requiring social change. As a way of encouraging the participation and commitment of the local neighborhood, a neighborhood core group should be employed as a key mechanism through which effective dialogue, resource mobilization, skill training, relevant needs assessment, strategic planning, and action resolution can be reached at the neighborhood level.[19]

Community driven. Active neighborhood members' participation is crucial for a project to accurately reflect the real interests, concerns, and needs of the community, to create a sense of ownership and commitment on the part of neighborhood members, and to gain credibility and legitimacy. Active participation is not the same as community outreach or getting information about residents and the neighborhood. The distinction must be made between a passive role as an advisory or information source and an active role as a neighborhood partner. This approach provides for community members having primary responsibility for the central decision-making role in prioritizing research outcomes in their communities, selecting the behaviors to be addressed in designing the methodology, and developing the most effective ways to disseminate results. Community participation and control are central principles that guide research planning, implementation, and data collection activities. Involvement of community members throughout the process is a component of community trust building and empowerment. As community members participate in different levels of the process, the results include the building of a level of trust, confidence, and success for community members.

Strengths based. This framework emphasizes natural supports, networks within the community, community empowerment, and individual self-reliance. In contrast to previous research models that have examined African American families and communities from a "deficit perspective," this approach looks at African American families from a strengths-based perspective. This strengths-based framework uses a research paradigm reported by Hill that involves strong kinship bonds, strong work orientation, adaptability of family roles, high educational achievement orientation, and a strong religious orientation.[20] This framework builds on the fundamental belief that African American individuals, families, and communities possess certain strengths, resources, and valuable assets.

The overall goal of a community-based research project is to promote solutions based on generic natural strengths within the community. The focus is helping local residents identify and amplify their own resources, which enhances the development of children and families in ways specific to that community. The strengths-based approach stresses community ownership of both the strengths and solutions. As the process unfolds, community members identify their strengths and their ability to overcome obstacles, which allows community members to become focused on enhancing their own identified assets. University researchers should work with neighborhood members and communities in helping them use natural supports and networks within their neighborhood. A strength-based approach allows researchers to work with families and communities by helping them discover and enhance strategies that can be used in raising healthy, productive, and successful children and families.

Capacity building. Change must take place over broad-based beliefs as well as social policies that will recognize and support community-level strategic planning, development, and quality of life.[21] Resources must be available to the people in the community for solving problems. The university team members can assist community organizations by providing technical assistance in the areas of program planning, implementation, and evaluation. They can provide immediate and ongoing technical assistance to the program or to the children and families in the community, thereby building human capacity. Residents must be well equipped to be more active in neighborhood life; they must be inquisitive, be aware of what is going on in the neighborhood, and develop skills of self-enhancement. As the process unfolds, families become more able to identify specific actions and strengths that can improve the quality of their lives.

Comprehensive services. Programs are often planned and implemented in a narrow and piecemeal manner, with little coordination across components or with other community-based and public programs. The system of care paradigm developed by Stroul and Friedman emphasizes the multiplicity and complexity of the needs of children and youth and their families,[22] and it underscores the necessity for intervention efforts to be multilayered and integrative. Following these principles of the system of care paradigm, community-based programs must include comprehensive frameworks and holistic conceptualizations of service delivery. The research team should recognize that children, youth, and families have multisystemic needs (i.e., health, social, educational, vocational, and recreational) and require supports, resources, and services to become self-sustaining.[23]

Multifaceted Research Methodologies

The emerging framework blends service-based principles and practices with research methodologies, yielding a data-based framework for informing community interventions. Effective research with African American communities requires a social-ecological perspective in which analysis is conducted in the natural environments of youth and families and involves multiple sources. This multifaceted framework blends community organization principles and practices with both quantitative and qualitative research methods into a framework for directing positive change among select audience segments. Strauss and Corbin's and Glaser and Strauss's grounded theory strategies serve to strengthen both residents and researchers.[24] The data are basically grounded in the reality of the lived experiences of African American families and are based on the notion that African Americans, like other ethnicities, are in the best position to articulate and represent their own unique experiences.

This approach is straightforward: create positive changes in the participants and improve the well-being of the community by addressing issues at the individual, child, adult, family, neighborhood, and comprehensive level. Research must focus on promoting solutions based on the goals of the stakeholders. Applied research is expected to promote solutions based on specific community application. This approach supports the involvement of community residents in identifying and strengthening their own natural supports, which will enhance the development of children and families in their own communities consistent with their own beliefs and values.

Examples of Implemented Culturally Competent Community-Based Research

Implementing this culturally competent community-based research approach grew out of the African American Family Supports Coalition in Tampa, Florida. A community–university partnership was established in 1997 to improve services for African American families by planning, coordinating, and implementing a program to identify strengths and family supports existing in four African American neighborhoods. This project adopted a multifaceted research approach for implementation. A culturally competent action research project emerged, involving strengths-based approaches with African American families and communities designed to enhance student academic achievement.

Three collaborative research projects involving several departments at the University of South Florida and community organizations were conducted to identify the strengths of African American children, families, and communities. This initiative, which included Richard Briscoe and Gwen McClain, was undertaken to increase the understanding of these strengths to support educational achievement, social development, and neighborhood development in African American communities. This is a community-driven research approach that was designed, planned, and conducted with the neighborhood residents. This research initiative is focused on providing data that will help researchers and practitioners better understand and assess the community-based family support systems to meet the needs of children and families in African American communities. Table 13.2 summarizes the following projects.

The first project, An Analysis of African American Family Supports: A Strength-Based Approach to Care in Hillsborough County,[25] was a community-driven research project to plan, coordinate, identify, and assess the strengths and resiliency factors that exist in African American families within four local communities in Tampa. Community stakeholders designed and conducted data collection that involved the following: summit meetings; in-depth census analysis; an examination of local data provided by African American organizations, individuals, governmental agencies, and universities; a review of the research literature; and asset mapping. Focus group data were collected directly from African American children, parents, senior citizens, residents-at-large, and education and community social service providers. The findings of the project were a synthesis of the different community-based data that were collected by the community stakeholders. The major findings of these analyses were identified by community members as "global strengths of African American families."[26] These community stakeholders developed specific action steps for use by school personnel and human service providers that built on the identified strengths. Stakeholders conducted work sessions to mobilize local communities to use strengths-based approaches.

The second project, Identifying Strengths of African American Families,[27] identifies the strengths of African American families in five national communities (Plant City, Florida; Savannah, Georgia; Baltimore, Maryland; Detroit, Michigan; and San Diego, California) to validate or nullify local findings of the first project and to develop a strengths-based assessment instrument. The project hired a local community liaison and collaborated with community residents in the design and implementation of the focus groups. Data were collected through in-depth, culturally sensitive interviews. Focus group interviews based

TABLE 13.2. Examples of Implemented Culturally Competent Community-Based Research

Study	Community Members Hired	Objectives	University and Community Partners	Neighborhood Driven with Timely Feedback	Strengths	Data Collected	Resource Buildings
African-American Family Support Analysis (1996–2003)	McClain 2 hired	Identify existing strengths, assets, and supports in four local communities Develop recommendations from findings	Social Work FMHI 31 Agencies, programs, and churches	Weekly and biweekly meetings with partners, neighborhoods, and a summit	Community and family strengths	Sythetsize research and local literature Census data Community meetings Asset mapping Focus groups and structured interviews	Program development Evaluation Organizational Grant writing
Identifying Strengths of African-American Families (2001–2005)	McClain 4 hired	Identify and strengths found in families and theircommunities in four national communities Develop an instrument to assess family strengths and resources	Social work FMHI 4 agencies	Scheduled and meetings with partners and summits in each national neighborhood	Child and family strengths	Focus groups Descriptive on sample and items and domain (scales) Reliability, discriminant, and factor analysis	Program development
Quality Use of Unknown Church Resources (2003–2005)	Favorite 1 hired	Develop a directory of churches Identify strategies and barriers related to services/programs Recommendations to strengthen services/programs	School of Business Social work FMHI 1 agency 8 churches	Scheduled and monthly meetings with partners	Educational, health, social services. and talents	Focus groups Semistructured interviews	Program development Evaluation Organizational Grant writing

(continued)

TABLE 13.2. (*continued*)

Study	Community Members Hired	Objectives	University and Community Partners	Neighborhood Driven with Timely Feedback	Strengths	Data Collected	Resource Buildings
West Tampa Telemarketing Initiative (1998–1999)	Tyson 1 hired	Investigate strengths and weaknesses of networking strategies to develop community partnership	Social work FMHI 8 programs School system 8 schools	Scheduled meetings with partners	Schools, services, and faith-based supports	Focus groups Structured interviews	Program development Evaluation Organizational Grant writing directory
East Tampa (2004–present)	Best 42 hired	Identify assets, resources, and programs offered by the schools Enhance capability of faith-based institutions Develop collaborative culturally competent research projects	College of Education FMHI 9 agencies, programs, and churches	Daily or weekly contacts by telephone, e-mail, or meetings	School, family and community assets	Focus groups Structured interviews	Program development Evaluation Organizational Grant writing

on a qualitative ethnographic protocol were held at specific community locations that were easily accessible to project participants. The project resulted in identifying fifteen major family strengths and it validated earlier local findings.

Community summits were held in the five sites, providing an opportunity for both community feedback and the dissemination of research findings. Another component of the study involved developing a twelve-hundred-item instrument using an adaptation of traditional test construction from the findings obtained from the focus group data collection phase.[28] The instrument will be a significant tool that will guide families in how they use their strengths in raising and nurturing healthy and successful children, and providers and researchers can use these strengths to establish more effective family supports and interventions. Pilot data from 2001 were analyzed and information from eight expert reviewers was summarized to examine the psychometric properties of the instrument.

The third project, Spiritual Educational Network Directory, examined the services for children and families that are provided by African American churches and the development of a directory of African American churches in the Tampa area. This was a collaborative partnership between the university and several faith- and community-based institutions. Representatives from these organizations participated in designing data collection procedures, developing the data collection instruments, analyzing data, and writing reports. A list of 340 churches were identified in the community. Fifty churches completed a questionnaire that was used to identify the specific educational, social, and health ministries and the church's resources, collaborations, and accomplishments. Most churches surveyed provided educational and social services programs; they provided their own resources to support these ministries and collaborated with other churches and community programs. According to data collected, these churches had a documented impact on individuals participating in these ministries.

The fourth project, West Tampa TeleNetworking Initiative, was initiated in an inner-city neighborhood in Tampa to investigate the strengths and weaknesses of networking strategies used to develop community partnerships.[29] An extensive engagement process was used prior to the initiation of this project and researchers met with various neighborhood community stakeholders regarding the development of the study proposal. Researchers and the stakeholders collaborated in the design and conduct of the project. A focus group methodology was used as the primary method to collect qualitative data for this project. Community representatives had an opportunity to review the questions intended to be used at focus group meetings, reflect on and provide feedback about the results of the focus group findings, and participate in the final preparation of the recommendations. This project documented the typical networking strategies used by schools, service providers, and faith-based organizations when serving the needs of children and families in an inner-city, low-income neighborhood. The focus group data illustrated attempts made by parents, school representatives, service providers, and faith-based organizations to communicate and exchange information with one another.

The fifth project, East Tampa Initiative, is a current initiative including Richard Briscoe, Harold Keller, and Gwen McClain, an ongoing service-learning, action research, and technical assistance project with several departments at the University of South Florida. This is part of the university's effort to foster collaborative research partnerships with schools and community agencies to transfer research into practice. One partnership, Service-Learning/Action Research Partnership: Applied Neighborhood-Based Research Projects, represents a long-term commitment to fostering a meaningful collaboration that will mutually benefit the university, community, and family partners, with specific responsibilities, time lines, and outcomes that were agreed on jointly. The partnership is fostered by two faculty members and one community member, who serves as a coinstructor of a service-learning and action research class. This class is centered on the strengths-based belief that African American families and communities possess resources and supports that should be recognized and sustained by others working with these families. Students are educated in this approach and the implementation of other culturally competent practices and are expected to produce contractually agreed-on project outcomes (e.g., written and oral presentations), that are consistent with the larger goals of the community partners. Each semester, students provide services in the East Tampa community and gather data as part of one of the ongoing projects in partnership with the community. These projects are concerned with the following: (1) school assets as they relate to community development and enhancing school–family–community interconnections; (2) enhancing the organizational capacity of faith-based institutions in East Tampa to further community development and children's achievement and development; and (3) technically assisting in the use of data from resident-driven needs assessments to inform decisions pertinent to the health, education, and social services infrastructure in East Tampa. One of the authors of this chapter, Evangeline Best, who is a community member engaged as a researcher, highlights the potential empowerment of the research data: "If I could have a wish, I wish all of East Tampa's assets could be bounded and put in every citizen's hand and everybody would be proud to say they are a product of East Tampa."

These examples are not meant to be prescriptive and are certainly not exhaustive. Rather, they illustrate that changing the frequent climate of distrust between African American communities and universities takes time and effort. This change requires strategic actions that clearly communicate the researchers' respect for community members and regard for the community members' contributions and may be contrary to the typical way universities operate. Each of these projects was implemented with the key elements listed in the following section and the lessons learned that enhanced the process and outcome of all of the community–university partnerships.

Establishing and Maintaining Trust Building

This conceptual framework emphasizes partnerships, mutual respect, and involvement of all stakeholders at all levels of projects. The aim of these principles is to recognize and value the strengths of all partners and reflect the understanding that partnerships are constantly evolving and thus require frequent assessments of lessons learned. Partnerships take time to develop and they evolve over time.[30] The ability to articulate the principles, statements of mission, and goals is an important aspect of successful partnerships. Sustained effort of trust building is crucial to the success of community-based research. Developing a trusting partnership takes time because individuals in the community may take a wait-and-see attitude. It is impossible to provide prescriptive strategies for building trust in African American communities, and there is little research that addresses this trust-building process. Each community and cultural context for community-based research must be examined for what strategies are effective or ineffective. Process notes and frequent participant dialogues conducted as part of all of these ongoing partnerships are important exercises for building trust. The results of those interactions provide examples of trust-building efforts, which are discussed more in the next few paragraphs.

Gain an understanding of the community. As faculty and students expressed a desire to engage with various communities, they connected with residents and local agencies to share interests and expertise. All university members (faculty and students) were invited to interact with community residents. They spent time working with residents to carry out activities, programs, and events in the community. Many hours were spent assisting community programs with fund-raising and grant writing to gather funds for the community. We assisted these activities by aiding with program implementation as well as the evaluation of program development.

In the East Tampa Initiative, members served on community–university partnership committees. They were taken on a tour of the neighborhoods by a lifelong resident of the community, which gave the university partners the opportunity to learn the history of the community and its assets and resources from the residents. Obtaining information directly from residents gave the university partners insight into the community that would not have been possible had they just driven through and looked at the neighborhoods from a car.

Take time to listen and engage in honest dialogue. In the East Tamp Initiative, faculty and students from multiple disciplines at the University of South Florida met with community partners and residents to discuss the projects to gain insight and establish a common "understanding and goals." Opportunities for open dialogue were made available throughout each project to clarify issues, nurture relationships, and perform and celebrate the projects' objectives. Faculty and students entering the neighborhoods worked on committees and with other agencies to address issues concerning the community. Considerable time was spent at research sites mutually processing and assessing what was going on among the research teams and how our interactions impacted the communities, university, and residents.

Establish a channel of communications to coordinate all activities. It is critical that engagement between the community–university partnerships involve ongoing communication so that individuals do not violate the tenuous trust that has been built. This communication must be responsive to and valued by the residents to maintain the trust building, while at the same time sustain progress on projects. Continuous communication between community and university partners is required in monitoring and managing all aspects of the projects without the traditional power differentials. Sometimes community partners have informed university partners when nonparticipating faculty were not following culturally competent practices. Similarly, university partners have moved quickly to include community partners when government entities have tried to exclude residents. Communications between university members and community were daily in the form of telephone conversations, e-mail correspondences, and in-person meetings. We were able to depend on one another to carry out our activities.

Timely feedback to the community. Researchers provided ongoing information to community residents for feedback and input. In addition to providing this information in a written report to the residents, presentations and other methods helped inform their respective communities and family members. This community-owned information is used to inform the local families and organizations as they plan various activities and services. Traditional studies have not valued the importance of sustaining community ownership of the data. The projects mentioned in this chapter ensured that this situation did not occur by using community meetings, civic board meetings, and other processes that the community partners deemed appropriate to share information. Finally, the university and community partners reported information together at these community settings and at professional conferences and venues.

Grants may allocate resources disproportionately. The projects all used applied research and were based on grounded theory and action research. One major intent was to implement actions or changes as knowledge was gained. In some cases, grants written for these projects were disproportionately allocated to the community, residents, or university. For instance, although the Identifying Strengths in African American Families project allocated funds to the community, most were allocated to the university because of the number of research staff required to complete a national project in multiple sites. However, the East Tampa coinstructors developed grants to conduct needs assessments via face-to-face interviews and focus groups with residents for data to inform future directions for committees. The interview and focus group scripts and questions were developed by residents, with Richard Briscoe and Gwen McClain facilitating and providing technical assistance. All monies in the initial grants were allocated to residents, with university personnel serving voluntary roles.

Open communication and commitment to trust building in the community–university relationships are critical to promoting understanding as subsequent grants are developed and focused on maximal benefit to the community.

The Mutual Impact of this Approach on African Americans, Research, and the University

Social scientists frequently express concern about the gap between research and its application. Within the context of education, a report from the National Research Council suggested that the gap is related to the manner in which research is traditionally conducted.[31] The report argued that questions must be framed, addressed, understood, and implemented by all participants for research to translate into application. Similarly, Rogers reviewed the literature on the diffusion of research into practice and identified the same mechanisms as the National Research Council.[32] These processes are consistent with the model being discussed here.

The potential mutual benefits of this approach are tremendous. Community questions and concerns are addressed, resulting in solutions that can be systematically implemented and evaluated. Community participants are invested in the solutions because they have been actively engaged in framing the questions and problems, defining the processes for addressing the questions, understanding the results, and implementing solutions. To the extent that human capital has been developed as part of the process, community resources, strengths, and assets have been enhanced in a manner that is likely to lead to sustainable changes. One of the authors of this chapter, Evangeline Best, a community researcher involved in the East Tampa Initiative project, noted the impact the research has on community members: "The research made the community become aware of their assets and not their shortcomings. Research helped the community focus on all the small and maybe insignificant things once taken for granted. Research helped us look at ourselves as special and unique, not different. Research helped us to realize that we have very valuable assets."

Universities and researchers also find benefits from their efforts. Faculty researchers have meaningful research agendas that are more likely to lead to action. Students' development as community-engaged and culturally competent scholars is enhanced. Research demonstrates that students involved in community-based learning opportunities are more motivated, perform better, and have higher retention rates.[33] A mutual benefit for both the community and the university is that residents of the community, African Americans specifically, are likely to feel less alienated from the university and are more likely to see the university as a viable institution to enroll in to pursue employment or education.

Holland described key organizational factors that indicate an institutional commitment to community engagement as the following: a mission statement; leadership commitment to a sustained engagement agenda; community-based research and teaching as criteria for hiring, promotion, and tenure; infrastructure and funding to support partnerships; community-based learning integrated across the curriculum; supported community research and collaborative work; and sustained partnerships with community stakeholders involved in defining, conducting, and evaluating community-based activities.[34] Such community–university partnerships provide the context that enables faculty to participate in culturally competent community-based research and gives community members in African American neighborhoods the ability to see faculty representatives of the university as committed to those stated values and actions.

Although the University of South Florida has had a clearly articulated mission statement that includes a commitment to community engagement, tangible progress is being made as a result of the ongoing and continually developing partnerships.[35] Campus engagement with the community is spreading across all units. The growing community–university partnerships and early outcomes were instrumental in the university being classified by the Carnegie Foundation as a major research university engaged with the community. The prestige accompanying this classification allows faculty to revise strategic plans incorporating both its research and community engagement missions. Legislative budget requests have been made to provide the necessary infrastructure to coordinate the university's commitment to community engagement via research and community-based teaching and learning. A paper on the explicit inclusion of community engagement into tenure and promotion criteria at all levels of the university has been drafted, and campus dialogue on the document has been initiated. These efforts further the institutionalization of community-based research.

Considerable growth and development of culturally competent community engagement is a major opportunity, with mutual benefits for all partners. Based on all five projects and our collective backgrounds, knowledge, and experiences as diverse people and academic scholars, we recognized that African American families are rich sources of everyday lived experiences and enhance the understanding of the overall realities of African American life and survival in America. We were able to build on our research modalities and purposefully tap into a direct source of energy and strength for individual, family, and community betterment, which creates strong and effective interventions and strategies. It is important that these strengths and contextual factors in conducting culturally competent community-based research are communicated in the professional research literature as well, rather than the typical de-contextualized methods sections of most of the research literature.

Notes

1. L. C. Jordan, G. A. Bogat, and G. Smith, "Collaborating for Social Change: The Black Psychologist and the Black Community," *American Journal of Community Psychology* 29 (2001): 599–620.

2. R. L. Williams, "The Death of White Research in Black Communities," in *Black Psychology*, ed. R. L. Jones (New York: Harper and Row, 1980), 403–17.

3. M. Singer, "Knowledge for Use: Anthropology and Community-Centered Substance Abuse Research," *Social Sciences and Medicine* 31 (1993): 15–25.

4. Jordan, Bogat, and Smith, "Collaborating for Social Change."

5. Jordan, Bogat, and Smith, "Collaborating for Social Change."

6. J. B. Cousins and L. M. Earl, "The Case for Participatory Evaluation," *Educational Evaluation and Policy Analysis* 14 (1992): 397–418; J. A. King and M. P. Lonnquist, *A Review of Writing on Action Research* (Minneapolis: Center for Applied Research and Educational Improvement, University of Minnesota, 1992); J. McKernan, "The Countenance of Curriculum Action Research: Traditional, Collaborative and Critical-Emancipatory Conceptions," *Journal of Curriculum and Supervision* 3 (1988): 173–200.

7. B. Glaser and A. Strauss, *The Discovery of Grounded Theory: Strategies for Qualitative Research* (Chicago: Aldine, 1967); A. Strauss and J. M. Corbin, *Basics of Qualitative Research: Techniques and Procedures for Developing Grounded Theory* (Thousand Oaks, CA: Sage, 1998).

8. R. Hill, *The Strengths of Black Families* (New York: Emerson Hall Press, 1972); Kretzman and McKnight, 1993; K. I. Maton, C. J. Schellenbach, B. J., Leadbeater, and A. L. Solarz, *Investing in Children, Youth, Families, and Communities: Strength-Based Research and Policy* (Washington, DC: American Psychological Association, 2004).

9. B. A. Stroul and R. Friedman, *A System of Care for Children and Youth with Severe Emotional Disturbances* (Washington, DC: Georgetown University Child Development Center, CASSP Technical Assistance Center, 1994); B. A. Stroul and R. M. Friedman, *A System of Care for Severely Emotionally Disturbed Children and Youth* (Washington, DC: Georgetown University Child Development Center, CASSP Technical Assistance Center, 1986).

10. Carnegie Foundation for the Advancement of Teaching, "The Carnegie Classification of Institutions of Higher Education," 2006, http://www.carnegiefoundation.org/classifications (accessed January 30, 2007); J. S. Vey, *Higher Education in Pennsylvania: A Comprehensive Asset for Communities* (Washington, DC: Brookings Institution, 2005).

11. Hill, *The Strengths of Black Families*; Kretzman and McKnight; K. I. Maton, C. J. Schellenbach, B. J., Leadbeater, and A. L. Solarz, *Investing in Children, Youth, Families, and Communities: Strength-Based Research and Policy* (Washington, DC: American Psychological Association, 2004).

12. Stroul and Friedman, *A System of Care for Children and Youth.*

13. Carnegie Foundation for the Advancement of Teaching, "The Carnegie Classification"; Vey, *Higher Education in Pennsylvania.*

14. A. Cablas, "Culturally Competent Methods Based on Evaluation and Research: How to Use Research Results in Systems of Care," in *Promoting Cul-*

tural Competence in Children's Mental Health Services, ed. M. Hernandez and M. Isaacs (Baltimore: Paul H. Brookes, 1998), 331–46.

15. The Carnegie Foundation for the Advancement of Teaching, "The Carnegie Classification."

16. Jordan, Bogat, and Smith, "Collaborating for Social Change."

17. T. Cross, B. Bazron, K. Dennis, and M. R. Issacs, *Towards a Culturally Competent System of Care* (Washington, DC: Georgetown University Child Development Center, Child and Adolescent Service System Program Technical Assistance Center, 1989), 11.

18. M. P. Benjamin, *Child and Adolescent Service System Program Minority Initiative Research Monograph* (Washington, DC: Georgetown University Child Development Center, Child and Adolescent Service System Program Technical Assistance Center, 1993), 35.

19. Jordan, Bogat, and Smith, "Collaborating for Social Change."

20. Hill, *The Strengths of Black Families*.

21. J. Albino and L. A. Tedesco, "Women's Health Issues," *Issues in Mental Health Nursing* 5 (1983): 157–72; R. Weissberg, M. Caplan, and R. Harwood, "Promoting Competent Young People in Competence-Enhancing Environments: A Systems-Based Perspective on Primary Prevention," *Journal of Consulting and Clinical Psychology* 59 (1991): 830–41.

22. Stroul and Friedman, "A System of Care for Severely Emotionally Disturbed Children and Youth" and "A System of Care for Children and Youth."

23. Stroul and Friedman, "A System of Care for Severely Emotionally Disturbed Children and Youth."

24. Strauss and Corbin, *Basics of Qualitative Research*; Glaser and Strauss, *The Discovery of Grounded Theory*.

25. R. Briscoe and G. McClain, *African American Family Support Analysis: Strengths of African American Families* (Tampa, FL: Children's Board of Hillsborough County, 2000).

26. Briscoe and McClain, *African American Family Support Analysis*, 72.

27. R. Joseph, R. Briscoe, A. Smith, J., Sengova, and G. McClain, *Strengths of African American Families: A Cross-Site Analysis of Families in Baltimore, Detroit, Plant City, San Diego and Savannah* (Tampa: University of South Florida, Louis de la Parte Florida Mental Health Institute, Child and Family Studies, 2001).

28. G. McClain and R. Briscoe, *Identifying Strengths in African American Families* (Tampa, FL: Children's Board of Hillsborough County, 2004).

29. P. Oullette, R. Briscoe, A. Jones, and C. Tyson, *West Tampa TeleNetworking Initiative: Towards the Development of a Technology-Supported School and Community Networking Strategy* (Tampa, FL: Children's Board of Hillsborough County, 2001).

30. Community-Campus Partnerships for Health, "Principles of Good Community-Campus Partnerships," 2006, http://depts.washington.edu/ccph/principles.html (accessed January 30, 2007).

31. National Research Council, *Improving Student Learning: A Strategic Plan for Education Research and Its Utilization* (Washington, DC: National Academy Press, 1999).

32. E. M. Rogers, *Diffusion of Innovations*, 5th ed (New York: Free Press, 2004).

33. A. W. Astin and L. J. Sax, "How Undergraduates Are Affected by Service Participation," *Journal of College Student Development* 39 (1998): 251–63.

34. B. A. Holland, "Analyzing Institutional Commitment to Engagement," *Michigan Journal of Community Service Learning* 4 (2004): 30–41.

35. J. Jetson, R. Jones, R. Ersing, and H. R. Keller, "Community Engagement's Role in Creating Institutional Change within the Academy: A Case Study of East Tampa and USF," paper presented at the Sixth International Service-Learning Research Conference, Portland, Oregon, 2006.

14

◆◆◆

Community Engagement and Collaborations in Community-Based Research

The Road to Project Butterfly

GiShawn Mance, Bernadette Sánchez,
and Niambi Jaha-Echols

Community collaboration and engagement in research is usually facilitated by the researcher seeking community partners in order to conduct research with populations that may have been traditionally excluded or erroneously represented in the academic literature.[1] However, when the community and researcher equally pursue one another, do the rules of engagement change? In this dynamic, is it possible for both parties to get what they need while holding the values of the community and intervention objectives sacred? These questions are particularly pertinent in African American communities,[2] where there is a deep skepticism toward institutions.

Given the history of unethical research conducted in African American communities, there is an inherent distrust of the medical and/or scientific research community.[3] Whether there is a realistic distrust or healthy paranoia, a multiplicity of contextual barriers exists in African American communities that make collaborations delicate and complex. With this history in mind, it is quite striking that an African American community organizer would deem an academician as a change agent and partner. This chapter highlights the road of engagement and collaboration among a community-based organization, two public elementary schools, and a university-based researcher. Although the road of engagement had many bumps and unexpected turns, ultimately, the journey, not the destination, was the most valuable experience. Within the context of an intervention, we will discuss (1) the role of African-centered values in community engagement;[4] (2) assumptions and expectations of community members and researchers when implementing an African-centered intervention; and (3) lessons learned.

Context of Community Engagement

Community engagement and collaboration are explored through an intervention that was implemented in an urban, low-income African American community in Chicago. The intervention, Project Butterfly, is an African-centered program designed to meet the needs of African American adolescent girls. African American adolescent girls living in inner-city, high-poverty neighborhoods in the United States are at risk for developmental difficulties, including behavior problems, depression, early sexual activity, and poor school performance.[5] Given that African American adolescents face stressful environments that place them at an increased risk for adverse emotional, intellectual, physical and behavioral outcomes,[6] Parham suggests that African American adolescents should develop a strong African American consciousness to rise above the social conditions that hinder their advancement.[7] Therefore, we expected that an intervention that promotes African-centered values would enhance African American adolescent girls' racial/cultural identity, and as a result, have a positive impact on their overall psychological well-being. Parham's suggestion forms the foundation of the current research.

Project Butterfly is rooted in African-centered philosophy and values and is dedicated to supporting young women and girls of African descent through the transitions of life. In order to help the reader better understand Project Butterfly, African philosophy and values are described.

African philosophy is the critical component that provides the foundation for traditional African-centered values. The basic assumption underlying African values reflects the notion of oneness between humanity and nature. This is represented by a collective sense of self; understanding and respect for self and other; a sense of one's spiritual connection to the universe; and a sense of mutual responsibility.[8] African philosophy emphasizes values such as cooperation, collective responsibility, interdependence, extended kinship, spiritualism, and reciprocity, all of which are embedded in African culture.[9] African-centered values are thought to enhance the African sense of self and prevent self-destructive behavior.

Afrocentric frameworks have been used to conceptualize, design, and implement services and programs for African Americans, with special attention directed at assessing the effectiveness of this approach.[10] Several African American scholars believe that an Afrocentric approach can provide a viable framework for theory, program development, and research within African American communities in general and with African American youth specifically.[11] Studies empirically support the positive role of African-centered values on African American youths' psychological well-being and development.[12]

Project Butterfly was devised by Niambi Jaha-Echols, one of the authors of this chatper, to help African American adolescent females better understand who they are and gain power and strength. She describes the mission of this program as a tool to provide an "internal awakening and begin the personal process of healing."[13] The concept of awakening and healing is relative to the need of each participant. The curriculum provides valuable information on African-centered values addressing identity, womanhood training (issues specific to females), and cultural knowledge.

Components of Project Butterfly include girls receiving an African Day Name, which lists characteristics of individuals born on a particular day of the week (e.g., Monday born—Adowa, the peacemaker), in order for girls to form a connection to their African lineage. Ancestors are identified through the completion of a family tree. Girls are introduced to the role of ancestors in traditional African philosophy and identify relatives and historical figures (e.g., Harriet Tubman) who have made a significant impact in the lives of African Americans. Rituals, such as relaxation techniques and journaling, are introduced as well as libations. Libation also allows girls to recognize their ancestors and give thanks to those who have made significant contributions to African Americans. Project Butterfly also emphasizes the African-centered values of respect for elders, collectivism, and reciprocity through the use of group cohesion exercises, family-oriented labels (e.g., Auntie or Mama instead of Ms. or Mrs.), and community involvement. The use of an African-centered framework is emphasized to promote African American girls' positive associations with their culture.

Nobles suggests that it is through African-centered prevention models that one develops the knowledge to understand and engage in culturally meaningful activity.[14] The premise of such models is that knowledge of one's culture and history will improve one's sense of self, which plays a positive role in psychological functioning.[15] By providing Project Butterfly as an example of an African-centered preventative model, we hope to illustrate the nuances within a collaborative relationship among an African American university researcher, an African American community activist and program developer, and an African American community.

Project Butterfly was implemented and evaluated in a public elementary school by a community member, Jaha-Echols, and a university-based researcher, GiShawn Mance (another author of this chapter). Jaha-Echols, the developer of Project Butterfly, is an entrepreneur in Chicago who conducts empowerment groups and artistry in the African American community. Project Butterfly was evaluated by Mance for her dissertation work. The other author, of this chapter, Bernadette Sánchez, was Mance's dissertation advisor who guided her in the research process. In order to assess the role of Project Butterfly in African American female adolescents, Mance conducted a quasi-experimental study in which sixth- to eighth-grade female students at an elementary school received the intervention while sixth- to eighth-grade female students at a nearby elementary school served as the control group. Both groups completed measures on a variety of outcomes (e.g., ethnic identity and psychological well-being) before and after the intervention. As a team, Mance and Jaha-Echols collaborated on delivering Project Butterfly in a manner that met the needs of the community and the dissertation. Before discussing the process of engagement and the issues that emerged, we will examine the role of African-centered values in the process of community collaboration and engagement in a low-income, urban African American community.

The Role of Culture in Community Collaborations

It is suggested that collaborations be strategically structured from the beginning, and this should be employed throughout the process.[16] However, in the midst of planning such an approach, it becomes imperative to consider the culture and context in which the collaboration exists. Specifically, engagement with an African American community that considers the construct of African-centered values adds unique dimensions to the process when understanding the "rules of engagement."

Culture is shared by a group but is harbored differently by each specific unit within the group, is communicated across generations, is relatively stable, and has the potential to change across time.[17] Quite often, culture is associated with race; however, as the previous definition suggests, culture refers to values, beliefs, and worldviews. On the other hand, although socially constructed, race often refers to physical characteristics, such as skin color, facial features, and hair types, which are common to an inbred, geographically isolated population.[18] For African American adolescents, race is a very salient aspect of identity and is related to psychological well-being.[19] These constructs are important to note because race is often used to describe culture, particularly in the African American community. A common example is when behaviors are described as "Black" rather than being attributed to culture. This differentiation between Black- and African-centered as cultural descriptors was quite visible in this collaborative relationship.

Although African American culture is varied and heterogeneous, there are some observed commonalities, such as values for cooperation and collective responsibility that are helpful to consider when engaging in community-based research.[20] The extent to which these values are present and how these values are manifested vary. Cooperation and collective responsibility represent working together and concern for the whole of nature.[21] From an African-centered paradigm, the collectivist orientation is reflected by the saying, "I am because we are; and because we are, therefore, I am."[22] In the process of engagement, a community may feel a collective responsibility to assist an African American researcher in answering questions that will help the larger whole. However, a community may display collective responsibility by protecting its members from greater political institutions and view an African American researcher as merely a player within a larger system.

In implementing Project Butterfly, it was imperative that the researcher respect the African-centered principles underlying the program while also being aware of the heterogeneity of values within the community. For example, although Afrocentric values played a role in acquiring a community partnership with Jaha-Echols, there appeared to be differences between the schools on their values and attitudes toward the current research.

Throughout the course of the project, each party appeared to have assumptions about the other's values and intentions, which played a significant role in the partnership. Some assumptions contributed to barriers while others opened doors to understanding. For example, although the researcher is African American, there was a sense of "otherness," which appeared to highlight the fact that the researcher was not from the community. Jordan, Bogat, and Smith highlighted that Black psychologists are typically trained in mainstream educational institutions, and out of necessity, master biculturalism whereby they adapt to both mainstream White settings and predominantly Black settings.[23] This biculturalism may not necessarily translate well in some low-income African American communities where certain behaviors may be interpreted as "acting White" and further serve to distance African American researchers from the community.

From the perspective of the community, there appeared to be a desire for evidence of Mance's authenticity. The community often identified their search for authenticity as "being real." Thus, there was a need for interconnectedness between Mance and the community by determining whether she could relate to community members and whether she was authentically "Black." Further, it was important for community members to feel that Mance was genuinely invested in the community and not simply out for personal gain.

Developing an Egalitarian Relationship

Community psychology, a field that has informed Mance's research training, embraces many values that can assist researchers in obtaining the cooperation, trust, and cultural perspective of community members.[24] The researcher's intention should include creating a relationship whereby the community contributes its knowledge and resources.[25] An initial challenge in the collaborative process is whether the researchers are too anchored in their own culture of scientific tradition to anchor their work in the culture of the community. Keys and colleagues suggest that the temptation of the researcher is often to seek the community's rubber stamp of approval for their own plans rather than including the voices of previously marginalized communities in a more egalitarian research process. Important to Mance was the process of sharing the voice and experiences of a community that has been historically excluded or viewed from a deficit model in the academic literature.[26] Therefore, Mance attempted to conduct her research in a collaborative and egalitarian manner while navigating multiple relationships in the project (i.e., Mance and Jaha-Echols; Mance, Jaha-Echols, and the control school; and Mance and the intervention school). This leads to initial research steps of Project Butterfly and how the researcher navigated the different collaborative relationships intertwined within the study.

Getting Started

Most community collaborations are multiphasic, are multifaceted, grow over time, and are influenced by persons, circumstances, and emerging changes in science or community needs.[27] The collaborative process of Project Butterfly began with the community's desire for an intervention for adolescent girls and Mance's interest and dedication to developing and implementing interventions for African American youth. Similarly, Jaha-Echols was influenced by a passion for culturally relevant interventions for African American adolescent girls. Thus, the researcher played a number of roles, such as initiator and later collaborator with the community school and primarily as the collaborator with Jaha-Echols.

Collaborations may take many forms, varying in purpose, structure, and process. Organized from lowest to highest in community involvement, these forms include (1) networking, (2) cooperation, (3) coordination or partnership, (4) coalition, and (5) collaboration.[28] Mance's relationship with Jaha-Echols reflected a collaboration whereby both individuals actively worked to define the problem and implement the intervention. However, our relationship with the community was less collaborative at times. The community often viewed us as the leaders and provided little insight or feedback. Throughout the course of the project, however, the relationship between Mance, Jaha-Echols, and the community shifted from a coordination of the intervention to a collaborative effort that allowed all parties to tailor an innovative program for the community.

Engaging the community and gaining entrée into a close-knit African American community must be done with great care. Establishing credibility in one's own cultural group can be quite a task. Given the close-knit, protective nature of the African American community due to their historical and current experiences, building on an existing relationship is a good approach. This allows the researcher to be presented as safe, and the community will be more apt to engage. The researcher's relationship with Jaha-Echols served to facilitate the engagement and collaboration with the intervention school.

The relationship between Mance and Jaha-Echols began with the mutual interest of providing psychosocial interventions for African American adolescent girls. Mance participated in an adult African-centered rites of passage to gain insight to culturally-based interventions. This provided entry into a subculture of the local African American community that was interested in developing and implementing similar interventions. When members of this Afrocentric community learned that Mance was interested in researching culturally relevant adolescent interventions, they directed her to Jaha-Echols. In a meeting, Jaha-Echols asked Mance to assist her in developing a cognitively appropriate board game to supplement a workbook titled *Project Butterfly*. During the development of the game, Mance and Jaha-Echols began to discuss future collaborations that included research.

Jaha-Echols developed Project Butterfly as a response to several local agencies' and schools' requests to provide a psychosocial intervention to address the increasing number of girls engaging in gang activity. She developed many strong relationships in the community and was well-known for her passion and commitment to African American women and girls. As Jaha-Echols worked with adolescent girls and developed Project Butterfly, self-esteem issues usually surfaced. Many of the girls revealed that they were in toxic relationships and/or situations and were unaware of the negative effects of these relationships on their well-being. Jaha-Echols soon realized that the girls represented a larger community of teen girls who were dealing with some of the same issues: cultural displacement, depression, and low self-worth/self-esteem. This is what ultimately inspired her book, *Project Butterfly*, which was written as a resource for girls. She wanted to give African American adolescent girls a more holistic approach to life so they know that they are more than the sum of their body parts. Jaha-Echols further aimed to help girls understand that transformation and change were always possible regardless of their past.

Mance and Jaha-Echols discussed the meaning and purpose of their collaboration as they began their journey in research. Although Mance decided to become a change agent through academia and Jaha-Echols chose the path of community advocacy, their common thread rested in their commitment to the African American community. This mutual value was instrumental in the partnership because it is imperative that partners identify common vision and goals and clarify expectations.[29] As the research collaboration evolved, the dynamics between Mance and Jaha-Echols experienced several shifts. As suggested by Mattessich and Monsey, collaborations are mutually beneficial.[30] Mance and Jaha-Echols each held different needs while the overall goal was the same— address the needs of the community. For example, the collaboration assisted the researcher in fulfilling her requirements for her doctoral degree and assisted Jaha-Echols in gaining documentation and empirical data regarding the intervention's effectiveness, which would allow Project Butterfly to receive future funding while also servicing more girls. Throughout the collaborative process, the researcher was quite clear in asserting that no guarantees could be made about the results. Establishing a trusting relationship was paramount in moving from volunteerism (e.g., assisting Jaha-Echols with the board game) to research. Given the common goals and relationship built between Mance and

Jaha-Echols, it became imperative for Mance to remain objective while conducting the research. To ensure this objectivity, Mance consulted with her dissertation chair, Sánchez, regularly in order to maintain the rigor of the study. Although the researcher had established significant credibility with Jaha-Echols, the success of the research was anchored in engaging the community.

Community Engagement

Project Butterfly was implemented in a couple of schools in Chicago prior to the research collaboration. It was quite successful in the community, well-known, and trusted that additional schools became interested. Word of mouth proved to be the largest endorsement of the program. Several school principals contacted Jaha-Echols requesting that Project Butterfly be implemented in their schools. Shared vision, which is an important characteristic for a successful collaboration, was a large determinate in identifying the two schools that would be willing to engage in the research. Taylor and Adelman define shared vision as the common vision focused on the good of the whole that unites stakeholders and provides momentum for moving forward.[31] All parties appeared to share the vision of providing support for African American adolescent girls.

The identified intervention school desired a program for their female students to address issues of character building, self-esteem, and violence. Given the principal's request of Project Butterfly at her school, Jaha-Echols felt that the school would be a good candidate for the research. The researcher entered into the school primarily based on the relationship between Jaha-Echols and the principal. The collaborative pair met consistently with the principal for several months to discuss the needs of female students. Additionally, the principal often met twice a month with her female students for a rap session whereby the girls wrote down life questions and dropped them in a basket for discussion. Mance and Jaha-Echols attended several of these discussions in an effort to create a presence in the school. Spending time with the students allowed the school community to become more familiar with Mance and Jaha-Echols. The pair introduced the idea of tailoring Project Butterfly to conduct research. Suarez-Balcazar et al. highlight that research collaborations should be based on the needs of the community.[32] Therefore, the researcher assessed the school's needs to ensure that research would be mutually beneficial. A meeting was conducted to specifically introduce the school principal to the research idea. This was followed by letters to the teachers describing the goals and procedures of the study. Regularly scheduled meetings were conducted with the principal and teachers for approximately six months, in which further explanations of the study were provided and questions answered. Teacher, student, and family engagement rested on the school leaders being committed to the research process. At certain points of the process, it appeared that some of the staff members at the intervention school were hesitant about implementation of the research because of Project Butterfly's philosophical framework.

Interestingly, this did not appear to be an issue in the control school located in the same neighborhood.

Although the schools were within walking distance of one another, there were cultural differences between the two, even though both schools were largely African American. The intervention school was uncomfortable with the African-centered nature of Project Butterfly. However, the control school was open to exploring an African-centered paradigm. Discussions at the intervention school revealed that the principal was more interested in a Black-centered approach that emphasized racial socialization and the Black American experience as a foundation to addressing community issues. From Mance's perspective, it appeared that the principal thought that an approach that reflected a communal orientation was appropriate but preferred that any references to Africa or anything African be excluded. Further, the perspective of the principal included the Black Christian experience and values as paramount in defining issues and solutions. The final request from the principal and teachers was that the Black experience in the United States is highlighted in the intervention.

The paradigm differences became increasingly important when the researcher was presented with the dilemma of conducting the study while honoring the school's interest and the original Project Butterfly program. Jaha-Echols consciously developed Project Butterfly from an African-centered perspective. Inherent in Jaha-Echols's development of Project Butterfly was the African-centered value of spirituality, which is not dependent on any doctrine, organization, or culture but on individual beliefs.[33] African Americans are of diverse faiths, and yet the majority is Christian.[34] Some African Americans of the Christian faith who are unfamiliar with an African-centered worldview may liken the africentricity as anti-Christian.[35] Jaha-Echols experienced this differentiation while she was developing credibility in her community. While forming relationships in her community, Jaha-Echols began to notice a variation in African-centered and Black-centered values. She gathered that community members who were in alignment with Black-centered values often mistrusted or devalued African-centered thought and values. Jaha-Echols focused more on the overall purpose of the intervention when introducing Project Butterfly to the community but remained true to her worldview.

Given the differences between the African- and Black-centered approaches as observed by Jaha-Echols, the researcher was faced with two questions: How do these differences influence the engagement process? Do they cause barriers or cohesion? Before addressing these questions, it is important to note that the impetus for developing Project Butterfly and later implementation of the intervention far exceeded the subtle nuances of both paradigms. Community members felt an urgency to address the maladaptive developmental pathways of their African American adolescent girls. The "how" of the intervention, African- versus Black-centered, became secondary to the overall purpose of the research.

Thus, engagement and collaboration rested on the collective responsibility that all partners felt for African American adolescent girls. This allowed the community to view the research as a form of advocacy. Thus, the community expressed pride that steps were implemented to address the needs of its girls. The community discussed concerns for their male students; however, the intervention school stated that they had limited resources and were unable to implement a program specifically for the male students. Mance and Jaha-Echols were familiar with a male prevention program that could address the community's concerns; therefore, the pair introduced the director of this program to the school's principal.

Although the concerns brought up by the intervention school about an African-centered approach to community intervention were at times stressful to Mance who was feeling anxious about completing her dissertation as originally planned and in a timely manner, it was important that Mance acknowledge these concerns. Exchanging resources can truly build a collaborative relationship in communities where there are competing needs. Each partner brings a set of resources and strengths to the relationship that need to be recognized and valued.[36] It was important that the researcher not only collect data but actually join and express concern for the community. By providing additional resources for the school communities, the researcher reiterated her authenticity to the community. However, there still remained some skepticism.

Addressing Barriers

In an effort to address the intervention school's hesitance to fully engage in a collaborative relationship, Mance and Jaha-Echols offered to share the content of the intervention with the principal and teachers. Mance provided research to school staff illustrating that culturally relevant values and beliefs were positively associated with psychological outcomes among ethnic minority youth.[37] Specifically, the promotion of culturally relevant beliefs and values provide mechanisms of change and positive behaviors for African American youth.[38] Although the school was familiar with the intervention and had seen several presentations, the willingness to discuss the content of each session proved to be quite beneficial for both parties.

Although Mance and Jaha-Echols were open to understanding the school culture and identifying its assets and strengths, over time the principal became more detached from the intervention research and ultimately turned the project over to the assistant principal. In contrast, the control school's principal remained active throughout the intervention research process and had no concerns about Project Butterfly and its theoretical framework. Several differences between the principals may account for their varied attitudes toward the research.

Beyond the differences in their openness to the intervention, the two principals also varied in age and approaches to addressing the presenting issues. The principal of the intervention school was older and identified herself as a strong Black Christian woman. Additionally, the school environment displayed less structure, which often led the principal to contend with pressing concerns. Although she had a genuine concern for addressing the issues of her students via an intervention, it appeared that Project Butterfly was not the type of intervention she desired. Mance and Jaha-Echols spent a considerable amount of time making presentations to teachers and the school's parent support network in order to gain buy-in and to address the principal's apprehensions. At this point, the research was no longer collaborative in nature but felt more like an effort to convince the school of the value and utility of the intervention. Contrastingly, the principal of the control school was younger and also identified herself as a Black Christian woman; however, she was interested in exploring a different approach to addressing the issues faced by the school's adolescent girls. This principal also appeared to be personally dedicated in assisting the researcher in completing her dissertation work. The principal expressed pride that the researcher was an African American woman interested in providing resources for African American girls. Additionally, she verbally expressed a personal commitment to assisting the researcher. Thus, the cultural value of collective responsibility was quite evident in the collaborative relationship between the control school principal and the researcher.

Implementation

The importance of effectively communicating research objectives to community members and building trusting relationships cannot be emphasized enough. The implementation of the research intervention had many unexpected bumps and turns. There were many competing circumstances that made implementation taxing at times and that shifted the research from an asset to a burden. Additionally, there were several challenges to implementing this research in a low-income, urban environment that was chronically exposed to violence. There was a lack of resources in the school as well as programmatic disruptions due to violence. Space and timing were often issues. The school was overcrowded, and therefore had little additional space to hold the intervention groups. Although the research was based on a time line, the needs of the students took precedence. For instance, the researcher cancelled intervention sessions when it appeared that students' and/or school issues should be a priority. This display of concern and care by the researcher created an authenticity to the researcher–community relationship. The community felt that the researcher was invested in the community (collective responsibility) and not simply the research (reciprocity) because of her willingness to allow the school's needs to take precedence over the research.

Lessons Learned

There were many valuable lessons learned from this experience that can serve as a guide to helping future university–community research collaborations and engagements with African American communities. Three key lessons learned from this experience are highlighted.

First, *clearly stating and addressing assumptions and expectations* will reduce skepticism when novel components of the research occur. By addressing assumptions and expectations, mutual respect can be established and can foster a positive experience for the researcher and the community.

Second, *displaying an appreciation of the culture is also important.* As an African American researcher engages an African American community, there may rest an assumption that one understands the culture. It is important to keep in mind that the manner that culture is displayed may vary. Thus, community partners will have a culture that must be respected, navigated, and learned before research can be adequately implemented.

Third, *give back to the community.* Giving back to the community reinforces the cultural value of reciprocity. It is important to make one's presence known and inquire about service needs of the community beyond the research. Building rapport is essential. Being present outside of the research demonstrates that the researcher cares and is invested in the community. Talk to community members and potential partners and be responsive to their needs. Listening to their voices and responding accordingly will offer a sense of empowerment such that participants feel they are involved in the design and implementation of the research. In the spirit of reciprocity, Mance implemented a tutoring program at the control school in appreciation for the community allowing her and Jaha-Echols to conduct research. Additionally, Jaha-Echols offered the opportunity for many of the research participants to attend Camp Butterfly, which is a one-week sleep-away camp where the workbook is emphasized.

Conclusion

Given that there are no systematic efforts or accumulated research that addresses how to build and maintain community collaborations,[39] particularly with African Americans, this chapter highlights the experience of a researcher–community collaboration while providing suggestions for future research and engagement. This chapter provides significant insight into the paradigm differences (African-centered/Black-centered) and heterogeneity that exist in African American communities. The road to Project Butterfly provides an honest example of the opportunities and challenges of conducting community-based research in African American communities. Overall, respecting the cultural considerations of African American communities is most valuable in the engagement process, which should also include practicing the cultural values of reciprocity, connectedness, and mutual respect.

Notes

1. S. Pokorny et al., "Prevention Science: Participatory Approaches and Community Case Studies," in *Participatory Community Research: Theories and Methods in Action*, ed. L. Jason et al. (Washington, DC: American Psychological Association, 2004), 87–104.

2. In this chapter, *African American* refers to individuals born in the United States who can trace his or her ancestry to an enslaved African in the United States.

3. V. L. Shavers-Hornaday and C. F. Lynch, "Why Are African Americans Under-Represented in Medical Research Studies? Impediments to Participation," *Ethnicity and Health* 2, no. 1/2 (1997), 31–46.

4. The term *African-centered* refers to traditional and historical cultural values based on the Akan culture of West Africa.

5. J. Brooks-Gunn, G. Duncan, and J. L. Aber, eds., *Neighborhood Poverty: Context and Consequences for Children* (New York: Russell Sage, 1997).

6. V. Stewart and A. Vaux, "Social Support Resources, Behaviors, and Perceptions among Black and White College Students," *Journal of Multicultural Counseling and Development,* 14 (1986): 65–72.

7. T. Parham, "Cycles of Psychological Nigrescence," *Counseling Psychologist* 17 (1989): 187–226.

8. J. L. White, *The Psychology of Blacks: An African American Perspective*, 2nd ed. (Englewood Cliffs, NJ: Prentice-Hall, 1984).

9. K. K. Kambon, *African/Black Psychology in the American Context: An African-Centered Approach* (Tallahassee, FL: Nubian Nation Publications, 1998).

10. F. Belgrave et al., "The Impact of Knowledge, Norms, Self-Efficacy on Interventions to Engage in AIDS-Preventive Behaviors among Young Incarcerated African American Males," *Journal of Black Psychology* 19, no. 2 (1993): 155–68.

11. F. Z. Belgrave et al., "The Influence of Africentric Values, Self-Esteem, and Black Identity on Drug Attitudes among African American Fifth Graders: A Preliminary Study," *Journal of Black Psychology* 20, no. 2 (1994): 143–56.

12. F. Z. Belgrave et al., "The Effectiveness of a Culture- and Gender-Specific Intervention for Increasing Resiliency among African American Preadolescent Females," *Journal of Black Psychology* 26, no. 2 (2000): 133–47.

13. N. Jaha-Echols, "Project Butterfly: Caterpillar Training Guide" (Ottawa, ON: Perfect Books, 2003), iii.

14. W. W. Nobles, "Psychological Nigrescence: An Afrocentric Review," *Counseling Psychologist* 17 (1989): 253–57.

15. Nobles, "Psychological Nigrescence."

16. R. Cohen, J. Linker, and L. Stutts, "Working Together: Lessons Learned from School, Family, and Community Collaborations," *Psychology in the Schools* 43, no. 4 (2006): 419–28.

17. D. R. Matsumoto, *Culture and Psychology: People Around the World* (Delmar, CA: Wadsworth Thomas Learning, 2000).

18. H. Betancourt and S. R. Lopez, "The Study of Culture, Ethnicity, and Race in American Psychology," *American Psychologist* 48, no. 6 (1993): 629–37.

19. J. S. Phinney, "Stages of Ethnic Identity Development in Minority Group Adolescents," *Journal of Early Adolescence* 9, no. 1–2 (1989): 34–49.

20. Kambon, *African/Black Psychology.*

21. Kambon, *African/Black Psychology.*

22. J. S. Mbiti, *African Religions and Philosophy* (Garden City, NY: Anchor Books, 1970), 108.

23. L. Jordan, G. A. Bogat, and G. Smith, "Collaborating for Social Change: The Black Psychologist and the Black Community," *American Journal of Community Psychology* 29, no. 4 (2001): 599–620.

24. C. B. Keys et al., "Culturally Anchored Research: Quandaries, Guidelines, and Exemplars for Community Psychology," in *Participatory Community Research: Theories and Methods in Action*, ed. L. Jason et al. (Washington, DC: American Psychological Association, 2004), 177–98.

25. Keys et al., "Culturally Anchored Research."

26. R. V. Guthrie, "The psychology of African Americans: An historical perspective," *in Black Psychology*, 4th ed., ed. R. Jones (Hampton, VA: Cobb and Henry): 41–52.

27. Pokorny et al., "Prevention Science."

28. Pokorny et al., "Prevention Science."

29. Y. Suarez-Balcazar et al., "University–Community Partnership: A Framework and an Exemplar," in *Participatory Community Research: Theories and Methods in Action*, ed L. Jason et al. (Washington, DC: American Psychological Association, 2004), 105–20.

30. P. Mattessich and B. Monsey, *Collaboration: What Makes It Work* (St. Paul, MN: Amherst Wilder Foundation, 1992).

31. L. Taylor and H. S. Adelman, "Connecting Schools, Families, and Communities," *Professional School Counseling* 3 (2000): 298–307.

32. Suarez-Balcazar et al., "University–Community Partnership."

33. F. Belgrave and K. Allison, *African American Psychology: From Africa to America* (Thousand Oaks, CA: Sage, 2006).

34. Belgrave and Allison, *African American Psychology.*

35. Y. A. A. Ben-Jochannan, *"African Origins of Major "Western Religions,"* (St. Paul, MN: Amherst Wilder Foundation, 1992).

36. Mattessich and Monsey, *Collaboration.*

37. J. S. Phinney, "The Multigroup Ethnic Identity Measure: A New Scale for Use with Diverse Groups," *Journal of Adolescent Research* 7, no. 2 (1992): 156–76.

38. Belgrave et al., "The Effectiveness of a Cuture."

39. P. Jensen, K. Hoagwood, and E. Trickett, "Ivory Towers or Earthen Trenches? Community Collaborators to Foster Real-World Research," *Applied Developmental Science* 3, no. 4 (1999): 206–12.

Final Word

African Americans and Community Engagement

The Challenge and Opportunity for Higher Education

Donald F. Blake

As a child, I grew up in a close-knit African American ghetto that was, at the time, located in one of the richest counties in the United States. The community was fairly homogeneous in that we were all poor; the impact of the Great Depression was still felt. The majority of the men were employed on Work Projects Administration (a program of Franklin Roosevelt's New Deal) projects, and the few women who worked were domestics. We did not know we were poor until a social service bureaucrat told us that we were, but the stark reality was that the community was an island of poverty surrounded by a sea of plenty. Much of the ability of the community and its individual residents to be successful was directly related to our being grounded in a fundamental Christian belief that we were "our brother's (and our sister's) keeper."

The principles of reverence, respect, politeness, good manners, and decency were well ingrained into the fabric of our characters along with the sense of caring for all members of the community. It was the strength of that caring as well as the lessons learned that contributed, in a large measure, to the success that we would achieve as professionals in adulthood. One indelible lesson that is still with me was taught to me by my parents. I was about eight years old and a senior citizen "hired" me to take her trash to the basement three times a week for a "salary" of twenty-five cents per week. I had no realization of the monetary value of my pay (bread was ten cents per loaf and milk fifteen cents per quart) and she did not work. When I got my first pay, I took it home and proudly gave it to my mother. She quizzed me thoroughly and said no more; however, I did note that Mom did not share my elation. When Dad came home that evening, they discussed my job and then Dad sent me to return the money with tacit instructions to let her know that I would continue to take her trash out for free. I was allowed to mark my missionary card at church as helping someone that week, and I continued that task until she moved away.

Historical Perspective

For many African Americans, community engagement was a way of life long before the concept became popular in higher education. It was this communal caring that helped sustain us during the cruel days of slavery; it was the essence of the nonviolent direct action that assisted Black Americans and those in other parts of the world to win victories over segregation, apartheid, racial hate, and discrimination. During the era of enslavement, we witnessed this commitment to community in the birth of babies, the care of children, caring for the sick, and support for the aged. In the television documentary *Roots*, the point was indelible that during slavery, women provided most of the leadership in sustaining the family and the community.

After Emancipation, the commitment to community continued to be an integral part of the fabric of African American society. This was most evident in the institutions of higher learning that sprung up after slavery. All were designed to provide these former salves with training and learning that would enable them to become productive citizens. Depending on which nomenclature one uses, there are approximately 120 historically Black colleges and universities in the United States today, and if you factor in the institutions that became White shortly after integration, the number is larger. Basically, none started out as liberal arts institutions. Many started out as secondary schools, while others were classified as industrial schools or manual training schools, but all had future visions to do for many Black folk what Harvard, Yale, and others were doing for Whites and a very limited number of Blacks.

While not the first of the historically Black colleges and universities to be established, the Negro Normal School in Tuskegee, Alabama, became one of the first, if not the first, institutions of higher learning to develop and promote those concepts revered today as community service and service-learning in a dignified manner. Authorized in 1881, its founding president was Booker T. Washington. In 1896, Washington hired a recent graduate of Iowa State, George Washington Carver, to develop an agricultural program at Tuskegee. Tackling problems related to poor farming productivity and poor nutrition, Carver and Washington established in 1904 a program called "Jesup Wagon" where instructors and students would take a monthly circuit visiting farms and teaching people how to farm using the latest techniques based on research methods designed and developed through scientific testing at Tuskegee. These were perhaps the earliest recorded instances of service-learning, community service, and community-based research in higher education. This helped define agriculture as a realistic and viable career option for former slaves and their progeny. Such practices as crop rotation and the use of the tomato, peanut, sweet potato, pecans, and soy beans as food items came from the Tuskegee programs, and the Jesup Wagon was also the precursor to the development of the extension programs by the U.S. Department of Agriculture.

I had the privilege of being taught and/or supervised by two of my instructors at Oakwood College who had worked with or worked for Dr. Carver at Tuskegee prior to 1920. One was Professor Robert L. Reynolds, a 1917 graduate of Ohio State University with a bachelor of science degree in agriculture, who took his first job at Tuskegee in Dr. Carver's department. Mr. Reynolds shared Carver's traits of frugality and not wasting anything and tried to instill similar characteristics in his students. He shared many of his experiences working with Carver in the rural areas around the school and he held clinics for local farmers (Black and White) on Oakwood's farm.

The other person was Chessie Harris. She went to Tuskegee as a preteen in 1917 and was assigned to work for Dr. Carver in his laboratory. She later worked also in his home. She held Dr. Carver in highest esteem. "Mom" Harris had taken home economics and was so skilled that Dr. Carver allowed her to accompany him on the excursions into the rural areas to teach the women home management skills. She did this until she finished high school and took some college work. I also learned "Carver" skills from her. She and her husband founded a home for orphaned black children in Huntsville, Alabama, and I served her as a consultant from 1965 until her death in 1997 at the age of ninety-one. The lessons of thrift and "waste not" that I learned from Reynolds and Harris are still integral parts of me today.

About the same time that Tuskegee was developing, a church group established Oakwood Manual Training School near Huntsville to educate Black youth. Oakwood had White administrators and faculty and Black students. This angered many of the local residents. However, when a crisis developed for one of the most vocal White neighbors, the Oakwood team became the Good Samaritan and brought their teams, wagons, farm implements, and Black students to harvest their antagonist's crops when he was unable to do the job. So Oakwood used community service to create supportive neighbors in a time and area of the country where the Ku Klux Klan terrorized Blacks and ruled them by intimidation.

America's Legacy in the African American Community

America continues to sidestep the reality of the debt that is owed to Black America. The leader of the free world and the greatest purveyor of democracy history has ever known, our nation adroitly avoids facing up to accepting full responsibility for much of the economic, educational, and social depravity that continues to plague the African American community. It also abdicates responsibility for designing methodologies that will be successful in ameliorating the conditions, plight, and blight of the Black communities. This is not to demean or denigrate the work of many honest and sincere people, but the truth is, with all of the improvement, too many Black Americans are neglected and deprived by today's standards.

Higher education has contributed to the problems that exist in the African American communities in a number of ways, but two in particular: (1) helping to perpetuate the myth regarding the inferiority of Blacks when it was popular to do so, and (2) when changes were made, higher education did not take a real leadership role in correcting the conditions that continue to trouble large sectors of the African American community. Now it is time for higher education to assert its leadership.

The Challenge and Opportunity for Higher Education

Noted American educator Ernest Boyer wrote, "I have this growing conviction that what is needed [for higher education] is not just more programs, but a larger purpose, a larger sense of mission, a larger clarity of direction in the nation's life."[1] One can interpret Boyer's "larger sense of mission" to include a commitment by higher education to redefine its role in solving some of the social ills of America, because they certainly do benefit from them. There have been some attempts to redefine higher education's role in the advancement of democracy and how it views the way it should play a pivotal role in "a larger clarity of direction on the nation's life." One of the most impactful set of suggestions came out of the Wingspread Conference of 2004.[2] The position statement from Wingspread is summarized here:

A. Integrate engagement into mission.
B. Forge partnerships as the overarching framework for engagement.
C. Renew and redefine discovery and scholarship.
D. Integrate engagement into teaching and learning.
E. Recruit and support new champions.
F. Create radical institutional change.

These are meaningful and exciting opportunities when fully implemented. But they do not go far enough. Others have stated parameters, but to date, the changes that have been posited by higher education have not produced changes needed in African American communities. Despite the fact that in the few instances of successful change models, access to higher education is always a key player.

The magnitude of the need for higher education to step up to the plate and use its resources, both human and financial, to address many of the inequities that continue to plague the minority communities was vividly highlighted by the election of an African American to the most powerful political position in the world. Now I am cognizant of the fact that some will state that Barack Obama's election indicates that racism is a dead issue. But the educational gaps that are omnipresent in communities that must educate diverse populations make a strong statement in favor of the need for much more assistance. Most educators admit to the racial differences in academic performance, but few want to speak to the challenge of the gaps related to expectations, opportunities, and available resources. Here is a thought for the proponents of financial reparations: that money could be used for tried and proven innovative programs in communities with large populations of African American children who go to school in public systems that still make short shrift of them and to establish endowments to fund their schooling in a variety of postsecondary programs.

The fact that Barack Obama is seen as an African American in spite of the reality that he is 50 percent White is indicative of an interesting perspective that Americans need to resolve. What makes a person Black? Higher education must be the leader in developing a different paradigm that defines race in this country. If America can tackle and resolve this malapropism successfully, it will be the shot that will be heard around the world.

However, Michelle Obama has a very different heritage. Some of her African American roots go back to a plantation in the low country of South Carolina on the banks of the Sampit River near present-day Geogetown.[3] Mrs. Obama's lineage can be traced at least one generation or more into slavery.

Many institutions of higher education, both in the South and in the North, benefited greatly from the egregious social institution of slavery. So these institutions, along with the rest of higher education, have a major indebtedness to the minority communities not only to ameliorate some of their ugly practices of the past, but also to sensitize and educate the students of today and the future, so that such praetorian, dastardly, and barbaric practices of the past will never again in all of human history even be thought of, much less put into practice.

There must be a meeting of the minds. Higher education must recognize that it must work in full partnership with the African American community to develop paradigms that will address community needs, and, at the same time, move the institution forward with its program of civic engagement.

Following is a set of eight challenges and opportunities for higher education, which, if adopted and implemented will result in a level of civic engagement that the African American communities can embrace. Higher education must:

1. Recognize and affirm that community (civic) engagement has been a linchpin for survival for African Americans since the first Africans came to America in 1619.

2. Recognize and operate on the premise that any civic engagement that does not result in community advancement and resident empowerment is worthless.
3. Learn to define and measure success in terms that are dictated by perspectives of the community.
4. Revise its rewards and recognition programs so that faculty will be encouraged to invest significant time and effort in civic and community engagement.
5. Commit to use portions of its endowments to fund and support civic and community engagement. This includes building civic and community engagement projects into major fund-raising campaigns.
6. Revise some instructional methodologies to take advantage of the strengths of the community and incorporate them into the structure of the education process so that students can value being civically engaged.
7. Devise programs that will significantly or totally eliminate a student's educational debt upon graduation.
8. Make a commitment to long-term sustainable programs and projects related to civic engagement.

All of life's experiences touch in two places: the horizon of the past and the horizon of the future. While we know a lot about the past, we can only speculate about the future. However, we can take the knowledge of the past and use it to design and deliver the actions of the present, which will help us predict, in a large measure, the outcomes of the future. Most African American communities do not have fond memories of their interactions with higher education. This makes the task of building trust and confidence in the future much more difficult, but not impossible. When African Americans were emancipated from slavery, higher education was a key player in developing the separate—but unequal—place for Blacks in the United States. Then, as African Americans became educated and demanded a fair share of the American dream that had been built in a large measure on their backs, America created a system of patronage and paternalism. "We are the doctors and we know what is best for you." But this position is not acceptable to Black people. What then should be done?

What is needed is to develop a collaborative partnership where all participants can come to the table as equal partners and work together for the common good of all people. In this volume you will have found concrete examples of how such collaborative partnerships can be and are being developed. We must always remember that as long as Americans go to bed (if they have one) hungry at night, or the performance gap continues to exist, those who sit at a bountiful table or those who do well academically should not feel comfortable.

Notes

1. E. L. Boyer, *Scholarship Reconsidered: Priorities of the Professorate* (San Francisco, CA: Jossey-Bass, 1990).

2. "CALLING THE QUESTION: Is Higher Education Ready to Commit to Community Engagement?" A Wingspread Statement 2004 by Mary Jane Brukardt, Barbara Holland, Stephen L. Percy, and Nancy Zimpher—on behalf of Wingspread Conference participants, University of Wisconsin–Milwaukee, 2004.

3. "From Slave Cabin to White House, a Family Rooted in Black America, TIMESONLINE (*London Times*), November 6, 2008.

Contributors

Editors

Stephanie Y. Evans, Ph.D., is a tenured associate professor in African American Studies and Women's Studies at the University of Florida. She is the author of *Black Women in the Ivory Tower, 1850–1954: An Intellectual History* (2007) and articles in journals such as *Thought and Action, International Journal of Africana Studies, African American Research Perspectives, Black Women, Gender and Families, GRIOT: Southern Conference on African American Studies, Florida Historical Quarterly, Feminist Teacher,* and *International Journal of Humanities.* She has practiced community service-learning since 1997 at California State University–Long Beach, Stanford University, the University of Massachusetts–Amherst, Brown University, and the University of Florida.

Colette M. Taylor, Ed.D., is an assistant professor of higher education at Texas Tech University. While working at the University of Florida from 1998 to 2006, she was responsible for the development of the community service and service-learning at the University of Florida, which was implemented as campus volunteer clearinghouse in the fall of 1998. Dr. Taylor served as a member of the cochair of Florida Campus Compact Advisory Council from 2002 to 2006 and a member of the Florida Campus Compact Consulting Corp from 2003 to 2006. She was a member of the board of advisors of the Florida Office of Collegiate Volunteerism from 1998 to 2001 and served as chair from 2000 to 2001. Dr. Taylor has taught several service-learning courses and has been a supervisor of the HUD Community Partnership Outreach Center at the University of Florida.

Michelle R. Dunlap, Ph.D., is a tenured professor and chair of the Human Development Department at Connecticut College, and an educational and community consultant who has worked collaboratively with educational institutions, corporations, state and local agencies, and nonprofits. She is author of *Reaching Out to Children and Families: Students Model Effective Community Service* (2000), and coeditor of *Community Involvement: Theoretical Approaches and Educational Initiatives* (2002) and *Charting a New Course for Feminist Psychology* (2002).

249

DeMond S. Miller, Ph.D., is a tenured professor of sociology and director of the Liberal Arts and Sciences Institute for Research and Community Service at Rowan University (Glassboro, New Jersey). His primary area of specialization is environmental sociology, disaster studies, the study of the social construction of place, community development, and social impact assessment. Dr. Miller has presented and published several professional papers; recent examples of such work can be found in *Researcher, Qualitative Report, Journal of Emotional Abuse, Space and Culture: An International Journal of Social Spaces, International Journal of the Humanities, Journal of Black Studies, Journal of Public Management and Social Policy,* and *Southeastern Sociological Review.*

Final Word

Donald F. Blake, Ph.D., is a retired academician who lives in Stanardsville, Virginia. with his wife, Vera, of more than forty-nine years. He has been an educator, corporate executive, executive director for several community-based non-profit organizations, and a partner in three consulting firms. He and Vera operate their own consulting firm, VDB Consulting Group, LLC. In higher education, he has served at every level from professor/researcher to president. Currently, Dr. Blake is serving as a consultant to the Community Relations Office at the University of Virginia in Charlottesville.

Authors

Evangeline R. Best is a native of the East Tampa, Florida, community. She is a retiree of the school district working with the Head Start Program. Ms. Best is a community leader recognized for her ability to motivate and organize people from diverse backgrounds.

Richard Briscoe, Ph.D., is a faculty member in the Department of Child and Family Studies at the Louis de la Parte Florida Mental Health Institute (University of South Florida). His interests are strengths, community-based and faith-based research with African American communities.

Jeff Brooks, Ph.D., is a sociologist who specializes in social psychology and gerontology. He earned his doctorate from Purdue University. He has an MSW from The University of North Carolina at Chapel Hill. Dr. Brooks is also involved in various community services.

Kendall M. Campbell, M.D., is assistant dean for minority affairs and assistant professor for community health and family medicine at the University of Florida College of Medicine. His special interests include cardiovascular disease, diabetes and teaching.

Richard Carifo is a member of a research team at California State University–Northridge.

John Fife is the director of counseling and student development at Virginia Union University in Richmond, Virginia. His research interests are the impact of spirituality and religiosity on behavior and attitudes toward HIV/AIDS; ethnic identity development; and substance abuse prevention.

Troy Harden, MSW, LCSW, received his master's degree in social work from Loyola University at Chicago, and is currently an Ed.D. candidate at DePaul University. He has over twenty years of experience serving in social service and community settings, and currently serves as gaculty and the director of field development for DePaul University's Masters of Social Work Program.

August Hoffman, Ph.D., currently teaches psychology at Metropolitan State University in St. Paul, Minnesota, and at the University of Wisconsin, River Falls. He has published several books and academic research articles, including the texts *Positive Psychology: An Applied Approach*; *Understanding Sport Psychology and Human Behavior*; and *29,051 Ways to Survive the College Experience*. He enjoys gardening in his time off with his family: his wife, Nancy, and his two children, A. J. and Sara.

Fleda Mask Jackson, Ph.D., is a principal investigator and faculty member at the Rollins School of Public Health. Formerly, the director of the HBCU Network of Campus Compact, she serves on the National Advisory Board on Health Disparities for the director of the Centers for Disease Control.

Niambi Jaha-Echols is the author of *Project Butterfly: Supporting Young Women and Gils of African Descent through the Transitions of Life*. She is also the founder and chief executive officer of two organizations that serve and support the transitional healing of women and girls: Project Butterfly and Camp Butterfly.

Monica Jones, M.S., is a doctoral candidate in the counseling psychology program in the Department of Psychology at Virginia Commonwealth University. Her clinical and research interests include community prevention and intervention programming, minority mental health, family psychology, and religion and spiritual values.

Harold R. Keller, Ph.D. is a professor in psychological and social foundations, and associate dean for academic affairs in the College of Education (University of South Florida). He is actively engaged in community-based research and community-based teaching/learning.

Dwayne A. Mack, Ph.D., is assistant professor of history at Berea College in Berea, Kentucky, specializing in the Civil Rights Movement. His publications include "Ain't Gonna Let Nobody Turn Me Around: Berea College's Participation in the Selma to Montgomery March," which appeared in the fall 2005 issue of *Ohio Valley History,*Fand "Crusade for Equality: The Civil Rights Struggle in Spokane during the Early 1960s," which appeared in the winter 2003/2004 issue of *Pacific Northwest Quarterly.*

GiShawn Mance, Ph.D., is currently a visiting assistant professor in the Department of Psychology at American University. Her research interests include child/adolescent mental health, community-based participatory research, race and culture, mental health disparities, and community/familial networks.

Jessica Mazza, M.S.P.H., is a research assistant at Northwestern University. She previously served as a research assistant at the Louis de la Parte Florida Mental Health Institute. Her research interests include mental health systems and community-based behavioral health services.

Gwen McClain, M.A., is a social and behavioral researcher in the Department of Child and Family Studies at the Louis de la Parte Florida Mental Health Institute (University of South Florida) and the president of R.I.S.E. Consultants. Her interests are culturally competent research and development strategies that promote social and economic justice.

Micah McCreary, M.Div., Ph.D., LCP, is a 2006–2007 American Council on Education Fellow, a tenured associate professor in the Department of Psychology at Virginia Commonwealth University, a licensed clinical psychologist in the State of Virginia, and an ordained Baptist pastor. He is the executive director and creator of the IMPPACT family intervention and conducts a small private practice in Richmond, Virginia. He has published articles and chapters in the areas of multicultural and family psychology.

Meta Mendel-Reyes, Ph.D., is director of the Center for Excellence in Learning Through Service and associate professor of general studies at Berea College, in Berea, Kentucky. She is the author of *Reclaiming Democracy: The Sixties in Politics and Memory* (1995), and has published articles and chapters on participatory democracy, community engagement, and service-learning.

David P. Moxley, Ph.D., is in the University of Oklahoma School of Social Work where he holds the Oklahoma Healthcare Authority Endowed Professorship in Health.

Lucy Mule, Ph.D., is associate professor in the Department of Education and Child Study, Smith College. Her research interests include multicultural education, teacher education, literacy education, and comparative education.

Joi Nathan currently serves as the coordinator of youth programs at the Center for Civic Education and Service at Florida State University. In addition to her duties with this program, Ms. Nathan is working towards a Ph.D. in educational policy, planning and analysis.

Bernadette Sánchez, Ph.D., is currently an assistant professor of psychology at DePaul University. Her research primarily focuses on youth mentoring relationships, race and culture, and academic achievement.

Eduardo Sanchez is an undergraduate student at California State University–Northridge and is currently studying psychology and research design. He plans to study psychology as a graduate student and continue his studies in race and ethnicity.

Raymond Tademy is a doctoral student in the social psychology program in the Department of Psychology at Virginia Commonwealth University.

Annemarie Vaccaro, Ph.D., is an assistant professor in the Department of Human Development and Family Studies at the University of Rhode Island. She earned her Ph.D. in higher education and an M.A. in sociology from the University of Denver and she earned an M.A. in student affairs from Indiana University of Pennsylvania. Her research interests include the intersections between higher education, student affairs, and social identities of race, class, gender, and sexual orientation. Issues of social justice, critical theory, and feminism are integral to her scholarship and pedagogy.

Julie Wallach graduated from California State University–Northridge and has coauthored several books and journal articles with Dr. August Hoffman addressing motivation, positive psychology, and procrastination. Her interests include health and exercise and fitness. She has two daughters and a husband and is very happy living in Malibu, California.

Olivia G. M. Washington, Ph.D., APRN, BC, NP, LPC, is a nurse scientist in the Wayne State University College of Nursing and in the Institute of Gerontology where she directs the Healthier Black Elders Center, a civic engagement project designed to improve the health of urban Black elders.

Kheli R. Willetts, Ph.D., is an assistant professor of African American art history and film at Syracuse University and academic director of the Community Folk Art Center, located in the city of Syracuse.

Index

❖❖❖

Made in the USA
San Bernardino, CA
19 December 2015